4/02

D1097560

ITALIAN CULTURE

A VIEW FROM AMERICA

PETER DORATO

SYLVIA DORATO

TSI Press   Albuquerque, New Mexico, USA   2001

Cover photograph: Torino, capital of Piedmont. View of Mole Antonelliana and the Italian Alps.

Copyright © 2001 Peter Dorato and Sylvia Dorato
All rights reserved. No part of this book may be reproduced, in any form or by any means, without permission of the authors.

TSI Press
P.O. Box 14126
Albuquerque, NM 87191-4126, USA
Phone: (505) 298-5817, Fax: (505) 291-0013
E-mail: tsi@cybermesa.com, http://cybermesa.com/~js

ISBN: 1-889335-15-0

Printed by GSI Documentation Management, 2428 San Mateo Place NE, Albuquerque, NM, 87110, USA.

945
DOR
2001

*This book is dedicated to the memory of **Nonno Fioretto** and **Nonni Rosina**, the first generation of Doratos in America, and to the success of the fourth generation: Shannon Rose, Bryce, Zachary, Alessandra, Serena Rose, Anne-Sophie, Lily Rayne, Gabrielle, and Skye Rosina.*

Preface

This book is based on lecture notes from an Italian Culture class that the first author has been teaching since 1993 in the Division of Continuing Education at the University of New Mexico. The course description reads as follows:

This course is designed for those who plan to visit Italy or who wish to become familiar with Italian culture. Topics will include: Basic elements of the Italian language; Italian dialects, as illustrated by the "Piemontese" dialect; Italian history and geography; evolution of the Italian language, from the Latin dialects to "Italian"; Italian literature, Dante and Manzoni; Early history, the Greeks, Etruscans, and Romans; Medieval and Renaissance Italy; Italian unification (Risorgimento), Garibaldi, Cavour, Mazzini; the House of Savoy; Turin, the first capital of modern Italy; famous Italian cities, Rome, Florence, Venice, etc.; Italian food and wine, and popular Italian songs.

There are no prerequisites for this course. No knowledge of Italian is assumed. Indeed part of the course is devoted to learning some of the basics of the Italian language. We include an appendix on Italian grammar for that purpose.

We have added to our title the phrase "A View from America" because we wanted to alert the reader that this is not a book written by two Italian scholars (Italian surnames not withstanding). Indeed we are not professionals in the Italian language, Italian history, or for that matter anything else Italian. Professionally we are Electrical Engineers. Culturally we are Italian-Americans, or as our relatives in Piedmont would say, Piedmontese-Americans. Our "Italian connection" started when *Fioretto Dorato* married *Rosina Lachello*, both from the village of *Villadeati* in the *Monferrato* region of Piedmont in northern Italy. Immediately following their marriage in Italy in 1931, they came to the United States. On the 17th of

December 1932 a son was born, *Pierino Dorato* (first author). In 1956, *Pierino* (Peter) married Madeleine Turlan, and on the 23rd of August 1960 a daughter was born, Sylvia Dorato (second author). That is our Italian connection.

Peter Dorato grew up in the lower west side of Manhattan, in a neighborhood known as the *Central Park West* district, an area just north of the *Hell's Kitchen* district. His first language was Piedmontese. Like most immigrants, the language spoken at home was not Italian, but rather an Italian dialect. Although the Dorato family visited relatives in Italy over the years, it was not until 1991, when Peter Dorato spent a sabbatical year at the *Politecnico di Torino,* that a strong interest in Italian and Italian culture developed in the family. One might expect that a book written by two Piedmontese-American engineers on Italian Culture would be different from your average book on the subject. Indeed, we hope this is the case, and that perhaps even Italian "scholars" will find things in the book that they would not likely find elsewhere, for example, a chapter on *Left-Brained Italians* or an appendix on *Piedmontese Grammar* and *Neapolitan Grammar.*

We feel it is important for anyone wishing to learn about Italian culture to understand that Italy is in reality a collection of many regions, each with its distinct language and its distinct culture. It should be noted that before 1861, when Italy was finally re-united, the Italian peninsula was a collection of independent nations. For this reason we have explored in some detail a particular region, Piedmont, and a particular dialect, Piedmontese, in some detail. We picked Piedmont because we know it best, but any region of Italy could have been chosen to illustrate the point.

We have included an extensive chapter on Italian popular songs in various dialects, another item not likely to be found in most books on Italian Culture, because we feel that one of the best ways to learn a language and the culture of a country is through its popular songs. When the Italian Culture class is taught at the University of New Mexico, one can often hear the class theme song *Parlami d'Amore Mariù* resonate in the hallway.

At the end of each chapter we have included a section on *Notes and References*, where we discuss various points raised in the chapter and discuss various relevant references. A complete list of references may be found at the end of the book.

The authors are extremely grateful to all the friends, family, and colleagues who supplied so many valuable inputs to this volume, written and oral inputs, books, cassettes, CD's, etc. etc. Thank you: *Salvatore Baglio, Carmen Ballati, Sergio Bittanti, Vito Cerone, Giorgio and Rita Cortellezzi, Luisa Del Giudice, Bianca Dorato, Christopher Dorato, Kathleen Dorato, Rachelle Duke, Roberto and Nadia Durante, Giovanni Fiorio, Luigi Fortuna, Francis Malpezzi, Massimo Menga, Laura Menini, Gigliola Mueller, Giovanni Muscato, Roberto Paolino, Armando Patrucco, Piera Raviola Pengo, Elvira Pulitano, Peter and Angela Roberto, "Cici" Mejnardi Rolando, Luigi Rolando, Armanda Selice, Rosa Lachello Sesso, Bruno Siciliano, Massimo Tartamella, Roberto and Cristina Tempo, Bruno Villata, and Josephine Weiss.*

We wish to thank the Club Culturale Italiano of Albuquerque, New Mexico for their support of the Italian Culture course, and all the students in the course who inspired the continued evolution of this volume. We also wish to express our special gratitude to Professor *Bruno Villata* for his help in editing our Piedmontese material (Professor Villata is a faculty member at Concordia University in

Canada, and is an editor of the Piedmontese-language journal *L'Arvista Dl'Academia*), and to the late Professor *Paolo Luggeri*, from Naples, Italy, for his help in editing our Neapolitan material.

Finally we would like to thank *Elvira Pulitano* for her careful review of the final draft of our manuscript, and Jila Salari Jamshidi of TSI Press and Gene Scanlan of GSI Document Management for expediting the final production of the book.

TABLE OF CONTENTS

CHAPTER 1. Some Preliminaries

1.1 INTRODUCTION

In this chapter, we will say a little something about the language, the geography, and the history of Italy. We will get into more details on these subjects in subsequent chapters. Since language is so central to any culture, we start with some comments on the Italian language and the basic rules for pronunciation. The physical environment of a people is also a determinant in defining its culture, so we will say a few things about the geography of Italy. Finally, the history of a people is obviously part and parcel of its culture, so we will present some of the highlights of Italian history.

1.2 THE ITALIAN LANGUAGE

Many people know that Italian evolved from Latin. But perhaps fewer people know that what is now Italian is in reality only one of the many dialects spoken in the different regions of Italy. In particular, official Italian is the dialect spoken in the region of Tuscany. Prior to 1861, when modern Italy became a united country, there was no common Italian language, and every region spoke its own separate dialect. Why was the Tuscan dialect selected as the official language? The reason for this probably goes back to the great literature that came out of Florence, the modern capital of Tuscany during the middle ages, e.g. the works of *Boccaccio*, *Petrarca*, and *Dante*. However, even as late as 1842, when *Alessandro Manzoni* completed his epic novel, *I Promessi Sposi* (The Betrothed), very few people outside of Tuscany spoke what we now call Italian. But *Manzoni*'s book had a tremendous impact on all of Italy. It played a key role in the final acceptance of the Tuscan dialect as the national Italian language.

1

In the next chapter, we will explore the history and evolution of the Italian language. We have included, in Appendix I, some of the basic elements of Italian grammar. In Chapter 3 we will explore an Italian dialect, Piedmontese, to provide some appreciation of the difference between dialects in Italy. Appendix II outlines the elements of Piedmontese grammar. It is interesting to note that the first king of a united Italy, *Vittorio Emanuele II,* spoke mostly Piedmontese. He was barely literate in the Tuscan dialect, which he adopted as the official court language.

Most Italian emigrants who came to America spoke only their dialect. Even to this day, if you go to any small village in Italy, you will almost surely hear the local dialect spoken, rather than Italian. In the cities the situation is different; very few people, especially young people, speak the local dialect anymore.

The first step in understanding a culture is understanding the language, and the first step in learning the language is learning to pronounce words properly. In the next section, we will highlight the main rules in pronouncing standard Italian.

1.3 PRONUNCIATION

Italian is probably the easiest language in the world to pronounce properly. Every letter is pronounced, and there are very few exceptions to the rules of pronunciation. Of course, to speak without an accent, like a native Italian, is a bit more difficult. Italian pronunciation is simplified further by the fact that the Italian alphabet is missing five letters, i.e. *j, k, w, x,* and *y*. Only foreign words or dialects may have these letters. We summarize below the pronunciation of vowels and consonants.

VOWELS

a– "a" as in "father", e.g. *casa* (house)

e - "a" as in "make", e.g. *sera* (evening)

i - "ee" as in "feet", e.g. *vini* (wines)

- "o" as in "note", e.g. *molto* (much)

u - "oo" as in "mood", e.g. *uno* (one)

   Most consonants are pronounced as in English. We list below only those that have pronunciations peculiar to Italian. This happens often when consonants are combined with certain vowels.

CONSONANTS

ci - "chee" as in "cheese", e.g. *ciao* (hello)

ce - "cha" as in "chair", e.g. *piacere* (pleasure)

chi - "key" as in "key", e.g. *pochi* (few)

che - "c" as in "cake", e.g. *perché* (why, because)

gi - "gee" as in "jeep", e.g. *giusto* (correct)

ge - "ge" as in "general", e.g. *gente* (people)

ghi - "gee" as in "geese", e.g. *funghi* (mushrooms)

ghe - "ge" as in "get", e.g. *Langhe* (Region in Piedmont)

gli - "li" as in "million", e.g. *figlia* (daughter)

gn -"ny" as in "canyon", e.g. *signore* (mister), or "ñ" in Spanish as in "cañon"

h - always silent

s - (between vowels) "z" as in "zero", e.g. *tesi* (thesis)

ss - (between vowels) "s" as in "sleep", e.g. *tessera* (card)

sc - (before a, o, u) "sk" as in "skip", e.g. *scala* (stair), *scopo* (object), or *scusa* (excuse)

sc - (before i or e) "sh" as in "ship", e.g. *scivolare* (to slip), *scendere* (to descend)

z, zz - "ts" as in "nuts", e.g. *piazza* (plaza), and of course *pizza*.

3

Sometimes pronounced "ds" as in "adds", e.g. *mezzo* (half)

Double consonants, e.g. *mamma* (mother), *bocca* (mouth), *nonno* (grandfather), *cappello* (hat), etc. are pronounced individually, i.e. *mam-ma, boc-ca, non-no, cap-pel-lo,* etc, in contrast to single consonants which are pronounced only once, e.g. *nono* (ninth). However, in ordinary speech it may be difficult to hear the difference between single and double consonants.

In general, the stress in Italian words is placed on the next-to-last syllable, e.g. *cucina* (kitchen), the stress is on *ci*. When the stress is the last syllable, an accent sign is usually added, e.g. *città* (city), *parlò* (he spoke). Sometimes an accent sign is used to distinguish words, e.g. *è* (is) and *e* (and).

Try your pronunciation on the following Italian names. How many of these names can you identify?

Marco Polo	*Giuseppe Buttafuoco*
Dante Alighieri	*Niccolò Machiavelli*
Giovanni Boccaccio	*Lorenzo de' Medici*
Leonardo da Vinci	*Galileo Galilei*
Amerigo Vespucci	*Alessandro Manzoni*
Cola di Rienzo	*Giuseppe Mazzini*
Girolamo Savonarola	*Francesco Sforza*
Vittorio Emanuele	*Elisabetta Gonzaga*

To practice your pronunciation you may want to sing along with Pavarotti.[1] Try the two following classical folk songs *Mamma* and *Parlami d'Amore Mariù.*

---

[1] Luciano Pavarotti, *Mamma,* London Records, 1984.

Mamma

> *Mamma, solo per te la mia canzone vola!*
> *Mamma, sarai con me, tu non sarai più sola!*
> *Quanto ti voglio bene!*
> *Queste parole d'amore,*
> *che ti sospira il mio cuore,*
> *forse non s'usano più.*
> *Mamma, la canzone mia più bella sei tu!*
> *Sei, tu, la vita,*
> *e per la vita non ti lascio mai più.*

Parlami d'Amore Mariù

> *Parlami d'amore Mariù!*
> *Tutta la mia vita sei tu!*
> *Gli occhi tuoi belli brillano,*
> *Fiamme di sogno scintillano!*
> *Dimmi che illusione non è!*
> *Dimmi che sei tutta per me!*
> *Qui sul tuo cuor non soffro più.*
> *Parlami d'amore Mariù!*

Comments and translations of these, and other, songs may be found in Chapter 6.

Finally, you should pronounce properly and memorize the following phrases, since they occur so often in Italian conversation.

Ciao - Hello/Goodbye

Arrivederci - Goodbye

Buona sera - Good afternoon/evening (any time after 2:00 p.m. in northern Italy)

Buona notte - Good night

Grazie - Thank you

Prego - You are welcome
Per piacere - Please
Come va? - How is it going?
Come sta? - How are you?
Bene, grazie, e Lei - Fine, thank you, and you (polite form).
Scusi - Excuse me (polite form).
Non parlo l'italiano - I do not speak Italian
Parlo solamente l'inglese - I only speak English
Lei parla l'inglese? - Do you (polite form) speak English?
Lei, come si chiama? - What is your (polite form) name?
Mi chiamo Pietro. - My name is Peter

Note that in most languages, besides English, there are two forms for addressing people, the "polite form" and the "familiar form." The polite form is used for people you do not know or people with respected positions, and the familiar form is used for family and friends. In Italian the two forms for "you" are *tu* (familiar) and *Lei* (polite).

1.4 A LITTLE GEOGRAPHY

Italy is divided into twenty "states" (*regioni*). However, only five of the states have the kind of political autonomy our states have here in the United States. Each state has a capital (*capoluogo*). We list below the twenty states with their capitals. Five states, indicted by asterics, have special autonomy, e.g. their own parliaments. See Map 1 for the location of the various states. You may recognize many of the state capitals, but are less likely to recognize the states. The autonomous states are indicated with dark shading. Note that the Italian island of *Pantelleria* is very close to the African coast.

ITALIAN STATES (*Regione*)

Regione (State)	***Capoluogo*** (Capital City)
1. *Abruzzo*	*L'Aquila* (L'Aquila)
2. *Basilicata*	*Potenza* (Potenza)
3. *Calabria*	*Catanzaro* (Catanzaro)
4. *Campania*	*Napoli* (Naples)
5. *Emilia-Romagna*	*Bologna* (Bologna)
6. *Friuli-Venezia Giulia**	*Trieste* (Trieste)
7. *Lazio*	*Roma* (Rome)
8. *Liguria*	*Genova* (Genoa)
9. *Lombardia*	*Milano* (Milan)
10. *Marche*	*Ancona* (Ancone)
11. *Molise*	*Campobasso* (Campobasso)
12. *Piemonte*	*Torino* (Turin)
13. *Puglia*	*Bari* (Bari)
14. *Sardegna**	*Cagliari* (Cagliari)
15. *Sicilia**	*Palermo* (Palermo)
16. *Toscana*	*Firenze* (Florence)
17. *Trentino-Alto Adige**	*Trento* (Trento)
18. *Umbria*	*Perugia* (Perugia)
19. Valle D'Aosta*	*Aosta* (Aosta)
20. Veneto	*Venezia*(Venice)

Map 1. Political Map of Italy

Map 2 shows the physical aspects of Italy. Note the most prominent are the Alpine (*Alpi*) mountain range that caps the northern part of Italy, and the *Appennini* mountain range that goes down the spine of the Italian peninsula. Note also the four major rivers (*fiumi*) of Italy, the *Po*, *Adige*, *Arno*, and *Tevere* (Tiber) that flow through the cities of Turin, Verona, Florence, and Rome, respectively; and the three major lakes (*laghi*) *Maggiore*, *Como*, and *Garda*, all in northern Italy. The seas (mari) that surround Italy include *Tirreno*, *Ligure*, *Adriatico*, and *Ionio*. The letters F, M, and L are often used on maps to indicate rivers, seas and lakes. Finally, note the two major volcanos of Italy, Vesuvius (*Vesuvio*) near Naples, and Etna near Catania.

Each state in turn is divided into "counties" (*province*). Counties are not likely to be familiar to foreigners, but they are important administrative units within each state, much like counties in the United States. We will not attempt to list all the provinces of each state, however we will list the provinces of Piedmont (*Piemonte*) as an illustrative example. The provinces of Piedmont are: *Alessandria*, *Asti*, *Biella*, *Cuneo*, *Novara*, *Torino*, *Verbania*, and *Vercelli*. Each province has its own capital city, usually with the same name as the province. See Map 3 for the location of the provinces of Piedmont. Note that the city of Turin (Torino) is the capital of both the state of Piedmont and the province of Turin. The governing body of a city is called *commune* in Italian. Small villages governed by a city are called *frazione*. Map 4 shows the physical aspecst of the province of Piedmont. Note that the Alps separate Piedmont from France and Switzerland. Piedmont includes three hilly areas, *il Monferrato*, *Le Langhe*, and *il Canavese* that are famous for their wines, and have their own cultural traditions that cut across provincial lines. Another famous area of Piedmont is the Po valley where rice and corn are grown in abundance. These are the ingredients used to make *risotto* and *polenta*, popular dishes in northern Italy. Other states in Italy are similarly divided into provinces and special areas.

Map 2. Physical Map of Italy

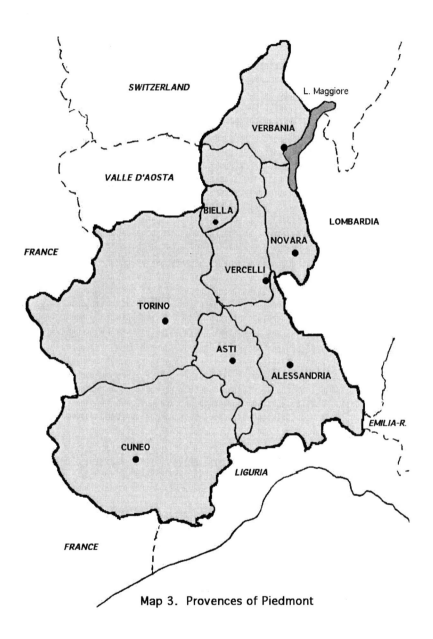

Map 3. Provences of Piedmont

11

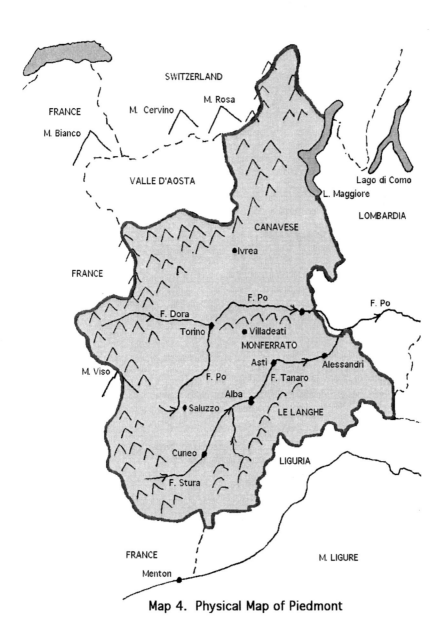

Map 4. Physical Map of Piedmont

1.5 A VERY SHORT HISTORY OF ITALY

In subsequent chapters, we will have more to say about certain periods of Italian history (*storia*). However, here we give a capsule view of the history of the Italian peninsula.

The Early Period (500 BC and earlier)

Among the early people to inhabit the peninsula were the Phoencians, the Greeks, the Celts, and the Etruscans. The Celts inhabited the northern part of the peninsula in the *Piemonte* area, the Etruscans the central portion, centered about *Toscana*, and the Greeks the southern part. The Greeks founded most of the cities in southern Italy, e.g. *Napoli* (Naples), *Crotone* (Crotone), *Siracusa* (Syracuse), etc. Many famous Greek mathematicians lived in southern Italy, e.g. Pythagoras (*ca.* 550 BC) in *Crotone*, and Archimedes (*ca.* 250 BC) in *Siracusa*.

The Roman Period (500 BC - 500 AD)

For about 1,000 years a small tribe, the *Latini,* ruled the peninsula, and most of the known world. They founded the city of *Roma*, and their language, Latin, became the basis of modern Italian. They constructed marvelous engineering structures, aqueducts, buildings, and roads, and gave civilization a system of law that is still in use in most of Europe. The Roman empire started with Caesar Augustus (27 BC) and ended with another Augustus, Romulus Augustus (476 AD).

The Dark Ages (500 - 1000)

In 238 AD, Germanic tribes (Visigoths, Ostrogoths, Huns, Vandals, Lombards) started to invade Italy. By 570 AD, the Lombards gained control of most of the peninsula. In 800 the Frankish ruler Charlemagne (*Carlo Magno*) was crowned Holy Roman Emperor by Pope Leo III. Venice was founded in 811 by people on the mainland trying to escape the invading Barbarians.

After the death of Charlemagne (814), there was total disarray in the peninsula and many rival city-states started to form. Arabs invaded Sicily and ruled the island for more than 200 years. They established Palermo as a center of arabic culture.

The Middle Ages (1000 - 1400)

This was the period of development of city-states and rule by Germanic emperors. Frederick I (*Barbarossa*) was crowned emperor of Rome in 1155. A rivalry between emperor and pope developed over who can name bishops and cardinals. Italy was divided into pro-emperor groups, the "Guibellines", and pro-pope groups, the "Guelfs". Normans, under Roger I, invaded Sicily circa 1036, and with the reign of Roger II, the Normans created a civilization in Palermo that was the envy of the world. Meanwhile, in northern Italy in 1056, *Umberto Biancamano*, originally from the region just south of Lake Geneva, invaded southern France and the Piedmont area. He initiated a dynasty, the House of Savoy, which ultimately became the ruling monarchy of a united Italy in 1861. This was a period of time when the peninsula became a battleground between competing foreign powers, in particular between France, Spain, and Germany. In 1282, the people of Sicily rebelled against their French rulers. The rebellion started with an episode that is now referred to as the "Sicilian Vespers" (*Vespri Siciliani*), made famous in one of Verdi's operas. A French soldier molested the wife of a Sicilian native during vesper services of Easter Monday. The natives slaughtered the French on the island. Few were spared. To identify anyone French, the natives made every doubtful person pronounce the Sicilian word *ciciri* (*ceci* in Italian, chickpeas in English). Most Frenchmen have difficulty pronouncing this word properly in the Sicilian dialect. Everyone mispronouncing this word was killed.

In 1347, *Cola di Rienzo* attempted to establish Rome as the capital of a united Italy, free of foreign domination, but ultimately failed and was murdered by a mob of his fellow Romans. About this same time the "Black Death" (Bubonic Plague) decimated the population of Italy. This was also a period of great achievements by Italians, e.g. the discoveries of *Marco Polo* (1298), the poetry of *Dante Alighieri* (*The Divine Comedy*, 1314), the art of *Giotto di Bondone* (1266 - 1337), and *Fra Angelico* (1387 - 1455), the life of *Francesco d'Assisi* (1181 - 1226), and the founding of the first University in Europe (University of Bologna, 1089). Map 5 shows the political status of Italy in the 1340s.

The Renaissance (1400 - 1500)

This period of time could also be called the "Florentine Period" because of the prominence of the city-state of Florence and the Medici family that unofficially ruled the city. The Medici dynasty was started by *Cosimo de' Medici*, who ruled from 1434 to 1464, and reached a peak during the rule of *Lorenzo de' Medici* from 1469 to the time of his death in 1492. Florence was nominally a republic, but the Medici, through their wealth, obtained mostly by banking interest, dominated the politics of the city and effectively ran the government. The Medici were very supportive of art and architecture, and during their rule art and architecture flourished. One of the major architects of the period was *Filippo Brunelleschi* (1377 - 1446) who designed the famous dome for the cathedral of Florence. Of course, sculptors and painters of the period are now legendary, *Donatello di Nicolo di Betto Bardi* (1386 - 1466), *Leonardo da Vinci* (1452 - 1519), *Michelangelo Buonarroti* (1475 - 1564), *Raffaello Sanzio d'Urbino* (1386 - 1466), to name a few.

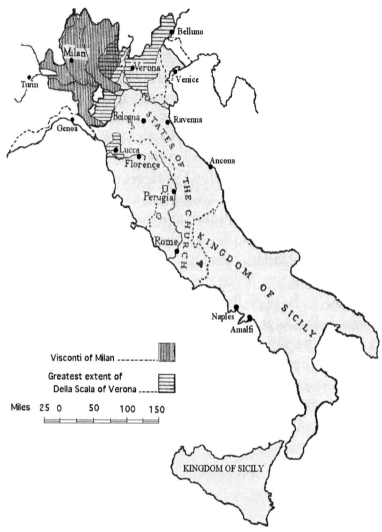

Map 5. Italy about 1340

Labels on map:
- Belluno
- Milan
- Verona
- Venice
- Turin
- Bologna
- Ravenna
- Genoa
- Lucca
- Florence
- Ancona
- Perugia
- STATES OF THE CHURCH
- Rome
- KINGDOM OF SICILY
- Naples
- Amalfi
- KINGDOM OF SICILY

Visconti of Milan --------
Greatest extent of
Della Scala of Verona _____

Miles 25 0   50   100 150

This was also a period of constant warfare between the city-states of Milan, Venice, Florence, Rome, Naples, etc. and between the city-states and foreign powers, in particular Germany, France, and Spain. This period witnessed new attempts to unite the peninsula into an "Italian" nation. One such attempt was by *Gian Galeazzo Visconti*, Duke of Milan (1379 - 1402). The attempt failed when he died in 1402. The peninsula was full of *condottieri,* soldiers for hire who fought for any city or country that paid enough. One such person, *Francesco Gonzaga*, Marquis of Mantova, almost destroyed the French army of Charles VIII at Fornovo in 1495, while employed by an "Italian" league of city-states. It is likely that if he had succeeded, Italy may have been spared the recurrent foreign domination it experienced in the years that followed. *Lodovico Sforza* (1451 - 1508), another Duke of Milan, also known as *Il Moro*, invited the French to invade Italy in 1494. Overall he was a disaster for Italy, but he did foster the arts and sciences, and it was he who invited *Leonardo da Vinci* to come and work in *Milano*. You can see a statue of Leonardo in front of *la Scala*, the famous opera house in Milan.

Florence was not only the center of the artistic and intellectual renaissance, but also the center of a moral renaissance created single-handedly by a Dominican monk, *Girolamo Savonarola* (1452 - 1498). Savonarola was born in Ferrara, entered a Dominican monastery in Bologna, and was then assigned to the monastery of San Marco in Florence in 1481. He was appalled by the immorality of the people and the clergy in Florence. While the arts flourished and bankers became wealthy, the poor starved women and children were regularly abused, and men were murdered for trifling. It was common to see bodies floating down the *Arno* river past *Ponte Vecchio*, the famous Florentine bridge. Right after the death of *Lorenzo de' Medici* in 1492, Savonarola's powerful sermons

GIROLAMO SAVONAROLA

Portrait by Fra Bartolommeo, in *Accademia di Belle Arti, Florence*

convinced the people to institute a democratic republic based on Christian principles. Florence became a "city of God." The poor were nurtured, the wealthy surrendered their luxuries, and the common people were given a say in running their city. But Savonarola had his enemies, the *bigi* who favored the return of the Medici family, the *arrabbiati* (the angry ones) who hated both Savonarola and the Medici, and, perhaps, most important of all, pope *Alessandro VI*. Savonarola's enemies called his followers the *piagnoni*, because they always left Savonarola's sermons crying (*piangere*, to cry in Italian). Perhaps it was too much to expect that a whole city would adhere to the stern moral principles of a monk for any extended period of time. His enemies ultimately triumphed and Savonarola was burned at the stake on May 23, 1498, in the *Piazza della Signoria*. To this day, every May 23rd people drop flowers on a plaque commemorating his death in the *piazza*.

Nicolo Machiavelli was a contemporary of Savonarola who had strong political ambitions. His philosophy of government differed radically from Savonarola's. Machiavelli believed that running a state was at total odds with living a moral life. He is probably best known for his philosophy that "the end justifies the means" ("*Nelle azione di tutti gli uomini, si guarda al fine*" – In the actions of all men they should look at the end result.) Just four weeks after the death of Savonarola, Machiavelli applied for the position of First Secretary to the *Signoria* (this term refers to the ruling body of Florence) and was awarded the position. Shortly thereafter, he was also appointed secretary to the *Ten of War*, the committee that dealt with military matters. These were purely administrative positions, but he performed his duties well and became well known both inside and outside the city. Savonarola and Machiavelli did share some common goals and experiences. They both wanted to see a democratic republic in Florence (although Machiavelli was willing to compromise for the right "prince"), and they both wanted to see all the foreigners driven out of Italy, and Italy united as a country.

SIMMS LIBRARY
ALBUQUERQUE ACADEMY

But, of course, the means to achieve these ends were very different. Savonarola based everything on God and the application of Christian principles, while Machiavelli based everything on force, intrigue, and the right "prince." In 1512, the Medici returned to power and the democratic republican government was eliminated, including Machiavelli's job. In 1513, Machiavelli was accused of participating in a plot to assasinate Giuliano de' Medici, and underwent the same torture that was applied to Savonarola, the *strapado*. The *strapado* was a common way to get a confession out of a prisoner in those days. A person was hung by the wrists behind the back and lifted to the top of a tall room, then dropped until just a few feet above the ground. This normally wrenched arms out of their sockets and produced the necessary confession. When applied to Savonarola, he confessed to being a heretic, but later recanted his confession. Machiavelli survived the ordeal, but was then exiled from Florence. During his exile, he wrote many books, among them: *The Prince*, *Discourses*, and *Florentine Histories*. *The Prince* is perhaps his most famous book. It deals with the things a ruler (a Prince) has to do to stay in power. Many feel *The Prince* still holds as a reasonable guide even for today's rulers, but not everyone is positive about the philosophy it contains. Bertrand Russell called it "a handbook for gangsters." Machiavelli dedicated *The Prince* to Giuliano de' Medici, in the hope that this would get him back his job. When Giuliano died in 1516, he rededicated it to Lorenzo de' Medici (the grandson of the Lorenzo who died in 1492), but he still did not get the job. In 1527 the Republic was reinstalled in Florence, but by this time many people felt that Machiavelli was too pro-Medici to be employed by the new republican government. Machiavelli died on June 21, 1527 and was buried in the Church of Santa Croce in Florence.

Nicolo Machiavelli, portrait by di Santi di Tito, Palazzo Vecchio, Florence

Finally, it should be noted that this was also a special period for Italian explorers, unfortunately for Italy, generally in the employment of some foreign country. Some well known examples include: *Cristoforo Colombo* (Christopher Columbus, 1451 - 1506) from Genova, working for Spain and discovering the "new world"; *Giovanni Caboto* (John Cabot, 1450 - 1498) from Venice, working for England and exploring the Canadian coast; and *Amerigo*

Vespucci (1454 - 1512) from Florence, exploring the north coast of the "new world" and ultimately bequeathing it his name.

The Spanish Period (1500 - 1800)

For the greater part of this three hundred year period, Spain was the major foreign power that ruled in Italy. In 1530, Charles V from Spain was crowned Holy Roman Emperor, and by 1559 the French were driven out of most of Italy, except for Turin and the Piedmont region. Map 6 shows the political status of Italy in 1559. The story of the Spanish domination of Milan in the early seventeenth century is vividly recounted in *Alessandro Manzoni's* classic novel *I Promessi Sposi*. The Spanish temporarily lost control of Naples to the Austrians from 1707 to 1735, but then Don Carlos from the Bourbon dynasty of Spain, regained control and ruled Naples from 1735 to 1759. He ruled as Charles III, King of Naples and Sicily. His Bourbon heirs were to rule southern Italy, until the arrival of *Garibaldi* in 1860.

At the beginning of this period, in 1526, Italy came close once more to ridding itself of foreign domination. That year *Giovanni de' Medici* was appointed Papal General in charge of an army of the "Italian League," supported by Rome, Florence, Venice and Milan, to fight the German Emperor. He was also known as *Giovanni dalle Bande Nere* (John of the Black Guards), and he fought with some success against the German armies. For his defense of the independence of the Italian peninsula, he became known as *Giovanni d'Italia*. Unfortunately, he was wounded in battle and died shortly thereafter. Once more Italy lost an opportunity for unification.

In 1706, *Vittorio Amedeo II,* a duke of the House of Savoy, defeated the French who were besieging the city of Turin. The victory established Piedmont as a strong and independent region, which ultimately was to provide Italy with its first king.

DUCHY
OF
SAVOY

P. OF
TRENTO

D. OF
MILAN

VENETIAN REPUBLIC

R. PARMA
OF GENOA

D.OF

HUNGARY

2

3

4

5

6

D.
OF
FLORENCE

STATES
OF
THE
CHURCH

8

KINGDOM
OF
NAPLES

KINGDOM
OF
SARDINIA

KINGDOM
OF
SICILY

50   0   50   100   150 Miles

Marquisate of Saluzzo 1
Marquisate of Monferrat 2
Mantua 3
Ferrar 4
Duchy of Mondana 5
Republic of Lucca 6
Duchy of Urbino 7
Stato dei Presidi 8

Venetian Republic ....

Spanish Possessions ....

Map 6. Italy in 1559

The Unification of Italy (1800 - 1900)

This is the period of the three R's, *rivoluzione* (revolution), *restaurazione* (restoration), and *risorgimento* (resurgence). In 1796, *Napoleone Buonaparte*, a Corsican, born one year after France acquired Corsica from Genova, invaded northern Italy, and brought the French revolution to the Italian peninsula. In 1799, France annexed the Papal States and banished various monarchs from their domains. *Vittorio Emanuele I*, king of *Sardegna e Piemonte* (Sardinia and Piedmont) was exiled to the Island of Sardinia and Ferdinand II, king of Naples and Sicily, was exiled to Sicily. Napoleon set up various "republics," e.g. the Cisalpine republic in the former papal states and the Parthenopean republic in the former kingdom of Naples. When Napoleon made himself emperor in 1814 these various republics were converted to kingdoms. The former Cisalpine republic became the **Kingdom of Italy,** even though it encompassed only a small fraction of the Italian peninsula. Piedmont remained under direct control of France. After Austria and their allies defeated France, all the Italian monarchs were restored to their former kingdoms. Austria gained control of Milan and Venice, and exercised strong control over the rest of the peninsula. When, in 1848, the Milanese revolted against their Austrian rulers, the Savoyan king of Sardinian and Piedmont, *Carlo Alberto*, came to their aid but was defeated at *Novara*. This effort to rid Italy of Austrian rule is often referred to as the "first war of independence." Although revolutionary France had been defeated, sentiment against absolute monarchies and for a united Italy increased. *Giuseppe Mazzini* (1805 - 1872) was a political activist who championed these two causes. He founded the secret society, *la Giovine Italia* (Young Italy), through which he advocated the unification of Italy and the establishment of a democratic republic. In 1848, *Carlo Alberto* was pressured into granting a constitution (*statuto albertino*), which ultimately became the constitution of a united Italy. After his defeat by the Austrians, he abdicated to his son *Vittorio Emanule II* (1820 - 1878). *Vittorio Emanuele II* appointed *Cavour* (*Conte CamilloBenso di Cavour* 1810 - 1861) to head his new constitutional monarchy. Cavour was an extremely astute politician and diplomat. He negotiated with Napoleon III of France, who had proclaimed himself emperor of France in 1852, to join forces with the Savoy monarchy and fight the Austrians in Lombardy. In 1859, the French and Piedmontese armies defeated the Austrians. This came to be known as the "second war of independence." As a consequence of their victory, the Piedmontese kingdom was extended to Lombardy, and the Austrian grip on the Italian peninsula was broken. Only Venice remained in the hands of the Austrians. The Piedmontese had to pay a price for French cooperation. They lost the city of Nice and part of Savoy on the French side of the Alps. However, by agreeing to plebiscites in Nice and French Savoy, the Piedmontese gained in turn French support for plebicites in other parts of Italy, and in 1859 the regions of Tuscany and Emilia-Romagna voted to join the Piedmont monarchy. The momentum for unification of Italy increased. In the spring of 1860, *Giuseppe Garibaldi* (1807 - 1882) collected a force of about one thousand soldiers, the famous *Mille*, initially with the thought of preventing the French from taking Nice, his home town, but then turning to the liberation of Sicily and Naples from the Bourbon King Ferdinando II. He defeated the Bourbon King, and turned over the kingdom of Two Sicilies to the Piedmont monarchy. Garibaldi was not a monarchist, but he felt that the Piedmont monarchy was the only feasible way to achieve a united Italy. Indeed, at the end of 1860, the Piedmont monarchy, under *Vittorio Emanuele II*, controlled all of Italy, except Rome and Venice. On March 17, 1861, *Vittorio Emanuele II* was proclaimed by the Piedmontese parliament, "king of Italy," and the first capital of the united Italy was established in Turin, the capital city of the House of

Savoy. But the Italians wanted Rome as their capital. The French were protecting the Pope and blocking the Italians from taking Rome. In 1864, another deal was struck with Napoleon III.

Giuseppe Mazzini

Giuseppe Garibaldi

Vittorio Emanuele II

Camillo de Cavour

The Italians would move their capital from Turin to Florence, and the French would eventually let the Italians enter Rome. Indeed, in 1866,the Italian capital was moved to Florence. Venice was outside the new kingdom of Italy and still remained under Austrian control. In 1866, the Italian kingdom signed a treaty with Prussia, an enemy of Austria, which led to a war known as the "third war of independence." The Italians did not do well in this war, but the Prussians soundly defeated the Austrians, and Austria was forced to cede Venice to Italy indirectly through France. This left only Rome outside the Italian kingdom. In 1867, *Garibaldi* lead a force to liberate Rome, but was defeated by the French at Mentana. Finally, on the 20th of September 1870, the Italian army, under the command of *Vittorio Emanule II,* took Rome, which was defended by only a small papal army. The French were too busy fighting the Prussians at the time. This date is so important in Italian history that just about every city in Italy has a street named *XX Settembre*. Of course there are also streets named after the heros of the *Risorgimento*, i.e. *Cavour, Vittorio Emanule II, Garibaldi*, and *Mazzini.* Map 7 shows the evolution of the unification of Italy. The dates on the map indicate the year each region was united to the kingdom of the house of Savoy. The pope at this time, Pius IX (*Pio Nono*), was deprived of all his temporal powers. He refused to recognize the new kingdom of Italy, and forbade all Catholics from participating in its government. It is a bit ironic that the same year that the pope lost all his temporal power, the Vatican Council declared the dogma of Papal Infallibility. It was not until the Fascist regime that peace was made between the Vatican and the Italian State. *Vittorio Emanuele II* died in 1878, and was succeeded by *Umberto I* who reigned until 1900 when an anarchist assassinated him. The end of this period witnessed an attempt by the new kingdom to obtain colonies in Africa. The Italians were defeated in Ethiopia, but obtained Eritrea as a colony and Somaliland as a protectorate.

27

Map 7. The Unification of Italy

Italy in the Twentieth Century

In July of 1900, *Vittorio Emanuele III*, son of *Umberto I*, became the third king of Italy. Italy was a constitutional monarchy with a democratically elected Parliament. However, the parliament was divided into many contending factions: federalists (who wanted a decentralized system of states) versus centralists, monarchists versus republicans, communists versus capitalists, north versus south (southern Italy is commonly referred to as *il Mezzogiorno,* in Italian), etc. On top of all these differences, there were groups that were happy to see parliament disappear, e.g. the Catholic Church (who after 1870 refused to recognize the Italian government), and the followers of *Vilfredo Pareto*, who preached government by the successful elite. *Pareto* graduated as an engineer from the *Politecnico di Torino* in 1870, but went on to become a world renown mathematical economist. His theory of multi-objective optimization is well known among modern systems engineers and mathematical economists. The Fascist dictator *Mussolini* admired *Pareto* greatly and claimed to have studied with him when he was teaching in Switzerland. Italy was not being governed very well at the time and the economic situation was desperate. Between 1900 and 1910, many Italians immigrated to North and South America. In particular, from 1910 to 1914 three million Italian immigrants were recorded entering the United States.

In 1917, the "Great War" (World War I) broke out. Italy joined the Allies (France, England, United States, etc.) against Germany. At *Caporetto* the Italians suffered a humiliating defeat, but a year later, in 1918, they won an important victory at *Vittorio Veneto*. After the war, Italy gained the city of *Trieste*, but few other concessions from either the Germans or the Allies. The disillusionment with parliament, the war, the economic situation, etc. provided fertile ground for the growth of Fascism. In 1922, *Benito*

Mussolini (1883 - 1945) and his followers, *le camicie nere* (the black shirts), marched on Rome. After the march, the king asked *Mussolini* to form a new government. This is the beginning of the Fascist period, ending only in 1945 with the death of *il duce* (the leader, as *Mussolini* was commonly called). During this period, *Mussolini* tried to convert the Italians into a nation of "Roman" warriors. He placed on the twenty *Lire* coin the motto, "*Meglio vivere un giorno da leone che cento anni da pecora*" (Better to live one day as a lion then one hundred years as a sheep). But even he had to admit that changing Italians was not easy. He is quoted as saying "*Governare gli italiani non è difficile, è inutile*" (Governing Italians is not difficult, it's useless).

Realizing that he needed the Catholic Church to consolidate his power, he concluded the Laterano treaty of 1929 that recognized, for the first time since 1870, the sovereignty of the Vatican. After some initial defeats, Italy conquered Ethiopia in 1935 and *Vittorio Emanuele III* was declared Emperor. In June 1940, Italy declared war on England and France and World War II began. In the beginning, the war went well for the Axis powers, Germany, Italy, and Japan, but then the tide turned and on July 25, 1943 the king dismissed *Mussolini* as Prime Minister. With support from the Germans *Mussolini* established a republic headquartered at *Salò* on the shores of Lake Garda (commonly referred to as the republic of *Salò*). But the republic was short lived and on April 28, 1945 *Mussolini* was executed near Lake *Como*, along with his mistress *Clara Petacci*, by Italian partisans as he attempted to escape Italy. As a consequence of its defeat in World War II, Italy lost Trieste.

In 1946, *Vittorio Emanuele III* abdicated in favor of his son *Umberto II* who reigned for only about one month. In a referendum on the monarchy, the Italians voted to reject the monarchy, with the only significant support for the monarchy coming from the south

(Naples voted 80% to retain the monarchy). In the general election that same year, the Communist party (*Partito Comunista Italiano*, PCI) won 19% of the popular vote while the new Catholic Christian Democratic party (*Partito Democrazia Cristiana*, PDC) won 31%. In 1948, George Marshall, U.S. Secretary of State, made it clear that Italy would stop receiving economic help from the United States if the Communists won in the general election. The Communists were defeated, but remained a powerful force in Italian politics, reaching a peak of popularity in 1976 when they received 34% of the popular vote, compared to 39% for the Christian Democratic party. Largely due to the Communist Party, divorce was legalized in Italy in 1970. The film *Alfredo, Alfredo,* starring Dustin Hoffman, takes a humorous view of the new divorce law.

The combined support of the United States and the Catholic Church kept the Christian Democratic party in control from 1946 to 1992. In a country where the law is not always taken very seriously (it is common to talk about "legal Italy versus real Italy"), it is not surprising that corruption ultimately gets out of control in a party that has ruled for forty six years. With the communist threat diminished, due to the downfall of communism in the former Soviet Union, the wide spread government and party corruption was finally exposed, and the term *tangentopoli* (bribe-city) became a common term in the press.

At the present time, the political situation in Italy is up in the air, however economically Italy is doing reasonably well, except for relatively high unemployment in the south. More Italians are enjoying *la dolce vita* (the sweet life) than ever before. Even though the cost of living is very high, Italians can cope because many have inherited housing, families pool their economic resources, and children put off marriage as long as possible.

Television has helped unite the country, both linguistically and politically. It has also introduced a large dose of American culture. English has replaced Latin as the language of the educated Italian. It appears that the regional customs and dialects are disappearing. But there are movements to preserve regional cultures. There are even some political movements, such as *la Lega Nord* in northern Italy, which advocates very strong autonomy for the regions. In any case, it is likely that future Italian history will revolve around the integration of Italy into the European community.

Some Historical Days of the Second Millennium

Italians are very sensitive to specific days in their history. As mentioned in the preceeding section, almost every city in Italy has a street named *XX Settembre* (20 September). This day commemorates the liberation of the city of Rome from papal forces in 1870. Following is a list of a few other memorial days of the second millennium.

On November 22 in 1220, Frederick II was crowned emperor of the Holy Roman Empire by Pope Honorius III. Frederick II goes on to become king of the two Sicilies (Sicily and Naples) and in 1224 he founded the University of Naples (now called in Italian, *Università degli Studi di Napoli, Federico II*).

On March 30 in 1282, the Sicilians in Parlermo revolted against their French rulers, and massacred all the French they could find. This event which occurred during vesper prayers the Monday after Easter day, is referred to as the Sicilian Vespers (*Vespri Siciliani*, in Italian*)*. *Guiseppe Verdi* wrote an opera about this day in Italian history.

On July 2 in 1465, the fleet of Alfonse of Aragone returned to Naples after defeating the French fleet off of Ischia. This event is celebrated in a famous painting in the Neapolitan Museum at

Capodimonte. This painting is available as a reprint in almost every souvenir store in Naples.

On April 8 in 1492, Lorenzo de' Medici died. Shortly after his death, Florence became a democratic republic under the inspiration of *Girolamo Savonarola*. Of course, all Americans know the year 1492 as the year Christopher Columbus discovered the "New World."

On July 6 in 1495, an army of the Italian league (Papal states, Milan, Naples, and Venice) led by *Francesco Gonzaga*, Marquis of Mantua, attacked the French army of Charles VIII near the town of *Fornovo* (located about 20 kilometers southwest of *Parma*). The French army escaped, but many historians agree that if this Italian army could have decisively defeated the French, unification of Italy would have occurred much earlier than 1861.

On May 23 in 1498, *Girolamo Savonarola* was burned at the stake for heresy in the *Piazza della Signoria* in Florence. A plaque identifies the exact spot where he was burned on the ground (which most tourists do not even notice as they wander through the famous Florentine Plaza). However, tourists should be reminded of Savonarola when they visit the huge hall (*Salone dei Cinquecento*) in the *Palazzo Vecchio*. This hall was built to handle Florence's expanded democratic government that was inspired by Savonarola.

On May 6 in 1527, Spanish and German troops started a brutal sack of Rome which lasted more than nine months. With the deaths of the commanding general of these troops the day before, all semblance of discipline was lost. In addition, most of the Germans were Lutheran, and they took special delight in sacking this capital city of Catholicism. Their Spanish comrades were just happy to get all the booty they could.

On September 7 in 1706, Prince *Vittorio Amedeo* II, from the House of Savoy, defeated the French in Turin. This is a very important date in Italian history since it signaled the start of a strong monarchy, the House of Savoy, which ultimately became the reigning monarchy of a united Italy. In 1720, the Piedmontese prince *Vittorio Amedeo* II became king as King of Sardinia.

On May 1 in 1797, Napoleon declares war on Venice. The last doge (elected ruler) of Venice, *Ludovico Manin*, is ousted from office, after more than one thousand years of republican rule. (The first doge, *Paolucio Anafesto*, was elected in 697.)

On September 7 in 1835, the religious feast day of the church of *Santa Maria di Piedigrotta*, celebrated with great pomp by the Bourbon royal House, was converted into a musical festival. The musical tradition of *Piedigrotta* lasted until 1954.

On March 4 in 1848, King *Carlo Alberto*, of the House of Savoy, accepted a constitution that limited the power of the monarchy. This constitution became the constitution of a united Italy in **1861.**

On June 4 in 1859, a French-Piedmontese army defeated the Austrians, liberating Milano from Austrian rule. This is a key date in the unification of Italy under the royal House of Savoy.

On March 17 in 1861, *Vittorio Emanuele* II, King of Sardinia, was declared king of Italy by the parliament of the House of Savoy in Torino.

On September 20 in 1870, the Italian army under the command of King *Vittorio Emanuele* II finally liberated Rome from papal control. Look for the street sign *XX Settembre* when you are in Italy.

On October 30 in 1918, the Italians defeated the Germans at *Vittorio Veneto* (a city about 50 kilometers north of Venice). This was a decisive battle in ending World War I. The armistice ending the war was signed November 4, 1918. *Quatro Novembre* (4th of November) is a common street name in Italy while *Vittorio Veneto* is a common plaza name.

On October 28 in 1922, the fascists marched on Rome. The next day King *Vittorio Emanuele* III invited Mussolini to form a government. Given the outcome of World War II, it is not surprising that there are no street names of XXVIII *Ottobere* in Italy. But one can imagine the situation, if the outcome had been different.

On June 2 in 1946, the Italian electorate voted in favor of disbanding the monarchy and moving to a republic form of government. The royal House of Savoy's "white-cross" symbol was removed from the Italian flag, and the males of the House of Savoy were banned from Italy.

On December 1 in 1970, divorce laws were passed. Divorce finally became a legal possibility in Italy.

1.6 EDUCATION IN ITALY

In Italy children go to elementary school (*scuola elementare*) and middle school (*scuola media*), as in the United States. However at the high school level one already starts to specialize. Those who plan to go onto college go to a *liceo* to pursue classical studies (*classico*), scientific studies (*scientifico*), or linguistics (*linguistico*). Those who wish to obtain some direct job training go to an *istituto tecnico* to focus on industrial (*industriale*) or commercial (*commerciale*) trades. There are no "community colleges" as we have here in the United States. This training is done at the high school level in Italy. The high school programs are of five years duration, and one normally finishes at age 18-19. There is a difficult national level exam (*Esame di Maturità*) required to obtain a high school "degree." However anyone who has passed the *Esame di*

Maturità is eligible to enter a public University of their choice, tuition free (only minimal fees are required to take exams). Almost all universities in Italy are public. The period of college education is normally five years, and the degree awarded is referred to as the *Laurea* (a degree which is somewhere between our Bachelor's degree and our Master's degree). To obtain a *Laurea,* one must write a thesis (*tesi*) and defend it in public, at graduation time! Graduation follows immediately after the defense of the thesis, and your college GPA, with the thesis grade averaged in is announced to the whole graduation audience (parents, family, friends, etc.) With the Laurea you are given the title *Dottore* (Doctor), so people with college degrees are often referred to as *dottore*, rather than mister or miss/misses. Recently, Italy introduced a research Ph.D. (*Dottore di Ricerca*), similar to our Ph.D., especially for those interested in academic careers. Those who wish to study law or medicine, do so directly from high school, while in the United States, professional education in law and medicine normally requires a pre-professional bachelors degree. Finally, it is interesting to note that in Italy, like most countries in the world, there is no such thing as "intercollegiate athletics" or "athletic scholarships."

1.7 NOTES AND REFERENCES

There are very few books with the term *Italian Culture* in the title. Indeed one may ask what topics should be included under such a title. Webster's New Collegiate Dictionary defines culture as, "the customary beliefs, social forms, and material traits of a racial, religious, or social group." The editors, David Forgacs and Robert Lumley, of the volume, *Italian Cultural Studies: An Introduction* include such topics as politics, linguistics, religion, gender relations, movies, music, and television, but they point out that the term *Italian Culture* would not be understood outside the United States, especially not in Italy. In any case, we have elected to include in our volume on *Italian Culture* topics such as language, food, history, science and mathematics, popular songs, geography, and something on the immigrant experience. The text of Cantarella, *The Italian Heritage,* traces Italian Culture over the last millennium. It covers a wide range of topics, including literature, politics, science, etc. by discussing the contributions of famous Italians such as Dante, Garibaldi, Marconi, etc. *Italy. A Cultural Guide,* by Ernest O. Hauser is a very valuable one-volume encyclopedic guide of terms and personalities associated with Italian culture.

One of the very best ways to learn Italian pronunciation is to listen to, and sing along with Italian popular songs. A number of such songs are collected in the chapter *Italian Culture through Popular Songs*, together with references to commercially available cassettes/CDs. There are also many language cassettes specifically designed to learn Italian pronunciation, too many to enumerate here. Of course, the best way is to have access to a native Italian.

There are also countless books on Italian history, many written by English historians. The English always had a special interest in Italy. One particularly prolific English writer on the subject of Italian history is Denis Smith. His books on the subject include *Mussolini: A Biography, A History of Sicily* (two volumes: *Medieval Sicily*, 800 - 1713 and *Modern Sicily*, After 1713), and *Italy and its Monarchy* (about the Piedmontese monarchy that ruled a united Italy from 1861 - 1946). Butler's book, *The Lombard Communes*, details the struggle between the city-states of Northern Italy and the German emperors, Frederick I (*Barbarossa*) and Frederick II, during the early middle ages. A detailed account of the reign of Frederick II may be found in Abulafia's book, *Frederick II: A Medieval Emperor.* For an account of the city-states in Italy during the Renaissance, see Lauro Martines' *Power and Imagination*, and for a description of the city-states in the southern Italian peninsula in the ninth and tenth centuries, see Barbara Kreutz's text, *Before the Normans.* Kreutz's book contains an excellent account of the interaction between the Lombard city-states of Naples, Amalfi, Solerno, the Byzantine empire, and the Muslim world just before the Norman conquest of southern Italy in the year 1036.

A very complete history of Venice may be found in Wiel's, *A History of Venice: From Its Founding To The Unification Of Italy.* One of the earliest and longest lived Republics in Italy, Venice was ruled by *Dodges* from 697 AD (*Paolo Lucio Anafesto)* to 1797 (*Ludovico Manin).*

A contemporary study of Renaissance Italy, from 1490 to 1534, may be found in Francesco Guicciardini's classic text, *The History of Italy.* Two short but very informative books on Italian history are Lintner's *A Traveller's History of Italy* and Hearder's *Italy: A Short History.* For a history of Italy after World War II, see Ginsborg's *A History of Contemporary Italy.*

The Jewish community of Piedmont played a significant role in supporting the house of Savoy in the unification of Italy. In return, many restrictions placed on Jews were removed. To celebrate these new freedoms, the Jewish community hired one of Turin's most famous architects, *Alessandro Antonelli,* to design a huge synagogue that could accommodate over 1,500 people. The project was started in 1863, but by 1877 funds had run out and the only partially completed structure was sold to the city of Turin. It was not until 1897 that the structure was completed. For many years it stood as the tallest brick structure in the world, at 167 meters tall. The building is called *Mole Antonelliana,* and is now a film museum. Turin was the original capital of movie films in Italy. The *Mole Antonelliana* is now one of Turin's most famous landmarks. A view of the *Mole* is captured in our cover.

38

Many famous authors traveled to Italy and wrote about their experiences, especially in the eighteenth and nineteenth centuries. A tour of Italy was the fashionable thing for the "rich and famous" to do at the time. The standard tour included Milan, Verona, Venice, Florence, Rome, Naples, Pompei, Palermo, and Syracuse. Some of the travelers included Charles Dickens (see *American Notes and Pictures from Italy*), Johann Wolfgang Goethe (see *Italian Journey*), David Herbert Lawrence (see, *Twilight in Italy: Sea and Sardinia; Etruscan Places*), Ralph Waldo Emerson (see, Barish's *Emerson in Italy*), and Henry James (see, *Italian Hours*). The travel accounts published by these famous authors provide an excellent way to learn about the geography, politics, and culture of the country.

An excellent contemporary account of a tour of Sicily may be found in Kubly's *Easter in Sicily*. Herbert Kubly, a well known author and reporter, recounts his coastal travels around the island of Sicily during an Easter period some ten years after the end of World War II. His stops included *Palermo* (capital of Norman and modern Sicily), *Erice* (spectacular mountain-top Norman village, now a popular site for scientific congresses), *Montelepre* (the hometown of the famous Sicilian bandit *Salvatore Giuliano,* the protagonist in Puzo's novel *The Sicilian,* who wanted to see Sicily become the 49th state of the United States), *Agrigento* (originally called *Girgenti,* site of many ancient Greek temples), *Piazza Armerina* (site of a famous Roman villa, still largely intact), *Siracusa* (capital of the early Greek civilization in Sicily), *Catania* (with nearby volcanic mount Etna), and *Taormina* (resort town located at the top of a cliff with a magnificent view of mount Etna and the Mediterranean). In his book , *American in Italy,* Kubly describes his travels to other cities in Italy a year earlier, including Turin, Florence, Naples, Rome, Milan, and Venice.

Runciman's text, *The Sicilian Vespers*, covers the complete story of this historic event, which took place in Palermo, March 29, 1282. The text also provides a detailed history of Sicily during this period of time. A wonderful book about Greek civilization in *Siracusa* (Syracuse) in the fourth century B.C. is the novel by Mary Renault, *The Mask of Apollo*. For a contemporary view of Sicily see Peter Robb's, *Midnight in Sicily*. It focuses on the 1995-96 Mafia trials in Palermo, but it also includes many observations about Sicilian culture, both modern and ancient.

The classic novel, *The Leopard*, by *Giuseppe Tomasi di Lampedusa*, provides a great deal of insight into the Sicily of the *Risorgimento*, a Sicily that for many centuries suffered domination from outside powers. To quote from the novel,

> *"For over twenty-five centuries we've been bearing the weight of superb and heterogeneous civilizations, all from outside, none made by ourselves, none we could call our own"*

Of course there are books written on all of Italy's major historical figures. For example:

•*Savonarola*

Romola, by George Eliot (a novel about a woman, *Romola*, and her life in the times of *Savonarola*).

Life and Times of Girolamo Savonarola, by Pasquale Villari (two volumes considered to be the definitive work on the life of *Savonarola*).

Savonarola, by William Van Wyck (a biography in dramatic episodes).

A Crown of Fire, by Pierre Van Paassen (an account of the life and times of *Girolamo Savonarola).*

The Elect Nation, by Lorenzo Polizzotto. (a study of the heritage of Savonarolian philosophy from 1494-1545).

•*Medici*

The Medici, by James Cleugh (a history about one of the most famous families of Florence, the *Medici*, including sketches of *Cosimo, Lorenzo, Alessandro*, and *Catherine de' Medici).*

•*Garibaldi*

Garibaldi and his Enemies, by Christopher Hibbert (an intriguing portrait of *Garibaldi* and his contemporaries, *Mazzini, Cavour, Vittorio Emanuele II*, etc. and the *Risorgimento* period).

•*Mussolini*

Mussolini, by Denis Mack Smith (this book is considered by many to be the standard English-language biography of *Benito Mussolini*).

My Rise and Fall, by Benito Mussolini (A recently published compilation of Mussolini's two autobiographies: *My Autobiograph*, published in English in 1928, and *The Fall of Mussolini: His Own Story*, published in English in 1948. The first volume covers the period of time from his birth, July 29, 1883, to the firm establishment of the Fascist regime by the late 1920s. The second volume covers the year of his decline, after the Grand Fascist Council voted him out of power on July 24, 1943.)

•*Machiavelli*

Machiavelli in 90 Minutes, by Paul Strathern (a very good 90 page summary of Machiavelli's life and works).

Machiavelli in Hell, by Sebastian de Grazia (a more detailed analysis of Machiavelli's life and works, with more emphasis on the "evil" aspects of both. A good illustration of the *strapado* torture can be found on page 37 of this book.).

The Life and Times of Nicolò Machiavelli, by Pasquale Villari (this is perhaps the most complete work on Machiavelli in two volumes).

The Man of the Rennaisance, by Ralph Roeder (this book also covers the life of Savonarola).

An engrossing novel about Italians fighting in the *Alto Adige* area of Italy during World War I is Helprin's novel, *A Soldier of the Great War.* It describes the nightmare of trench warfare and the lasting effect this war had on a whole generation of Italians. In a letter to his parents the hero of the book, *Alessandro,* writes,

> *"I don't care about our claims on the Alto Adige, so I'm fighting for nothing, but so is everyone and that's not the point. A nightmare has no justification, but you try your best to last through it, even if that means playing by the rules. I suppose a nightmare is having to play by rules that make no sense, for a purpose that is entirely alien, without control of either one's fate or even one's actions. To the extent that I do have control, I'll do what I can. Unfortunately, the war is ruled inordinately by chance, to the point almost where human action seems to have lost its meaning. They're executing soldiers not only for theft and desertion, but*

sometimes, for nothing. I believe that after the war, for a long time, perhaps even for the rest of the century, the implications of this will reverberate throughout almost everything...."

The Great War certainly reverberated in the life of our father/grandfather, *Fioretto Dorato*, who fought in the battle of *Vittorio Veneto* as a boy of nineteen. The war scarred him psychologically for the rest of his life, which he ended, on March 22, 1978.

The economic and political chaos in Italy, just before and after the "Great War", resulted in a mass immigration of Italians to the United States in the period 1900 - 1930, and resulted in the birth of fascism. Patrucco's scholarly book, *The Critics of the Italian Parliamentary System, 1860 - 1915* chronicles the difficulty Italians were having with "democratic" institutions during this period of time.

Two Jewish-Italians from Turin, *Carlo Levi* and *Primo Levi* wrote of their experiences in Italy during World War II. In *Primo Levi*'s book, *The Periodic Table*, each chapter has a title taken from the name of an element in the periodic table of elements, from Argon to Carbon. *Primo Levi*, a chemist by profession, linked the subject matter of each chapter to the chemical properties of the particular element. For example, in his first chapter titled Argon, he discusses the hidden nature of the Jewish community in Piedmont, hidded like the inert element Argon. *Carlo Levi*, a medical doctor by profession, wrote the book *Christ Stopped at Eboli*. In 1935 he was exiled to a primitive village in *Basilicata* for his opposition to the Fascist regime. The village, *Gagliano*, was about seventy miles south of the city of *Eboli*. It was such a God-forsaken place that the natives would often say, "Christ stopped short of here, at *Eboli.*"

Two excellent novels that tell the story of Italian immigrants in the United States are Chay's *Pilgrims Pride* and Puzo's *The Fortunate Pilgrim*. It is interesting that both these books have the word "Pilgrim" in their titles. Indeed, Italians were one of the many modern "pilgrims" that immigrated to the United States from Europe. Chay's book recounts the story of a Piedmontese family that settles in a mining town in Southern Colorado at the turn of the century, while Puzo's book is a story of a Neapolitan family that settles in the lower west side of Manhattan (Hell's Kitchen) in the late 1920's.

Must reading for anyone who wishes to understand Italy and Italians is Barzini's *The Italians: A Full-Length Portrait Featuring Their Manners and Morals*. The chapter titles of this book provide an excellent outline for a course on Italian Culture, i.e.

•**The Peaceful Invasion**. A chronicle of tourism in Italy from ancient to modern times.

•**The External Pilgrimage**. Pilgrimages to Rome, the Holy City throughout history.

•**The Fatal Charm of Italy**. The attraction of Italian art, music, and the sweet life (*la dolce vita*).

•**The Importance of Spectacle**. The importance of "looking good" (*fare una bella figura*) to Italians.

•**Illusion and Cagliostro**. The tendency for some Italians to deceive, personified by Count *Alessandro di Cagliostro* (born Giuseppe Balsamo, in Palermo in 1743). *Cagliostro* was a con artist par excellence. His most famous swindle was doubling the size of a diamond ring. *Casanova* and *Mussolini* could be cited as other examples of this characteristic.

•**The Other Face of the Coin**. The problem of "adjusting" (*sistemazione*) in Italy, to too many laws, too much injustice. The first author was once told by an Italian policeman, when he complained about someone going through a red light, "what do you want, we're Italians."

•*Cola di Rienzo* **or the Obsession With Antiquity**. An entertaining account of Cola di Rienzo's attempt to make Rome the center of a united Italy in 1347. The obsession with the recreation of a Roman Empire in Italy is exemplified further by *Mussolini's* regime.

•*Mussolini* **or the Limitations of Showmanship**. A short account of *Mussolini's* career and the key reason for his ultimate downfall, more "show than substance."

•**Realism and** *Guicciardini*. In Italy, "realism" has a history of meaning to live with corruption, foreign invasions, and tyrants. Two Florentines, *Machiavelli* (born in 1469) and *Guicciardini* (born in 1482) show how it is possible to live with "realism" and still succeed. This chapter is their story.

•**The Pursuit of Life**. A short dialog on the daily struggles of life in modern Italy.

•**The Power of the Family**. To quote Barzini directly, "*The Italian family is a strong hold in a hostile land: within its walls and among its members, the individual finds consolation, help, advice, provisions, loans, weapons, allies, and accomplices to aid him in his pursuits.*" The Popes took care of their families, just as the Mafia does today. And of course, *La Mamma* is the center of the family.

•**How to Succeed**. In a nutshell Barzini says, " belong to the right organization."

•**The *Problema del Mezzogiorno*.** The problem of southern Italy (*Mezzogiorno*), generally meaning the Italian peninsula south of Naples, and the islands of Sicily and Sardinia. Traditionally this has been the poorer part of Italy. Contrast is made between the North's emphasis on economic success and the South's emphasis on political success.

•**Sicily and the Mafia.** The Mafia, both in Sicily and the United States, as a reaction to a hostile environment. *Gli amici degli amici* (Friends of "the friends" as the *Mafiosi* often call themselves), as an example of the "right organization" for success.

•**Forever and After.** A tale of the battle at *Fornovo* in 1495 between a League of Italian States and the army of the French monarch, Charles VIII. The Italian League almost defeated the French invaders in this battle. As Barzini points out, if the Italian league had defeated the French, it is likely that the course of Italian history would have changed significantly. Italy could well have become a united country at that point and might well have avoided all the subsequent foreign invasions. One dramatic event that occurred "after" that is described in this chapter, is the sack of Rome in 1527 by the German Emperor Charles V.

•**The Perennial Baroque.** A short history of the few centuries after the sack of Rome in 1527. The domination of the Spanish in southern Italy and Milan.

An amusing view of Italians may be found in Giorgio Bocca's *In Che Cosa Credono Gli Italiani* (What Do Italians Believe In)? Basically, he claims Italians are very schizophrenic. They believe in God, but they love to sin. They believe in united Europe, but they can drum up real enthusiasm only for their local village or city. He concludes, however, that there are two things that all of Italy believes in. One is yelling (the title of chapter VI is *Urlo dunque sono* - I yell therefore I am), and the other is **not** waging war.

Another book which attempts to define Italy and Italians is Paul Hofmann's *That Fine Italian Hand*. There is a great deal of overlap between Hofmann's book and Barzini's; however, Hofmann provides an "outsiders" (non-Italian) view of Italy, while Barzini provides the "inside" view. Also by Hoffman is the book *Cento Città: A Guide to the "Hundred Cities & Towns" of Italy*. This book covers the smaller cities and towns of Italy.

Someone planning to travel extensively or do business in Italy would do well to read Flower and Falassi's, *Culture Shock, Italy - A Guide to Customs and Etiquette*.

An excellent book that deals with the translation of Italian culture to America is the text of Malpezzi and Clements, *Italian-American Folklore*. This book deals with the Italian immigrant communities in the United States and covers such topics as customs, recreation, songs, food, etc. They stress the fact that Italians brought with them the campanilismo[2] culture that prevailed in Italy, especially at the turn of the century. See also Del Giudice's *Studies in American Folklore* and, for a personal account from the lives of such famous Italian-Americans as Mario Cuomo, Francis Coppola, Yogi Berra, Alfonso D'Amato, Michael Andretti, Rudolph Giuliani, Tony Bennett, Geraldine Ferraro, etc., see Brandi Cateura's *Growing Up Italian*.

An interesting study of the evolution of Italian culture within the Italian-American community in the United States may be found in Alba's *Italian Americans*. Alba's thesis is that by the third

---

[2] A term that derives from the word *campanile* (church bell tower). The implication is that the loyalty of Italians is limited to only that part of Italy that can be seen from the tops of their local church bell tower.

generation, most links with the culture of the "old country" are gone. This proposition is captured in the subtitle of the book, *Into The Twilight of Ethnicity*. Indeed typically what happens is that the first generation's (those born and educated in Italy) knowledge of English is very minimal. The second generation's (the first generation born and educated in the United States) knowledge of Italian is minimal. In fact, in many cases knowledge of "official" Italian is zero. There is only oral familiarity with a regional dialect. By the third generation, knowledge of Italian, or even an Italian dialect is just about zero. Of course, there are exceptions to this pattern, especially for those who remain in Italian-speaking enclaves (Little Italies). There are also third-and-latter generation "Italian-Americans" who rediscover their roots, visit Italy often, and become very knowledgeable in the Italian language and in Italian culture. But these tend to be the exceptions that prove the rule. Of course this pattern of "lost ethnicity" is common to most immigrant groups in America. The final chapter in William Murray's book, *The Last Italian. Portrait of a People*, chronicals the life of a first -generation Italian-America living in retirement in the North Beach area of San Francisco by the name of *Giuseppe Ciardullo*. The North Beach area was once a thriving Italian community, but now most of the Italians are gone. Even a first-generation Italian-American like *Ciardullo* can become a "last Italian".

Many articles about Italy have appeared in the magazine, *National Geographic*. Some examples, most relevant to this chapter are: Kenny's article, "United Italy Marks Its 100th Year" (Nov. 1961), LaFay's article, "Sicily, Where All The Songs Are Sad" (March, 1976), Ellis' article, "Surviving Italian Style" (Feb., 1984), and Gore's article, "When The Greeks Went West" (Nov. 1994).

Finally, we would like to note an interesting book that expounds the virtues of Italian Culture. The book is James Walsh's *What*

Civilization Owes to Italy. This book was written shortly after the Great War (World War I). The author is frustrated at the focus of the big powers on military strength and material things. He admires Italy, a minor military power during the Great War, and for most of its post-Roman history , but a country that has contributed so much to civilization. He covers a long list of contributions, including contributions to music, the arts, architecture, the sciences, universities, medicine, law, mathematics, literature, etc.

CHAPTER 2. Food and Wine

2.1 INTRODUCTION

Cibo e vino (food and wine) are very important elements of Italian culture, as eating traditions are in any culture. Also, as can be expected by the long history of a fragmented peninsula, many dishes are regional in nature. However, the drinking of wine during meals is fairly universal, a habit that dates back to pre-Roman times. Italy has ideal geography and climate for growing grapes, hilly country sides with lots of sun. In this chapter we will explore Italian eating habits, regional dishes, and Italian wines. It is interesting to note that Italian cuisine is the most popular non-native cuisine in the world, with *pizza* now essentially an international dish.

2.2 ITALIAN EATING HABITS

The three main meals in Italy are:

> *La prima colazione* - Breakfast
> *Il pranzo* - Lunch
> *La cena*- Dinner

Unlike breakfast in the United States, breakfast in Italy is a very small meal, usually *un cappuccino* (frothy coffee and milk) and some *biscotti* (biscuits). At one time, lunch was the main meal. Everyone would quit work at noon and come home to a full Italian meal, take a nap, and then return to work about 3:30 p.m. But now this custom has changed, at least in the big cities, and dinner is generally the main meal. A full formal Italian meal (normally served for special guests or occasions) consists of the following components:

Aperitivo - Before dinner drink.

Antipasto - Variety of hot or cold meat or vegetable dishes (Hors-d'oeuvres in French).

Primo - First course, generally a choice of *pasta, gnocchi* (potato dumplings), *risotto* (rice), or *zuppa* (soup).

Secondo - Main course, generally a choice of *carne* (meat), *pesce* (fish), or *pollo* (chicken).

Contorno - Hot vegetable side dish.

Insalata - Salad.

Formaggio - Cheese.

Dolce - Dessert.

Frutta - Fruits.

Caffè - Coffee, generally an *espresso*.

Digestivo - After dinner liqueur. (Pousse-café, in French).

Not long ago, everyone drank wine with their meals, even young children (diluted with water). But now many people, especially young people, have stopped drinking wine. Instead they now simply drink *acqua minerale* (mineral water) or *una bibita analcolica* (a non-alcoholic soft drink).

By far the most popular meat in Italy is *vitello* (veal). American style steaks are unusual. The closest one can get to an American steak is *bistecca alla Fiorentina,* basically a rare T-bone steak.

Italy has the best *gelato* (ice cream) in the world and Sicily the best in Italy. Most *Gelaterie* (ice cream stores) make their own fresh ice cream. In the evenings, especially in the summer, you see people lining up at the *Gelaterie* for just one more *gelato*. And at all times of the day you will see people in *il Bar* drinking *espresso* coffee or *un aperitivo*.

Drinking coffee is always a special event in Italy, especially in Naples. The classical Neapolitan song (see Section 6.3), *'A tazza 'e cafè* (A cup of coffee), is about this fellow who is in love with a waitress (Brigeta) at a bar. He compares her to a cup of coffee, "like sugar on the bottom, but bitter on top." There are many ways to have coffee in Italy besides the classic *espresso*. We summarize some of the different ways coffee is served:

Caffè ristretto – A very strong espresso.

Caffè lungo – Espresso with more water than usual.

Caffè latte – Coffee with milk, pretty much American style.

Caffè macchiato – Espresso coffee stained (*macchiato* in Italian) with a few drops of milk.

Cappuccino – A foamy mixture of coffee and milk.

Caffè corretto – An espresso "corrected" with a *digestivo*, usually *grappa*.

Caffè granite – Cold coffee served over crushed ice. A specialty of Naples.

Italians eat dinner much later than we do in the United States, and the further south one goes the later one eats dinner. It is not unusual to see people in Sicily entering a restaurant at 11:00 p.m.

While Americans are very familiar with many Italian dishes, e.g. *pizza*, *spaghetti*, *ravioli*, *lasagne*, etc., there are many Italian dishes, even delicacies, that are probably unknown to most Americans, for example:

Cervelli fritti - Fried brain of lamb or veal.
Polenta e coniglio - Corn meal and rabbit.
Gnocchi - Potato dumplings.
Bollito misto - Mixed boiled meats, including beef tongue.
Testarelle arrosto - Roast lamb's head.
Trippa - Tripe (intestines).

53

Uccelli allo spiedo - Birds on the split.

Cozze gratinate - Stuffed mussels.

Carciofi ripieni - Stuffed artichokes.

Prosciutto con melone - Prosciutto (raw ham) with melon.

Anguilla con peperoni - Eel with peppers.

Fegato alla veneziana - Veal liver with onions.

Fritto misto - Mixed fried meats and vegetables.

Finally, we list some phrases you are likely to hear during an Italian meal.

Mangiamo - Let's eat!

Ma prima un aperitivo - But first a cocktail.

Vermouth, va bene? - Is Vermouth okay?

Sì grazie, salute. - Yes thanks, cheers.

Allora, buon appetito. - Well, here is to a good meal. (It is traditional to wait for someone to say *buon appetito* before starting to eat!)

Per secondo, abbiamo della carne. Spero che vi piaccia. - For the main course, we have meat. I hope you like it.

Chi vuol bere del vino? Bianco o rosso? - Who would like to drink some wine? White or red.

Posso avere un bicchiere d'acqua? - May I have a glass of water?

Prenda ancora un po' di carne! - Have some more meat!

No grazie, va bene così. - No thank you, I have enough.

Tutto era cosi delizioso. Grazie per la cena. - Everything was so delicious. Thank you for the dinner.

2.3 REGIONAL ITALIAN DISHES

Just like there are many languages in Italy, there are many regional dishes. Obviously, from Italian regions that border on the sea you can expect good seafood. Rice is more popular in the north than in the south, and so on. The same dish may even go by another name in a different region. For example in *Piemonte, ravioli* are called *agnolotti* (*agnolòt,* in the *Piedmontese* dialect).

Of course, the most famous Italian dish in the world is *pizza.* The origins of *pizza* go back to the early Greeks and Romans. The Romans ate a plain white "pizza" with raw onions, which they called *moretum.* The term *pizza,* which evolved from *picea,* came into the Italian language during medieval times. Naples is the "capital" of Italian *pizza,* and a famous story about Neapolitan *pizza* is about the *pizza* called *Pizza Margherita.* In 1889, when King Umberto I and his wife Queen Margherita were in Naples, the queen decided to serve a "patriotic" *pizza* that included the colors of the Italian flag, green, white, and red. She had the cook prepare a *pizza* with basil (green), *mozzarella* (white), and tomatoes (red). This combination is now the famous *Pizza Margherita.* Here in the United States, we tend to make our *pizza* with lots of complicated toppings. Most restaurants here do not even list *Pizza Margherita.* When you visit Italy, do not forget to order a "simple" *Pizza Margherita.* It's the patriotic thing to do.

Before describing a few typical regional dishes, we would like to say something about *pasta,* since it is so popular in all parts of Italy. *Pasta* in Italy comes in a large variety of shapes. The regional differences in pasta dishes are generally in the sauces that are added to the pasta. When pasta is served with a sauce, it is called *pastasciutta* and when served in a soup, *pasta in brodo.* Some of the different pasta forms are:

Lumachini - Small snail (*lumache* in Italian) shaped pasta.

Tagliatelle - Flat noodles.

Farfalle - Butterfly (*farfalla* in Italian) shaped pasta.

Maccheroni – Tubular-shaped pasta.

Penne - Pen (*penna* in Italian) shaped pasta.

Rigatoni – Tubular-shaped pasta with ridges (*righe* in Italian).

Ravioli –Square-shaped paste dumplings with meat or cheese stuffing.

Tortellini - Small triangular-shaped ravioli.

Cappelletti - Small hat (*cappello* in Italian) shaped ravioli.

Vermicelli - Thin spaghetti (*vermicelli* in Italian means, literally, "little worms").

Cannelloni - Large tubular-shaped pasta filled with meat.

Most pasta sauces are tomato (*pomodoro*) based, and almost all have the three basic Italian cooking ingredients **oil**, **garlic**, and **onion** (*olio, aglio, e cipolla*).

Rice is another dish that may be found in all parts of Italy, although it is especially popular in the north (*Piemonte, Lombardia, e Veneto*). Rice dishes are called *risotto*. Rice may be cooked in a number of different ways depending on the region, one of the most famous being *risotto alla milanese*. *Polenta*, a corn meal mush, is another favorite in northern Italy. It is generally eaten in the winter. Traditionally it was a common dish of the poor people. It has its origins in Roman times when soldiers cooked gruel of crushed millet and wheat seeds and called it *pulmentum*. Next, we describe a few specific regional dishes.

Campania

Pizza Margherita – This is a classic pizza of Naples, created in 1889 for the Queen of Italy, *Margherita*. The ingredients were selected to show the colors of the Italian flag, basil for **green**, mozzarella for **white**, and tomatoes for **red**.

Pizza alla napolitana – Actually if you ask for this pizza in Naples, they will be confused. In most of Italy, outside of Naples, this means pizza with anchovies. But, in Naples, *pizza alla napolitana* is likely to be interpreted as *pizza alla marinara*, an old favorite of the sailors (*marinaio*) of Naples. It is made up of oil, tomato, garlic, and oregano. No Mozzerella! To make things even more confusing, if you ask for *pizza alla marinara* outside of Naples you get a pizza with seafood topping.

Spaghetti alla puttanesca – Spaghetti "prostitute style" (puttana – prostitute). The hot spicy sauce in this dish is made of garlic, dried chili, anchovies, tomatoes, black olives, oil, and capers.

Vermicelli con le cozze - Thin spaghetti with mussels.

Sfogliatelli – Crisp sheets of cooked dough filled with *ricotta* cheese and candied fruit.

Emilia - Romagna

Tagliatelle alla bolognese - Tagliatelle with a special meat sauce called *ragù bolognese*.

Tortellini - Cappelletti served with *ragù bolognese* or in a broth..

Cotechino con lenticchie- Pork sausage (boiled) with lentils.

Lazio

Spaghetti alla carbonara - Spaghetti in a butter, cheese and bacon sauce.

Abbacchio alla romana – Young roasted lamb with herbs (rosemary and sage) and garlic.

Saltimbocca alla romana – *Saltimbocca* means "jump in the mouth." It is that good, made of slices of veal and prosciutto rolled up together in a Marsala sauce.

Pagliata – Calf intestines with the mother's milk still included. This classic Roman dish is not easy to find in restaurants. One needs to go to the *Testaccio* section of Rome to find restaurants that serve it.

Cannelloni - Large tubular pasta filled with meat and topped off with a cheese, butter, and cream sauce.

Liguria

Fritto misto di mare - Mixed fried fish.

Zucchini ripieni - Zucchini shells filled with a egg and cheese sauce.

Buridda – Classic Genovese fish stew cooked with onions, carrots, celery, anchovies, pine nuts, and tomatoes.

Linguine con pesto – Linguine with pesto sauce. Pesto is a sauce made of garlic, pine nuts, olive oil, basil, and parmesan cheese.

Trofie – Gnocchi (potato dumplings) with pesto sauce.

Lombardia

Risotto alla milanese - Arborio rice with onions, beef marrow, and saffron.

Costolette di vitello alla milanese - Breaded veal cutlets served with lemon wedges.

Panettone - Fruit cake from Milano, especially popular at Christmas time.

Piemonte

Polenta e coniglio - Polenta with rabbit.

Bagna cauda - Hot oil, anchovie, and garlic dip with fresh vegetables.

Bollito misto - Mixed boiled meats (tongue, beef, veal, chicken, salami, etc. served with *salsa verde*, a parsley, garlic, and anchovie sauce).

Gnocchi alla bava – Potato dumplings with cheese sauce.

Grissini - Famous bread sticks from *Torino*.

Bugie – Fried flour, covered with fine sugar. Popular at carnival time.

Bonet – Baked cake made of crushed amaretti cookies, chocolate, sugar, and eggs.

Sicilia

Capponata - An eggplant based vegetable antipasto.

Spaghetti alla siciliana - Spaghetti with tomato meat sauce topped off with slices of fried eggplant.

Cassata alla siciliana - A ricotta based dessert.

Toscana

Arista – Pork loin pierced with holes then filled with rosemary, pepper, and salt.

Bistecca alla fiorentina - Rare T-bone steak.

Trippa alla fiorentina - Tripe with potatoes and tomato sauce.

Veneto

Anguilla con peperoni alla veneta - Eels with peppers.

Zuppa di pesce - Fish soup (much like the French bouillabaisse).

Fegato alla veneziana - Onions and liver (but no bacon!). Often served with polenta.

A word about Italian ham. What we call **ham** here in America is called *prosciutto cotto* (cooked prosciutto) in Italy, and what we call prosciutto is called *prosciutto crudo* (raw prosciutto). In Italy, the default meaning of prosciutto is *prosciutto crudo*. A very popular *antipasto* throughout Italy is *prosciutto con melone* (prosciutto with cantaloupe melon) or *prosciutto con fichi* (prosciutto with figs). Also what we call "bologna" here in America is actually *mortadella* from Bologna. Although Italians are not as fanatical cheese eaters as the French, cheese is usually served at the end of the meal, and many Italian cheeses are well known throughout the world, e.g. *mozzarella, ricotta, parmigiano, gorgonzola, provolone, pecorino,* *fontina,* etc. Speaking of French cuisine, it should be noted that Catherine de' Medici from Florence is generally credited with the introduction of fine cooking to France in the 16th century.

Finally, it should also be noted that a number of ingredients, which we commonly associate with Italian cooking, were introduced to Italy from the new world, e.g. the tomato (*pomodoro*), corn (*granturco* for *polenta*), red peppers (*peperoni rossi*), and the potato (*patata,* for *gnocchi*).

2.4 ITALIAN WINES

Of course, like food, wines in Italy are regional. To insure that wine comes from a given grape variety, you should look for "DOC" (*Denominazione di Origine Controllata*) on the label. A "G" (*Garantita*) added to DOC, means special quality control for that particular grape variety wine. Very fine distinctions are made even for wines of a given variety. For example, *Barbera,* a hardy red wine made from the *barbara grape,* can be *Barbera d'Alba, Barbera d'Asti,* or *Barbera del Monferrato.* To insure a wine comes from a given region, the designation IGT (*Indicazione Geografica Tipica*) is used. Of course wines are divided into the usual categories of red (*rosso*), white (*bianco*), and rosé (*rosato*).

Below we list a few of the better known regional wines. You may note that a large number of wines are listed under the *Piemonte* region, many of which you will probably not recognize. *Piemonte* is perhaps the largest wine-producing region, but many of its wines are not exported, thus not as well known outside of Italy. In the list below, "Garantita" wines are identified with a "G."

Piemonte

Asti Spumante (G) - Very sweet sparkling white wine made of Moscato variety of grapes.

Barbera - Hardy red wine, made of Barbera grapes.

Barberesco (G) - Aged red wine made of the Nebbiolo grapes.

Barolo (G) - Aged red wine made of Nebbiolo grapes.

Dolcetto - Red wine made of Dolcetto grapes.

Erbaluce di Caluso - Dry white wine made of Erbaluce grapes.

Freisa - Light red wine made of Freisa grapes.

Gattinara (G) - Light red wine made of Nebbiolo grapes.

Grignolino - Light red wine made of Grignolino grapes with up to 10% Freisa grapes.

Moscato - Very sweet white wine, made of Moscato grapes.

Toscana

Brunello di Montalcino (G) - Robust red.

Chianti (G) - Light red wine made of a mixture of black Sangiovese and white Malvasia grapes.

Vin Nobile di Montepulciano (G) - Aged red wine.

Vin Santo - Sweet dessert wine.

Trentino - Alto Adige

Pinot Grigio - Dry white wine.

Merlot - Red wine.

Veneto

Bardolino - Light red wine.

Soave - Dry white wine.

Valpolicella - Dry red wine.

Lazio

Frascati - Dry semi-sweet or sweet white wine.

Est! Est! Est! - Dry white wine.

Campania

Lacrima Christi - Dry white wine.

Emilia - Romagna

Albana di Romagna (G) - Dry white wine.

Lambrusco - Fizzy red wine.

Sangiovese - Fruity red wine

Sicilia

Corvo di Salaparuta - Dry white wine.

Etna Rosso - Red wine made form vineyards on the slopes of Mount Etna.

Marsala - Sweet wine from the city of Marsala.

Regaleali - Dry white wine.

In addition to its wines, Italy is famous for its before and after dinner drinks. Torino is the birthplace of *Vermouth*, a common *aperitivo* made of wine flavored with herbs from the nearby Alps. There is sweet and dry Vermouth, and red and white Vermouth. In Italy, white Vermouth is sweet, while in the United States white Vermouth is usually of the dry type (mixed with Gin to make the famous American dry martini). Other well-known *aperitivi* are *Punt e Mes* and *Campari.* *Fernet Branca* is a famous after dinner *digestivo*, together with *Grappa* (strong, clear liqueur made from grape stems), often added to espresso coffee. Some of the more popular liqueurs from Italy include *Strega* (*Strega* means "witch". A figure of a witch on a broom appears on the label of this yellow liqueur.), *Amaretto di Saronno* (almond based liqueur), and *Sambuca* (clear anisette flavored liqueur). Finally, we should note that the *digestivo* that is currently most popular in Italy,is *Limoncello* (lemon flavored liqueur). Some of the best *Limoncello* is produced in areas around Naples, e.g., Sorrento, Amalfi, etc., where lemons grow in abundance.

2.5 NOTES AND REFERENCES

There are many books that have been written on Italian food and wines, too many to try to cover in just a few pages. So we will limit ourselves to four books that are typical of what is available on the subjects.

An excellent book on Italian cuisine in general is Laura Busini Birch's book, *Traditional Italian Food.* This book contains a wide range of recipes from various Italian regions. The book also contains a nice introduction to Italian "feast" days and markets in addition to wines, special herbs, cheeses, and breads.

The book by Alberta Lantermo, *La Cucina Delle Regioni D'Italia: Piemonte*, describes dishes from the state of Piedmont. Recipes are given in Italian, Piedmontese, and English. This book is a part of a series of twenty volumes that describe the cuisine from different states and cities in Italy, e.g. *Valle D'Aosta, Milano, Liguria, Friuli e Trieste, Trento, Bolzano, Veneto, Emilia, Romagna, Toscana, Umbria, Marche, Roma, Abruzzi e Molise, Napoli, Puglie, Calabria e Lucania*, *Sicilia e Isole*, and *Sardegna*.

The book by Daniel Halpern, *Halpern's Guide to the Essential Restaurants of Italy*, provides a comprehensive guide to major restaurants in Italy. Each restaurant is evaluated by "class", atmosphere, service, wine, and price. "Class" relates to decor, glassware, presentation of food and wine, etc. It also lists suggested dishes and wines for each restaurant. Regional dishes and wines are discussed in some detail for each of the states of *Abruzzi*, *Emilia-Romagna*, *Lazio*, *Liguria*, *Lombardia*, *Marche*, *Piemonte*, *Toscana*, *Umbria*, *Valle d'Aosta*, and *Veneto*.

Valentina Harris' book, *Traveler's Guide to the Food of Italy*, contains detailed information on local dishes and wines from all of the various regions of Italy. Harris' book includes interesting historical accounts of the regions and their local specialties. Two other cook books that focus on regional dishes are Alda Boni's *Italian Regional Cooking*, and Lorenza de' Medici's *Italy.The Beautiful Cookbook*. The de' Medici book also includes many stunning photographs of the various Italian regions.

Finally we would like to cite Sophia Loren's recently published cookbook, *Recipes and Memories*. It not only contains recipes for classic Neapolitan dishes, but also includes a great photo collection of her Neapolitan family and her movie career.

CHAPTER 3. Evolution of the Italian Language

3.1 PRE-LATIN LANGUAGES

Before Latin became the universal language of the Roman Empire, many languages were spoken on the Italian peninsula. In the south, Greek was common; in the north, Celtic, Ligurian, and Venetic were the spoken languages; and in the center, Etruscan and Umbrian dominated. Unfortunately, most of these languages were only spoken, so we have no written records of these languages, except, of course, Greek. The Etruscans had a written language, but only limited examples exist today, mostly proper names inscribed on tombs.

3.2 WRITTEN VERSUS SPOKEN LATIN

Classic "written" Latin is a fairly complex language. Proper names are declined to distinguish their role in a sentence. For example, the name Paul becomes:

> Paulus - subject
>
> Paulum - direct object
>
> Paulo - indirect object.

This makes it possible to use any word order in a sentence, without causing ambiguity. For example:

> *Paulum mordet lupus*
>
> *Lupus mordet Paulum*

mean the same thing, that is "the wolf (lupus: subject) bites (mordet) Paul (Paulum: direct object)." There is an extensive collection of written Latin including poems, legal documents, plays, historical records, etc. However, even at the height of Roman influence, not everyone spoke a Latin corresponding to the official written language. By the year 300 AD, spoken Latin had dropped many of the word endings that distinguished various declinations and began to resemble modern Italian in a very striking way, as can be seen by the table shown below.

Classical Written Latin	Spoken Latin	Modern Italian
paucum (a little)	*pocu*	*poco*
corpus (body)	*corpu*	*corpo*
caput (head)	*capu*	*capo*
lupus (wolf)	*lupu*	*lupo*
dabit (will give)	*dare a*	*darà*
aqua fontis (water from the fountain)	*aqua de illa fonte*	*acqua della fonte*
equus (horse)	*cavallu*	*cavallo*
pullus (chicken)	*pullu*	*pollo*

Note that by dropping final consonants, many words end up with vowel endings. Therefore, spoken Latin must have sounded very much like modern Italian. However, note also that some words changed completely from the written to the spoken, e.g. equus to cavallu.

Many Greek words were incorporated into Latin, especially religious terms since Greek was the language of the early Christian church. Some examples are:

Greek	Latin
pascha (Easter)	pascha
parabole (word)	paravola
diabolos (devil)	diabolus
barbaros (barbarian)	barbaro
papas (father)	papa
stadion (stadium)	stadium
theatron (theater)	theatrum
problema (problem)	problema
cathedra (cathedral)	cathedra
politikos (politics)	politicus
diskos (disc)	discus

3.3 END OF THE ROMAN EMPIRE

The year 476 AD, when Odoacer was pronounced emperor of the Gothic Kingdom of Italy, generally marks the end of the Roman empire. Starting in 401 AD, the Italian peninsula experienced invasions from the Visigoths (401 AD), the Huns (452 AD), the Vandals (455 AD), the Ostrogoths (493 AD), the Byzantines (533 AD), the Lombards (568 AD), the Franks (774 AD), the Saracens (800 AD), and the Normans (1036 AD). Of course, with all these invasions and no central government to enforce a common language, spoken Latin quickly deteriorated into a large number of distinct "dialects." Because many of the invaders admired the old Roman empire, they adapted Latin as their official "written" language. But their spoken languages were distinct from the "Latin dialects," and relatively few of their words were incorporated into the dialects. We list below, however, a few examples of Italian words that have come from various invading nations.

Words of Arabic Origin

Arabic	Italian
narangia (orange)	*arancia*
limun (lemon)	*limone*
qahva (coffee)	*caffè*
sifr (zero)	*zero*
tasa (cup)	*tazza*
al-giabr (algebra)	*algebra*
dar-sina-a (arsenal)	*arsenale*
sukkar (sugar)	*zucchero*
diwan (customs house)	*dogana*

Words of Frankish Origin

Frankish	Italian
strappon (to tear)	*strappare*
brun (dark)	*bruno*
frisk (fresh)	*fresco*
gris (gray)	*grigio*
want (glove)	*guanto*

Words of Lombard Origin

Lombard	Italian
balk (balcony)	*balcone*
banka (bank)	*banca*
flasko (flask)	*fiasco*
skerzon (to joke)	*scherzare*
wankja (cheek)	*guancia*
palla (ball)	*palla*
rihhi (rich)	*ricco*

Words of Gothic Origin

Gothic	Italian
haribairg (hotel)	*albergo*
bandivo (band)	*banda*
suppa (soup)	*zuppa*
blank (white)	*bianco*
fani (mud)	*fango*
nastilo (ribbon)	*nastro*

After 1000 AD, there was very little left of the Latin spoken during the days of the Roman Empire. Only the Catholic Church and universities continued with spoken Latin. Written Latin however persisted in legal documents and scholarly publications. Universities in Italy continued to use Latin as the language of instruction up to the 1850s. In 1852, Latin was abolished at universities in the Kingdom of Piedmonte and Sardinia. The Catholic Church did not abolish Latin as the official church language until 1967.

Even as early as 1000 AD the dialects spoken on the Italian peninsula were very close to their present form, but there were very few written examples. Almost all written material was in Latin, even if somewhat removed from the classical Latin of the Roman period. The Latin-based languages spoken by the common people were referred to as the *vulgar tongues*.

3.4 DEVELOPMENT OF WRITTEN "ITALIAN" DIALECTS

The period 1000 - 1300 witnessed the development of written vulgar tongues. Since few people understood Latin, many legal documents ultimately had to be written in local dialects. For the same reason religious sermons had to be written in local dialects. Indeed two of the first examples of written dialects were the poetic praises (*Laude*) of Saint Francis of Assisi (1182 - 1226) written in an Umbrian dialect, and sermons (*Sermoni Subalpini*) written in a Piedmontese dialect, about the same period of time. We list below two short examples of these early written writings.

Laude Delle Creature a Dio
by *San Francesco d'Assisi*

Laudato sii, mio Signore, con tutte le tue creature
specialmente messer lo frate Sole
il quale, il giorno, allumini per noi;
Ed ello è bello e radiante con grande splendore;
di te, Altissimo, porta significazione.

Sermo in Nativitate Domini vel cotidianus
from *Sermoni Subalpini* (unknown author)

Or vos en direm un isemple qui ben s'i conven.
El fo un reis qui avea un anel d'or o avea un pera preciosa.
Or aven que el era andà per isir fora a chambra,

70

si li chai lo pera de l'anel en la forana.
Or comande a un so serve qu'el i intras e si l'en
traes.

One may recognize many words in the above writing as modern Italian words, or at least close to modern Italian words, e.g. *mio Signore* (my God), *frate Sole* (brother sun), *il giorno* (the day), *per noi* (for us), *è bello* (is beautiful), *Sermo* (*Sermone*-sermon), *isemple* (*esempio* - example), *reis* (*re* - king), *un anel d'or* (*un anello d'oro* - a gold ring), *fora* (*fuori* - outside), *chambra* (*camera* - room), etc. Note that some of the Piedmontese words are actually closer to French than Italian, e.g. *chambra* (chambre in French). Other major sources of early written dialects were the songs and poems written for royalty. An especially active court was the court of Frederick (*Federico*) II. Frederick II (1194 - 1250) was the grandson of Frederick I, called Frederick Barbarossa, from the Hohenstaufen dynasty in Germany, who in 1152 became Holy Roman Emperor and king of Italy. Frederick II was himself crowned Holy Roman Emperor in 1215. He was born in Sicily of a Sicilian mother, *Constance of Sicily* (1146 - 1198) and established his court in Palermo. The court he established was one of the most admired of the time. It was famous for its support of intellectual pursuits and its tolerance for the many diverse people, Hebrews, Normans, Greeks, Muslims, etc. that lived in Sicily at the time. The Sicilian court poetry was influenced by the dialect spoken in southern France, *Provençal* or *Langue d'Oc* (Language of "yes" = *oc*). In northern France, the dialect was referred to as *Langue d'Oil* (Language of "yes" = *oil*, or in modern French *oui*). Frederick II himself wrote poems in the local Sicilian dialect, and the written dialect that developed in his court became known as the vulgar tongue from the *Scuola Siciliana* (Sicilian School). A short example of his poetry follows:

Dolze mea donna lo gire
non è per mia volontate,
che mi convene ubbidire
quelli che m'a 'n postestate.

Here too one may recognize "Italian" words, e.g. *Dolze* (*dolce* - sweet), *mea donna* (*mia donna* - my woman), *per mia* (for my), *mi convene* (*mi conviene* - it is convenient for me), *ubbidire* (obey), etc.

The written language of the court of Frederick II greatly influenced the poets in Florence and became the basis of a written Florentine dialect referred to as the vulgar tongue of the "*Scuola del dolce stil novo*" (School of the new sweet style). The greatest of these poets was Dante Alighieri (1265 - 1321). Through his monumental works, in particular *La Divina Commedia* (Divine Play), he perfected this written dialect. It is basically this written dialect of Dante that became the official language of Modern Italy. Dante's poetic epic *La Divina Commedia* is divided into three parts *Inferno* (Hell), *Purgatorio* (Purgatory), and *Paradiso* (Heaven). Perhaps, the most stirring lines in this epic poem are those where the poet describes the words on a sign above the gates of hell.

Inferno (Canto III)

"Per me si va nella citta dolente,
per me si va nell 'eterno dolore,
per me si va tra la perduta gente.
....
Lasciate ogni speranza, voi ch'entrate."

72

The sign reads:

> "Through me, one enters into the city of sadness,
> through me, one enters into eternal pain,
> through me, one goes amongst the lost people.
> ....
> Abandon all hope, ye that enter."

Dante politically was a "white" Guelf, a faction of the Guelphs (individuals who favored the Pope over the emperor) who were much more liberal than the "black" Guelphs. In 1302, he was permanently banished from Florence by the black Guelphs. This was the beginning of his odyssey through the Italian peninsula, which brought him in contact with all the various dialects that were spoken at the time. He pondered the possibility of a perfect Italian dialect that would be a synthesis of all the existing dialects. He wrote a book on the question of the perfect Italian vulgar tongue. The book was written in Latin, with the title *De Vulgari Eloquentia* (On the Illustrious Vulgar Tongue). It is interesting to note that Dante found none of the existing dialects, even his own Florentine, satisfactory and instead suggested the creation of an "Italian" language that incorporated the best of all the dialects. It is also interesting to note how critical Dante was of the existing dialects. We summarize below some of his comments on various dialects.

The Dialect of Rome

"Of all vernaculars the Roman tongue, no vernacular but a dismal, disagreeable noise, is the worst of all."

The Dialect of Sardinia

"We also reject the Sardinians, who are not Italian but who have to be classed with the Italians, for they alone are without their own dialect, imitating Latin as apes imitate people."

The Dialect of Puglia

"The Apulians, either because of their own roughness or because of the influence of their neighbors of Rome and Maches speak barbarically."

The Dialect of Romagna

"Entering the Romagna, I note that I have found two dialects in Italy with perfect contrary features. One of them seems so feminine because of softness in vocabulary and pronunciation, that a man, even with a masculine voice, is mistaken for a woman when he speaks it."

The Dialect of Venetians

"The Venetians should not believe either that they have the vernacular we are seeking."

The Dialect of Tuscany

"Let us come now to the Tuscans, who mired in their vast stupidity, claim for themselves the honor of possessing the most illustrious vernacular. ..... And so if we examine Tuscan dialects and consider how and in what ways the aforesaid men have diverged from their own, there can be no doubt that the vernacular we are seeking is not among those which the Tuscan people have attained."

Even Dante's own dialect was not satisfactory! The only dialect Dante had something good to say about was the Sicilian dialect. In particular he says, "I say that if by 'Sicilian vernaculars' we mean the language as it is spoken by the ordinary native, from whose mouth our judgement should proceed, then this dialect does not deserve preference, because it takes up so much time with those long extra sounds, as in the line 'Tragemi d'este focoro, se t'este a boluntate,' for instance. But if we mean by Sicilian the language that comes from the mouths of the most distinguished Sicilians - as may be observed in the poems cited above - it differs in no way from the most praiseworthy vernacular, ..."

To provide an illustration of the variations between various Italian dialects we list below the conjugation of the verb "to be" (*essere*, in Italian).

Singular

English	Italian	Piemontese	Sicilian	Neapolitan
I am	Io sono	*Mi i son*	*Iú sugnu*	*I' songo*
You are	Tu sei	*Ti it ses*	*Tu si'*	*Tu sì*
He, she is	Lui, lei è	*Chiel,chila a l' é*	*Iddu, idda è*	*Isso, essa é*

Plural

English	Italian	Piemontese	Sicilian	Neapolitan
We are	*Noi siamo*	*Noi i soma*	*Nui semu*	*Nuje simmo*
You are	*Voi siete*	*Voi i seve*	*Vui siti*	*Vuje site*
They are	*Loro sono*	*Lor a son*	*Iddi sunnu*	*Loro songo*

It should be noted that letters are sounded differently in each dialect, and dialects contain many sounds and letters not found in Italian. For a discussion of pronunciation in Piedmontese, see the chapter *Piedmontese, the King's Italian*. Also there are strong variations within a dialect. For example, in Piedmont, the dialect spoken in *Torino* has some serious variations from the dialect spoken in *il Monferrato*.

The ideal "Italian" that Dante dreamed of was never realized. Instead the Florentine dialect ultimately became the official Italian language. The works of two other Florentine writers, the poet *Francesco Petrarca* (1304 - 1374), and the novelist *Giovanni Boccaccio* (1313 - 1375) helped establish the Florentine dialect as the written language of Italy. Boccaccio's novel *Decamerone*, a story of a group of noble men and women who flee the plague of

1348 by holding out at a villa in the Tuscan Hills, is perhaps one of his best known works. However, even though the Florentine dialect became the written Italian dialect of choice, few people could read or write it, and Latin continued as the "official" written language for hundreds of years after the death of Dante. Indeed, at the beginning of the 1800s the Florentine dialect was spoken and read only in Tuscany. In other parts of the peninsula common people spoke their local dialects, intellectuals read and wrote in Latin, and foreign rulers spoke their native tongues, e.g. French, Spanish, German, etc. If it were not for the decision of the novelist *Alessandro Manzoni* (1785 - 1873) to re-write his book *I Promessi Sposi* (The Betrothed) in the Florentine dialect in 1842, it is likely that another dialect may have become the national language. Perhaps Piedmontese would have ended up as the national language given that the country was reunited under the Piedmontese monarchy. *Manzoni's* novel had a incredible impact on the people of the peninsula, and is now standard reading for every student in Italy. *Manzoni's* novel takes place near lake Como during a period of Spanish domination (1628 - 1630) and is about two people, *Renzo Tramaglino* and *Lucia Mondella*, who are engaged to be married (betrothed). But a local nobleman, *Don Rodrigo*, wants *Lucia* for himself, and uses his thugs (*bravi*) to prevent the consummation of the marriage. The segment of the book we list below deals with the encounter of the thugs and the local priest, *Don Abbondio*, in which the thugs warn the priest that he is not to marry *Renzo* and *Lucia*. The priest is reading a book while returning home from a walk. Two thugs stop him and the following conversation ensues.

I Promessi Sposi
L'incontro di don Abbondio coi bravi

"*Signor curato,*" *disse un di quei due, piantandogli gli occhi in faccia.*

"Cosa comanda?" rispose subito don Abbondio, alzando i suoi dal libro, che gli restò spalancato nelle mani, come su un leggìo.

"Lei ha intenzione," proseguì l'altro con atto minaccioso e iracondo di chi coglie un suo inferiore sull'intraprendere una ribalderia, "lei ha intenzione di maritar domani Renzo Tramaglino e Lucia Mondella!"

"Cioè ..." rispose, con voce tremolante, don Abbondio: "cioè. Lor signori son uomini di mondo, e sanno benissimo come vanno queste faccende. Il povero curato non c'entra: fanno i loro pasticci tra loro, e poi ... e poi, vengono da noi, come s'andrebbe a un banco a riscuotere: e noi ... noi siamo i servitori del comune."

"Orbene," gli disse il bravo, all'orecchio, ma in tono solenne di comando, "questo matrimonio non s'ha da fare, nè domani, nè mai."

The Betrothed
The encounter of Don Abbondio with the thugs

'Your Reverence!' said one of them, staring him straight in the eyes.

'What can I do for you?' replied Don Abbondio immediately, looking up from the book, which remained open in his hands, as if on a lectern.

'And so you have it in mind,' said the bravo in the threatening manner of a man who has caught a subordinated in the act of committing a blackguardly crime, 'you have it in mind to marry Renzo Tramaglino and Lucia Mondella tomorrow!'

'Well!' said Don Abbondio in a trembling voice, 'well, you see ... you gentlemen are men of the world, and realize how these things go. It's nothing to do with the poor curé; these people make their own muddled arrangements, and then ... why, they come to us just as they might go to a bank to draw money ... we are ... just the servants of the community.'

'Very well,' said the bravo, speaking into the priest's ear, quietly, but in a tone of impressive command, 'that wedding is not to take place. Not tomorrow, and not any other time either.'

3.5 A COMMON ITALIAN LANGUAGE

In 1868, after the unification of Italy, *Manzoni* headed a commission to study the adoption of a common Italian language. Their choice was the Tuscan dialect of Dante. However, it was only during the 1930s, under the Fascist regime, that public schools became common and Italians started reading and writing one language. Of course with the advent of television and immigration between different regions, the Tuscan dialect was finally established as the "Italian language." In every major city, one now speaks the same dialect, *Toscano*. But in small villages the local dialects can still be heard.

3.6 NOTES AND REFERENCES

A very complete study of the evolution of the Italian language may be found in Migliorini's *The Italian Language*. He traces the development of the language from Latin, to Italian vernaculars, to recent modifications in the language (1915 -1965). Another excellent book on the subject is Pulgram's *The Tongues of Italy*. In Pulgram's book, the evolution of Italian is tied in very closely to the history of the peninsula. As may be noted from the title, he focuses on the many dialects that actually constitute the "Italian" language. An extensive collection of poems written in various dialects, with English translations, may be found in Haller's *The Hidden Italy*. The term "hidden' in the title characterizes the fact that outside of the regions where the dialect is spoken, little is known of this poety.

As noted previously in this chapter, Dante was very interested in the "Italian" language. The recent book by Shapiro, *De Vulgari Eloquentia - Dante's Book of Exile*, includes a translation of Dante's famous book on the subject, *De Vulgari Eloquentia* together with comments and notes on Dante's life and works.

Of course, there are many textbooks on the Italian language. See, for example, Speroni et. al. , *Basic Italian*. Mario Constantino's *Italian at a Glance* is a valuable language pocket book for the traveler. It contains many useful phrases, a quick grammar guide, and a short dictionary. There are also books on various Italian dialects. See for example Brero and Bertodatti's *Grammatica della Lingua Piemontese*, Pitrè's *La Lingua Parlata del Dialetto Siciliano*, or Fierro's *Grammatica Della Lingua Napoletana*. Unfortunately, none of the books on dialects are available in English.

At the time of Italy's unification in 1861, less than 3% of the population was literate in the "standard" Italian language (Tuscan dialect). Dictionaries had to be written to translate various dialects to standard Italian. See, for example (References), the dictionaries of *Andeoli* (Neapolitan-Italian), *di Sant'Albino* (Piedmontese-Italian), and *Traina* (Sicilian-Italian).

Finally, if you want to hear some of the Italian dialects, the text, *Italian Traditional Song*, edited by Luisa Del Giudice, includes a cassette with songs from all over Italy sung in the local dialects.

CHAPTER 4. Piedmontese: The King's Italian

4.1 INTRODUCTION

In 1860, the year before the unification of Italy, the only languages you were likely to hear in Piedmont[3] were French and Piedmontese[4]. At the royal court of the House of Savoy in Turin, French was the official language, but Piedmontese was almost always the spoken language. Indeed the first king of Italy, *Vittorio Emanuele II*, from the House of Savoy, was only marginally familiar with "Italian" (the Tuscan dialect), and always preferred speaking Piedmontese. His three great loves were hunting (*la caccia*), war (*la guerra*), and women (*le donne*). These activities often brought him in contact with the common people, whose only language was Piedmontese. He had a long list of mistresses including *Laura Bon*, *Virginia Rho*, *Vittoria Duplessis*, *Claudia Cucchi*, *Rosita Mauri*, *Caterina Sirtori*, and *Emma Ivon*, but his favorite was *Rosina Vercellana* (*la bela Rosin*, as she was called in Piedmontese). They met when she was about fifteen. She was a simple, uneducated girl who always spoke to the king in Piedmontese and who regularly cooked *bagna cauda* for him during their quiet evenings together. After his wife *Maria Adelaide* died, he married *Rosina Vercellana* in a civil ceremony, but the marriage was never officially recognized. *Cavour*, the king's Prime Minister, was very unhappy with the king's liaison with *Rosina*. At one point Cavour had a treasury bond (*buono di tesoreria*) made out as a bribe to the king to entice him to give up Rosina. The king had lots of debts and needed all the money he could get. But when Cavour offered him the *buono* (*bon* in Piedmontese), the king was reputed to have said in Piedmontese, "*Mi*

---

[3] Piedmont - *Piemonte* in Italian, and *Piemont* in Piedmontese.

[4] Piedmontese - *Piemontese* in Italian, and *Piemontèis* in Piemontese.

im ten-o cost bon e anche la Rosin, ch'a l'é na gran bela fija" (I am going to keep the bond and Rosina also, who is a very beautiful woman, in English; *Mi tengo questo buono e anche Rosina, che è una gran bella ragazza,* in Italian). When the king's army finally captured Rome in 1870, the official record quotes him as saying in Italian "*Finalmente ci siamo*" ("Finally we made it"), but people present at the time say he actually spoke these words in Piedmontese, "*Finalment i-i soma*".

Rosina Vercellana with Vittorio Emanuele II

4.2 PIEDMONTESE PRONUNCIATION

Piedmontese is an Italian dialect with close links to the French Provençal dialect. In the next section, we will further explore the development of the Piedmontese language. Below we summarize the rules for pronunciation and introduce some of the special letters that appear in Piedmontese. A short summary of Piedmontese grammar is given in Appendix II.

Most of the vowels in Piedmontese are pronounced as in Italian. However there are some notable exceptions.

o - pronounced like Italian "u" e.g. *toe* (*tuoi* - your)

u - pronounced like French "u" as in "tu", e.g. *un* (*uno* - one), same as German "ü"

eu - pronounced like French "eu" as in "peu", e.g. *eut* (*otto* - eight) same as German "ö"

There are also a number of special symbols to distinguish other pronunciations. For example:

ò - pronounced like Italian "o", e.g. *scòla* (*scuola* - school)

ë - pronounced like English "e" as in "the", e.g. *ël* (*il* - the)

é - pronounced like Italian "e", e.g. *mangé* (*mangiare* - to eat)

j - pronounced like English "y" as in "yes", e.g. *i veuj* (*voglio* - I want)

Unlike Italian, many Piedmontese words end in consonants. The pronunciation of consonants is generally the same as Italian. However, there are certain double-consonants endings that have special pronunciations. For example:

cc - pronounced like English "ch" as in "lurch", e.g. *svicc* (*vivace* - vivacious)

ch - pronounce like English "k" as in "bike", e.g. *mach* (*solamente* - only)

gg - pronounced like English "g" in "George", e.g. *ragg* (*raggio* - ray)

In Piedmontese, when an article starting with a vowel comes after a word ending in a vowel, the vowel in the article is replaced by an apostrophe, e.g. *chiel a ciama ël fieul* (he calls his son) becomes *chiel a ciama 'l fieul*; *a-i é gnanca un can* (there is not even a dog) becomes *a-i é gnanca 'n can*. Finally, it should be noted that hyphenated words and letters are common in Piedmontese, while non-existent in Italian. For example, *i-j diso* (I say to him), *it ven-e* (are you coming).

Unfortunately, the use of special symbols to distinguish Italian pronunciation from Piedmontese is not standard, and the reader may find Piedmontese written with symbols other than those listed above. For example the symbol "ô" is sometimes used to denote the Piedmontese "o", which is pronounced like the Italian "u". For example, *fomna* (woman) is sometimes written *fômna*. We follow here the notation in Brero's *Grammatica della Lingua Piemontese* where for example, "o" is pronounced like the Italian "u" and appears without any special symbols. This confusion in symbols occurs when Piedmontese is written so that it can be properly

84

pronounced in Italian. Things get worse when one tries to write Piedmontese so that it can be properly pronounced in English. There are few instances where Piedmontese is written for English speaking readers. However, there is a well known novel by Marie Chay, entitled *Pilgrim's Pride*, about a Piedmontese family that comes to settle in a mining town in southern Colorado in the 1890s. The text is loaded with Piedmontese words spelled so that they can be pronounced by English speaking readers. Below we list a few examples from the book.

English-Piedmontese (Chay)	Piedmontese-Piedmontese (Brero)
garcigns (bread sticks)	*ghërsin*
padrugna (female boss)	*padron-a*
poulanta (corn meal)	*polenta*
tumigns (Piedmontese cheese)	*tomin*
taliarigns (flat pasta)	*tajarin*
risotte (cooked rice)	*risòt*

It is interesting that Chay felt obliged to add an "s" to plural nouns. This is not done in either Piedmontese or Italian. It should be noted that the Piedmontese dialect varies from one part of Piedmont to another. There are at least four notable variations of Piedmontese, e.g. the Piedmontese from *Torino*, *il Monferrato*, *il Canavese*, and *le Langhe*. Finally, it should be noted that the Piedmontese dialect includes many words that are closer to French than Italian, as illustrated by the table below:

English	Italian	Piedmontese	French
to work	*lavorare*	*travajé*	travailler
cow	*mucca*	*vaca*	vache
fire	*fuoco*	*feu*	feu
woman	*donna*	*fomna*	femme
apple	*mela*	*pom*	pomme
to go out	*uscire*	*surtì*	sortir
mister	*signore*	*monsù*	monsieur

4.3 PIEDMONTESE LITERATURE

After the fall of the Roman empire, the Catholic church maintained Latin as the official church language, but the number of people who understood Latin became smaller and smaller. Thus to preach to the people, the clergy had no choice but to use the local "vulgar" Latin, i.e. the local Italian dialect. To prepare their sermons, the clergy therefore had to put in writing a dialect the people could understand. This then was the impetus to the development of written "vulgar tongues." Thus, in about the year 1100 in the Piedmont area there appeared a collection of sermons written in the "Piedmontese" dialect called *i Sermoni Subalpini* (the Subalpini sermons). We list below the first few sentences of one of the sermons entitled (in Latin) *Exemplum de tribus amicis* (Example of three friends).

> *Un eisemple direm d'un hom qui ot tres amis. L'un era ric, e l'autre era ric, mas non era si ric cum era lo premer. Lo terz era povre. Or quest bon hom, qui avia questi trei ami, si era gastaldo d'un alt hom.*

Below we compare some of the words that appear in these sentences, between the "modern" Piedmontese dialect and modern Italian, i.e. the Tuscan dialect.

Sermoni Subalpini (English)	Modern Piedmontese	Modern Italian
un hom (a man)	*n' òm*	*un uomo*
ric (rich)	*rich*	*ricco*
amis (friends)	*amis*	*amico*
l'autre (the other)	*l'autr*	*l'altro*

In the fourteenth century, more religious literature appeared, written in the Piedmontese dialect, the so-called *Laudi Sacre* (Sacred Praises). The theme of these "praises" was generally the passion of Christ on the cross and the agony of his mother, Mary. We list below the first paragraph of one of these "praises" entitled, in Latin, *Lamentatio Lacrimosa* (Tearful Lamentation).

> *Oy me car figl, ti hay vist morir*
> *e li toy bey ogli non pos più obir,*
> *a toa mare non poy pi parler.*
> *Oy me dolenta, che debi più may fer?*

Again, we list some comparisons with modern Piedmontese and Italian.

Laudi Sacre	Modern Piedmontese	Modern Italian
me car figl (my dear son)	*mè car fieul*	*mio caro figlio*
toa mare (your mother)	*toa mare*	*tua madre*
parler (speak)	*parlé*	*parlare*
fer (to do)	*fé*	*far*

Another area where it became important to have a written language was in legal agreements. Below we give an example of a "surrender" document, involving the surrender of the *Pancalieri* castle in the year 1410.

La Presa di Pancalieri

Nota que lo castel de Panchaler
que tuyt temp era fronter
e de tute malnestay fontana;
per mantenir la bauzana
e al pays de Peamont trater darmage,

gli segnour de chel castel n–avén lor corage.
Ore lo bon princi de la Morea, Loys,
gli à descazà e honevolment conquys;
que o gl-à so host fermà
e tut entorn environà
de gent de pe e de gent d-arme,
unt eren trey coglart e quatre bombarde.
ma per la vertuy de Madona Luysa
chel castel ha cambià devysa,
sì que l-an mille CCCCX, circa le XXII hore,
lo mercol ady' vint nof de ottovre,
chigl del castel se son rendù
e ala marcy' del dit princi se son metù,
que gli a dedintre soe gent mandà
e la soa bandera sussa lo castel àn butà,
la qual n-à la banda biova traversa,
en criant aute vox: «Viva lo princi a part versa».

Al qual Dee per la soa bontà
longament dea vitoria e bona santà. Amen.

However, the first examples of serious writings in Piedmontese are probably the *tòni*, satirical poems set to music. The term *tòni* means "songs" (*canzoni*, in Italian). We list below a few stanzas of a *tòni* written (unknown author) in the sixteen hundreds.

Canzone di Madonna Luchin-a

Luchin-a va a la piassa
con lo cavagn al brass,
e treuva una cabassa
pien-a 'd ramolass.
Cand a j'ha vist,
na buta tre da banda,
peui dis a l'ortolanda:
«Vàire veul-lo 'd chist?»

«Deme na parpaiola
ch'a l'han bon savor
e sté su mia paròla
ch'a-i n'é pa gnun mijor.
Se pensesse për sòrt
ch'mi 'v men-a baie,
veuj deve j'ortolaie
e lo sëstin e l'ort.

Un carluss vë veuj deve
sensa sté a mërcandé.
Se veule contenteve
tiré ij mei dné,
o sù, velà,
n'veuj mai ch'a sea dita!
A Dio bon-a vita,
bon-a vita, bon ann.

Anyone who knows modern Piedmontese would have no difficulty understanding this *tòni*. It is about a lady *Luchin-a* who goes to the plaza (*piassa*) to buy some vegetables (*ortolaie*), with her basket in hand (*cavagn al brass*).

After poetry came plays, and one of the most famous early Piedmontese play writers was *Carlo Giambattista Tana* (1649 - 1713). His most famous play is entitled *Ël Cont Piolèt* (Count Piolet). It is about the amorous adventure of a count, *Piolet*. We list below part of a dialog by the count found in scene twelve of this play.

From: *Ël Cont Piolèt*

> Amor, it im ciampàire,
> it im ciampàire, Amor.
> O ti o l'anfreidor
> im lasse nen mangé,
> im peuss nen durmi vàire;
> it im fas core a pé
> com un can màire;
> sansa saveje ancor
> s'Rosëtta 'm veul për sò sfojor.
> I son vënù a pòsta
> da mëssé Bias për avèje na rispòsta,
> ma a dis ch'a l'ha la ca
> pien-a dë forësté,
> ch'a j'hà ancor nen podù parlè.
> I avria bin gust d'avèj la fia,
> e costa vigna si dapress ida mia ...
> ma! cos'é-lo mai, chi ved?
> Rosëtta! I lo cred.
> O guarda ampò ch' bela garsonëtta;
> com a l'é dësvia;

90

a l'é lì viva, viva,
mi dío la vrità,
dë vòte am fà travonde la saliva.

He talks about his love for *Rosëtta*. He says "love, you are chasing me down" (*Amor, it im ciampàire*); "either you love, or a cold" (*O ti, o l'anfreidor*); "have taken away my apetite for food" (*im lasse nen mangé); etc.* The dialog ends with his reaction on seeing *Rosëtta*. He says, "Oh look what a beautiful young girl" (*O guarda ampò ch' bela garsonëtta*); "how she stands there alive, alive" (*com a l'é li viva, viva*); "to tell the truth" (*mi dio la vrità*); "sometimes she makes me drool" (*dë vòte am fà travonde la saliva*).

Perhaps, one of the most famous Piedmontese writers was Father *Ignazio Isler* (1702 - 1788), a parish priest (*La Crocetta* parish in *Torino*) who wrote poetry about everyday life in Piedmont, and titled these poems "*Canzoni Piemontesi.*" In the segment of a poem, entitled *Il paese della cuccagna*, listed below, he writes about some of the dishes people from Piedmont like to eat, and when they should be eaten.

Il Paese della Cuccagna

An fiocand, a-i ven 'd lasagne
Larghe tre travers ëd di,
E 'd michëtte a gran cavagne
Con dij bon maron candì.
Quand a-i ven, peui, la tempesta,
Tuti, anlora, a fan gran festa:
Che l'é tuta mach 'd bombon,
D'ale e 'd cheusse dë capon.

91

Dla polenta bela e consa
Ij fossaj son pien a ras:
E na pije fin ch'av pias;
Basta andé con una bronsa
Squasi gnun j'é ch'a na toca
Bin ch'a fonda tuta an boca,
Fòra 'd costi sensa dent
Ch'a na mangio alegrament.

The poem starts, "When it snows, comes the lasagna" (*An fiocand, a-i ven 'd lasagne*). He then goes on to write about "wings and thighs of capon" (*D'ale e 'd cheusse dë capon*), which one eats when a storm (*tempesta*) comes. Finally, he writes about *Polenta*, the classic Piedmontese corn meal dish, which of course can be eaten any time.

With all this literature being written, it was inevitable that "grammar" should evolve, and indeed in 1783, the first Piedmontese Rules of Grammar (*Grammatica Piemontese*) appeared, compiled by *Maurizio Pipino*. However, with the unification of Italy, interest in Italian dialects faded. It was only through the efforts of a group of poets-including *Amilcare Solferini*, *Oreste Fasolo*, *Alfonso Ferraro*, and *Arrigo Frusta*, who published a journal called *Birichin* (meaning "naughty one" in Piedmontese)-that written Piedmontese was kept alive. Then in the 1920s there was a renewed interest in the Piedmontese dialect, generated largely by the poet-writer *Pinin Pacòt* (*Giuseppe Pacotto*) and his journal *Ij Brandé*. We list below a small segment of an article he wrote in *Ij Brandé* in 1927. It is on the subject of preserving the Piedmontese dialect (language?) and starts out "We write Piedmontese because we speak it, and we speak and write it really from the heart..." (*I scrivoma 'l piemontèis përchè ch'i lo parloma, e i lo parloma e i lo scrivoma pròpi 'd cheur,...*). It ends "Our journal, little and poor as it is, is born to defend it, our dialect, and with it our tradition, our history, our character, so that, we Piedmontese-Italians, will learn to be good Italians when we learn to be good Piedmontese" (*Nòstra arvista, pcita e pòvra coma ch'a l'é, a nass apòsta për difendlo, nòstr parlé, e con chiel nòstra tradission, nòstra stòria, nòstr caràter, përchè, noi italian e peimontèis, i savroma esse 'd bon italian quand ch'i l'abio 'mparà a esse 'd bon piemontèis).* Remember, if you try to read this passage, the Piedmontese "ò" is pronounced like the Italian "o" while the Piedmontese "o" is pronounced like the Italian "u."

> *I scrivoma 'l piemontèis përchè ch'i lo parloma, e i lo parloma e i lo scrivoma pròpi 'd cheur, adess ch'a smija ch'a vada perdendse, dëspresià e dësmentià da jë stess piemontèis ch'a lo arnego.*
>
> *S'a l'é vèra ch'a staga për meuire, e bin, noi i voroma nen ch'a meuira! Con tut nòst sentiment e con tuta nòstra fòrsa i s'oponoma.*
>
> *Nòstra arvista, pcita e pòvra coma ch'a l'é, a nass apòsta për difendlo, nòstr parlé, e con chiel nòstra tradission, nòstra stòria, nòstr caràter, përchè, noi italian e piemontèis, i savroma esse 'd bon italian quand ch'i l'abio 'mparà a esse 'd bon piemontèis*

Pinin Pacot

So far the Piedmontese dialect, like other Italian dialects, is still alive. Outside big cities the dialect is the Italian of the people, the new vulgar tongue. Piedmontese songs are celebrated by the folk singer, and now politician (Activist in the *Lega Nord*, the political party seeking a more autonomous league of northern Italian states) *Gipo Farassino*. He has recorded a collection of his Piedmontese songs in *Gipo a sò Piemont* (Gipo, to his Piedmont). The song listed below is from this collection. It is a song about a "sad neighborhood" (*na borgà 'd malinconia*) of Turin, just "beyond the railroad bridge" (*'Dla dal pont, ëd la feròvia*) on the wrong side of the tracks. With "gray houses with many courtyards, where children born old, play" (*le ca grise con tante cort, andoa a gieugo ij cit, ch'a nasso vej*). "But luckily there is *Maria*" (*ma për fortuna a-i é Maria*). "It is difficult to live on poetry, if the Po is far away, and the hills a dream" (*A l'é dificil vive 'd poesìa, se 'l Pò a l'é lontan e la colin-a 'n seugn*). The river Po runs by Turin, with hills on the other side, both far away from this poor neighborhood. "Maria, if she's a little cold she comes real close. Maria, she's a little girl and I love her so" (*Maria, sa l'a 'n pò freid am ven visin. Maria, a l'é na cita e mi i veuj bin*). In this sad neighborhood, the "trees look like they are made of cement" (*le piante ch'a smijo 'd ciman*), and "around them there are only dogs" (*E intorn a lor a-i é mach ij can*) that "sniff a bit and turn away" (*ch'a nufio 'n pòch e a tiro via*).

Dla Dal Pont

Dlà dal pont, ëd la feròvia
a-i é na borgà 'd malinconìa.
un giornalé, na drogheria,
e le ca grise con tante cort
andoa a gieugo ij cit, ch'a nasso vej
E se na fija a basa 'n fieul
a l'é na còsa tanto normal,
ch'a son nen bon a sbassé j'euj.

A l'é na borgà sensa poesìa,
ma për fortun-a a-i é Maria.
Maria, a chërd ancor an nòstr amor.
Maria, a s'entusiasma a vëdde 'n fior.
E quand surtoma a serca la mia man,
e seugna 'd parte ansem a mi doman.

Maria, a l'é sicura che j veuj bin,
a l'é mia, ancheuj 'nt ës mond pien ëd sagrin.
E quand la nebia a stërma soa borgà,
a sorid sempre come na masnà.

A l'é dificil vive 'd poesìa,
se 'l Pò a l'é lontan e la colin-a 'n seugn.
Nojautri i l'oma 'l pont ëd la ferovia,
che sota a-i passo ij treno ch'a subio e coro via,
al sol, al mar, che noi i vedroma mai.

Maria, sa l'a 'n pò 'd frèid am ven visin.
Maria, a l'é na cita e mi i veuj bin.

Dlà dal pont, ëd la ferovia,
a-i é na borgà 'd malinconia.
Anche da 'd di a smija andurmia,
con j'euj sarà dij sò pogieuj,
con ij fornej ch'a fumo mai,
e con le piante ch'a smijo 'd ciman.
antorn a lor a-i é mach ij can,
ch'a nufio 'n pòch e a tiro vìa.

De Magistris

Other Piedmontese songs may be found in the chapter, *Italian Culture through Popular Songs*.

There are also poets still writing in Piedmontese. One such poet is *Bianca Dorato* (No relation to the authors). *Bianca*, or Italians would say *la Bianca*, writes poems about the mountains (Alps) which cap Piedmont, and the spectacular lights (*lus*, in Piedmontese) that permeate the mountains. We list below a poem entitled *Për Sòn* (For This), taken from her collection of poems *Drere 'd Lus* (Paths of Light). A poem can never really be translated from one language into another. However, to give the reader some idea of the sentiment being expressed by this poem, a loose translation into English is also listed.

Për Sòn

A-i son dij leu, là amont --
solengh ëd fiòca àuta,
barsaj nèir anchërnà
da speje avusse,
fiare 'd giassa brusanta.
A-j fà la lus, a l'alba:
con ròche nuitere a batiss
na ca për la s-ciandor.
Per sòn i ven-o da leugn
ciamanda ver se drere --
ch'a-i sio për mi
lame 'd giassa tajenta
a travërseme 'l cheur,
a dreube stra a la lus.

Bianca Dorato

For This (*Per sòn*) / There are places up there / lonely places of high snow drifts / black steep splintered places / of sharp swords / flames of burning ice / making light (*lus*) for the dawn / with nocturnal rocks build / a house of brilliance / **For this** I come from far away / crying towards the paths (*drere*) / that they be for me / cutting blades of ice / cutting the heart (*cheur*) / to open paths to the light.

96

It is not clear how much longer Italian dialects will survive. Perhaps Italian, French, Spanish, German, etc. will become themselves dialects of a United States of Europe. But for now dialects are an integral part of Italian culture. We have attempted to give the reader some flavor of one of the many dialects of Italy.

4.4 NOTES AND REFERENCES

Unfortunately, there is very little literature available on the Piedmontese dialect, or for that matter any Italian dialect, written in English. The book by Brero and Bertodatti, *Grammatica della Lingua Piemontese*, provides an excellent introduction, not only to Piedmontese grammar, but also to Piedmontese culture and literature. However, this volume is only available in Italian. A very complete account of Piemontese literature, from the twelfth to the eighteenth century, may be found in Brero's volume, *Storia della Letteratura Piemontese - Primo Volume*. Brero has also compiled a two-volume Piemontese - Italian dictionary, *Vocabolario Italiano - Piemontese*.

For those who read Italian, the recent book by Roberto Gervaso, *La Bella Rosina*, provides a very entertaining account of life and times of *Vittorio Emanuele II* and his famous mistress/wife *Rosina Vercellana*.

The text of Hermann Haller, *The Hidden Italy*, contains a good collection of poems by Piedmontese poets, e.g. *Edoardo Calvo* (1773-1804) and *Nino Costa* (1886-1945). Included in the collection is *Costa's* poem titled, *Ai Piemonteis ch'a travajo fòra d'Italia* (To the Piedmontese who work abroad). It is an ode to hard working Piedmontese who had to leave Piedmonte to find employment. One line goes, *S'aj pias gargarisè quaich bota 'd vin, j' è gnun ch'a bagna 'l nas për travaié* (even if they like to drink a few bottles of wine, no one works harder than they do). Another poem by *Costa* in the collection has as its theme a bombing of Turin by the Allies during World War II. The title of the poem is *14 Luj 1943: Complenta për la sità 'd Turin* (July 14, 1943: lamentation for the city of Turin). The first line of the poem goes, *"Pioroma ant l'ora neira dël destin, pioroma gent, për la sità 'd Turin* (Let's cry in the dark hour of our destiny, let's cry people for the city of Turin).

Throughout Italy dialects are on the decline, mainly due to use of standard Italian in the mass media and easy travel from one region to another. However, efforts are being made to preserve local dialects and cultures. To help preserve the Piedmontese language and culture, in 1969 the *Centro Studi Piemontesi* (Center for Piedmontese Studies) was founded in Turin. The center publishes a journal titled, *Studi Piemontesi.*, which covers the whole spectrum of Piedmontese culture, from history, to language, to literature, etc. In 1991, *l'Academia dla Lenga Piemontèisa (*the Piedmontese Language Academy) was founded by Professor Bruno Villata in Montreal, Canada to promote the Piedmontese language, especially in the new world, where countries such as Canada, the United States, and Argentina have large populations of people with Piedmontese origins. The academy publishes a journal, *l'Arvista dl'Acaemia* (the Academy Journal), which is written mostly in the Piedmontese dialect. Finally, in Turin, a newsletter is published with the title, *Gioventura Piemontèisa* (Piedmontese Youth) written almost exclusively in Piedmontese.

CHAPTER 5. Left-Brained Italians

5.1 INTRODUCTION

They say that the left part of our brain is the part that deals with logical/scientific thoughts, and that the right part of our brain deals with our intuitive/artistic thoughts. Most books on Italian culture focus on right-brained Italians, the artists, the musicians, the poets, etc. Since right-brained Italians are so well documented, we have elected to present in this chapter some of the famous left-brained Italians, the mathematicians, the scientists, and the engineers.

In the United States, mathematics, science, and engineering do not command the respect found for these disciplines in most other countries and in Italy in particular. Outside of *Euclid*, have you ever run across a street in the United States named after a mathematician? As a matter of fact the reason the street name *Euclid* appears in so many cities in the United States is not out of respect for Greek mathematics, but because whenever a surveyor runs out of street names, *Euclid* comes to the rescue. In Italy streets named after mathematicians, scientists, and engineers are fairly common. The first author recalls two such streets that he encountered daily on his way to the *Politecnico di Torino* during a sabbatical leave from 1991 to 1992. At the crossing of the two streets were the signs reading: *Via Giuseppe Peano, Matematico 1858-1932 and Via Corrado Segre, Matematico 1863 - 1924.*

If one counts Greeks who lived in Sicily and southern Italy, famous left-brained "Italians" go a long way back. *Pythagoras* (569 - 590 BC), a name known to all high school students in the world, founded his mathematical cult in *Crotone*, a city in what is now the Italian state of *Calabria*. Of course, he is most famous for the Pythagorean theorem on right triangles, which states that $a^2+b^2 =$

c^2, where "a" and "b" are the sides of a right triangle, and "c" is the hypotenuse. Another Greek-Italian, *Archimedes* (?? - 212 BC) was born in Sicily, e.g. *Siracusa.* *Archimedes* was a fantastic mathematician/scientist /engineer, the ideal of a left-brained person. He is known for many things, but perhaps best known for his discovery of the area of a circle being equal to πr^2, where r is the radius of the circle, and his approximation of π, i.e.

$$3\frac{10}{71} \leq \pi \leq 3\frac{1}{7}.$$

It is said he was killed by a Roman soldier while contemplating a mathematical problem he was writing in the sand. The Romans were great engineers, but few names of famous Roman engineers remain. The Romans, unlike the Greeks, were not interested in creating new mathematics or science and by the time the Roman Empire fell, a long dark age in science and mathematics ensued in Italy, as well as the rest of the Western world. It was not until increased commerce with the Arab world, during the middle ages, that interest in science and mathematics was renewed.

We distinguish between left and right-brained people, but of course we all have two-sided brains, and there is one well known Italian, *Leonardo da Vinci* (1452 - 1519) whose two sides were equally well developed. He was an artist, scientist, and engineer, the original "renaissance Man." However, with the evolution of time, one had to become more focused to make significant contributions in a given field. So in the sequel, we will present separately some famous Italian mathematicians, scientists, and engineers.

5.2 MATHEMATICIANS

Before discussing particular mathematicians, we should perhaps make some observations about mathematicians in general. First of all it was the Greeks, Euclid in particular, who created the discipline of mathematics, with its definitions, postulates/axioms, logical arguments, and theorems. Next, one should know that mathematics is generally divided into three main branches: Geometry (Study of points, lines, and surfaces), Algebra (Study of "finite" equations and operations), and Analysis (Study of infinite operations and limiting processes, e.g. derivatives and integrals). Finally, it should be noted that most mathematicians gain their fame only after their results are applied, in science or engineering, sometimes many centuries after their deaths. However, pure mathematicians are interested primarily in abstract mathematical results, and not the applications of mathematics. A good example is the British mathematician Godfrey Harold Hardy who was so proud of the fact that no applications were likely to be found for his abstract theory of complex functions. How disappointed he would have been to know of the application by engineers of his theory, known as Hardy spaces, to the design of control systems in the early eighties.

In any case, let us look at some of the contributions Italians have made to mathematics.

Fibonacci (1175 - 1250)

Born *Leonardo da Pisa* (Lenny from Pisa, not to be confused with Lenny from Vinci), *Fibonacci* was most famous for the book he wrote in 1202 entitled *Liber Abaci*. In it he posed a problem of rabbit population growth which lead to the sequence of numbers 1, 1, 2, 3, 5, 8, 13, 21, 34, 55, 89, 144, ..., now called the *Fibonacci* sequence. It is obvious that the nth term in the sequence, F_n, is simply the sum of the two previous terms, algebraically

$$F_n = F_{n-1} + F_{n-2}.$$

An equation of this type is referred to as a difference equation and one can show (the left-brained reader may want to fill in the details) that its solution is of the form

$$F_n = \frac{(\alpha^n - \beta^n)}{\alpha - \beta}$$

where $\alpha = (1+\sqrt{5})/2$ and $\beta = (1-\sqrt{5})/2$. The ratio $(1+\sqrt{5})/2 = 1.618033989...$ (recall that irrational numbers must have non-repeating decimal representations) appears in many applications and is called the **golden ratio**. When Lenny from Vinci (*Leonardo da Vinci*) illustrated *Luca Pacioli's* book *De Divina Proportione*, he included a figure of a man which contains a number of rectangles whose sides are in proportion to the golden ratio. This figure, referred to as *Vitruvian Man*, is probably one of *Leonardo da Vinci's* most famous illustrations, and is found on many souvenir T-shirts from Italy.

A more recent application of Fibonacci sequences, developed by J. Kiefer in 1953, involves the problem of searching for the maximum of a function f(x) over an interval $x_1 \le x \le x_2$. Kiefer developed an algorithm, now called a *Fibonacci search*, where after n-steps the location of the maximizing value of x is restricted to an interval of length $\dfrac{L}{F_n}$, where $L = x_2 - x_1$ is the original length and F_n is the nth *Fibonacci* number. See Wilde's text, *Optimum Seeking Techniques*, for more details.

In his time, Fibonacci was known only to a very small circle of co-workers. Now he is known to a large group of scientists and systems engineers. This is an excellent example of applications making the mathematician famous.

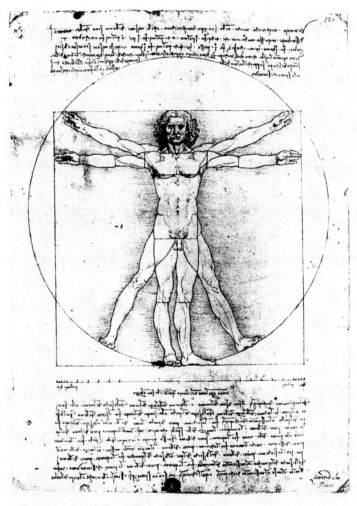

Leonardo, *Vitruvian Man*. Accademia, Venice

103

Girolamo Cardano (**1501 - 1576**)

During the sixteenth century, Italian mathematicians played a dominant role in algebraic developments. *Girolamo Cardano*, although perhaps not the most creative of the Italians at the time, wrote a manuscript entitled *Ars Magna* which included the solution of cubic and quartic polynomial equations. Most readers probably recall the quadratic equation

$$ax^2 + bx + c = 0$$

and its solutions

$$x_1 = \frac{-b + \sqrt{b^2 - 4ac}}{2a} \quad \text{and}$$

$$x_2 = \frac{-b - \sqrt{b^2 - 4ac}}{2a}$$

from high school algebra. This solution was known at the time. However, general solutions to the cubic

$$ax^3 + bx^2 + cx + d = 0$$

or quartic

$$ax^4 + bx^3 + cx^2 + dx + e = 0$$

were unknown. Actually it was *Sciopine da Ferro* (1465 -1526) and *Nicoló Fontana* (1500 - 1557), also known as *Tartaglia*[5], who independently discovered methods for solving the cubic equation. Both wanted to keep the method a secret, but *Cardano* (also known as *Cardan* or *Cardanus*) tricked *Tartaglia* into giving him the solution, which he then included, without permission but with acknowledgement, in his book. The quartic, or biquadratic equation was solved by *Cardano's* student *Luigi Ferrari* (1522 - 1565).

Cardano referred to complex roots, that is roots that involve the square root of a negative number such as $\sqrt{-1}$, as "impossible" roots. However, he was the first to actually use complex numbers in computations. For several centuries after *Cardano*, mathematicians tried to find explicit solutions to polynomial equation of degree greater than four, but always failed. It was not until 1826 that the German mathematician Abel proved that it was impossible to analytically solve a polynomial equation of order greater than four.

Giovanni Girolamo Saccheri (1667 - 1733)

In the field of geometry, the name of Saccheri stands out for his attempt to prove the "parallel postulate" of *Euclid*. A key postulate in *Euclid's* geometry was that, *through a point, not on a given line, there exists one and only one line parallel to the given line.*[6] Over the centuries mathematicians were concerned about the independence of this postulate from the other postulates of *Euclid*.

---

[5] *Tartaglia* comes from the Italian *tartagliare* (to stutter). As a child *Fontana* was slashed across the mouth by an invading French soldier in his home town of *Brescia*. This wound caused a speech impediment which lasted the rest of this life. He accepted in good humor the nick name *Tartaglia*.

[6] Actually the postulate in question, the fifth postulate, is a bit different, but can be shown to be equivalent to the postulate cited here.

Many felt that the "parallel postulate" could actually be proven from the other postulates. In 1733, *Saccheri* wrote a book entitled *Euclides Vindicatus* (*Euclid* Vindicated, in Latin). In this book Saccheri attempted to prove that the parallel postulate followed from the other postulates of Euclid. He approached the problem by assuming the parallel postulate was false and then attempted to arrive at a contradiction with the other postulates. His contradiction was equivalent to assuming that instead of *only one line parallel to a given line*, there could be *two distinct lines parallel to a given line*. He was lead to many "strange" geometric results, but never a contradiction. Rather illogically, he finally concluded that eventually a contradiction would be reached, and there was no other geometry but "Euclidean" geometry. This lapse in logic was a bit ironic since Saccheri was a Jesuit priest who specialized in teaching of logic. While a professor at the *Collegio dei Gesuiti di Torino* (Gesuit College of Turin), he wrote a book on logic entitled *Logica Demonstrativa*. Perhaps for Saccheri the Gesuit priest, admitting that there could be geometries other than Euclidean geometry, was like admitting that there was more than one God. Indeed, when in 1831 the famous German mathematician *Gauss* came to the conclusion that based on *Saccheri's* negation of *Euclid's* fifth postulate, other geometries were possible, he kept his discovery secret for fear of the reaction for suggesting there could be more than one geometry. Unknown to *Gauss*, it was the Russian mathematician *Lobachevsky* who was prepared to fully develop a "new geometry" based on the negation of Euclid's fifth postulate. He developed a geometry based on the postulate that *through a point not on a given line there exists two or more distinct lines parallel to the given line*. He published his results as a series of memoirs in the years 1829 - 30. This "non-Euclidean" geometry became known as *Lobachevskian geometry*. Those only familiar with Euclidean geometry will find the results of Lobachevskian geometry very surprising. For example, that the sum of the angles in a triangle is always <u>less</u> than 180° (In Euclidan geometry, the sum is always <u>equal</u> to 180°). A simple model of Lobachevskian geometry can be constructed by thinking of points inside a given circle, where "straight lines between two points are defined as arcs of circles going through the given points while intersecting the given circle at right angles. Finally, in 1854 the German mathematician *Riemann* suggested a geometry in which *no two lines* are parallel. The geometry based on this parallel line postulate is now referred to as *Riemannian geometry*. In *Riemannian geometry*, the sum of the angles in a triangle is always greater than 180°. A simple model for *Riemannian geometry* is the surface of a sphere, where lines are defined as arcs of great circles (circles created on the sphere when the sphere is intersected with a plane going through the center of the sphere). One knows that the shortest distance between two points on a sphere is defined by such arcs. Obviously all such lines on a sphere intersect when extended, hence no "lines" can be parallel.

Jacopo Francesco Riccati **(1676 - 1754)**

Riccati was born in Venice and studied law at the University of Padua. He was a wealthy count who instead of practicing law did research in mathematics. His mathematical results, four volumes simply entitled *Opere*, were published in 1756, two years after his death. What has made *Riccati* incredibly famous in the world of modern systems engineering is his investigation of *differential equations* of the form

$$\frac{dx}{dt} = ax^2 + bx + c.$$

Jacopo Francesco Riccati

It turns out that equations of this form, generalized to the matrix (rectangular array of variables) case, play a key role in the design of navigation and automatic control systems. The differential equation,

$$\frac{dX}{dt} = A'X + XA + Q + XWX,$$

where X is a symmetric n x n matrix, is now universally known as the *matrix Riccati differential equation*. It was the American scientist/engineer Rudolf Kalman who, in the early sixties, showed that many navigation and automatic control problems could be reduced to the solution of this matrix differential equation. In the text *Linear Quadratic Control* by Dorato et. al., where Kalman's design theory is presented, the name *Riccati* is cited over ninety times. Unfortunately, when most people hear this name they are more likely to think of an Italian cheese than a famous Italian mathematician.

Maria Gaetana Agnesi (1718 - 1799).

Italy has a history of being much more accepting of women in science and mathematics than the rest of Europe. During the Dark Ages, through the Renaissance, and even after, most European countries severely stifled women's educational opportunities.

Maria Gaetana Agnesi

The only opportunities were available through monasteries and nunneries. Italian women were making their mark before the end of the Middle Ages. It was even said that Italian women during the Renaissance were more accepted as equals in nontraditional fields than they are today. This opened mindedness lead to a number of exceptional women mathematicians and scientists in the 17th and 18th century.   Perhaps the most remarkable is *Maria Gaetana Agnesi*.   She was born in *Milano* in 1718 to wealthy, well-educated parents.   Her father, Dom Pietro Agnesi Mariami, a professor of mathematics, occupied a chair at the University of Bologna.

Maria Gaetana Agnesi is best known for her work on differential and integral calculus entitled *Analytical Institutions*, published in 1748. It was the first and most complete book on infinitesimal analysis and was considered one of the most important mathematical publications of the time. She pulled together works from various mathematicians including Newton's method of "fluxions" and Leibniz's method of differentials. In one part of her book she discusses a "versed sine curve" $xy^2 = a^2(a-x)$. This curve was studied earlier by Guido Grandi and Fermat. It became called *aversus* - a latin word meaning to turn. But, in Italian it sounded like the word *versiera* which means she-devil or witch. During translation of her book, the curve discussed by Maria became known as the "witch of Agnesi." Today, Maria Agnesi's name is synonymous with the "witch of Agnesi." This is very ironic considering the saint-like life lead by Maria. She is remembered for her charitable work with poor and destitute people.

Maria was elected to the Bologna Academy of Sciences and through an invitation of Pope Benedict XIV, was given an appointment as honorary lecturer in mathematics at the University of Bologna in 1750. She retired in 1752 and devoted her life to helping others. In 1762, the University of Turin asked her opinion of the

110

young Lagrange's articles on the calculus of variations, but she was totally emerged in social efforts and declined to answer. She died in 1799, and at the one-hundredth anniversary of her death, Milan named a street in her honor.

Giuseppe Luigi Lagrange (1736 - 1813).

Lagrange was born in *Torino* (Turin) of a French father and Italian mother. Incredibly brilliant as a child, he was appointed professor of mathematics at the Royal Artillery School in Turin (now a military school called *Scuola di Applicazione*) at the age of 18. In those days there were no schools of engineering. Engineering and applied mathematics were taught in military schools. Lagrange was interested in developing a calculus for the minimization of functions which depended not on points, but entire curves. He played a key role in developing the theory now called the *calculus of variations*. The basic problem he considered was to find a "curve" y(t) such that the integral:

$$\int F(t, y, y')\,dt$$

is minimized, where y' denotes the derivative of the curve y(t) with respect to t. The equation that characterizes the optimal curve

$$F_y - \frac{d(F_{y'})}{dt} = 0$$

where F_y and $F_{y'}$ denote partial derivatives of the function $F(t, y, y')$, is now commonly called the *Euler-Lagrange* equation. The calculus of variations was used extensively in designing optimal trajectories for various space missions in the early sixties. *Lagrange* applied his theory to problems in mechanics and in 1788 published his classic book, *Méchanique Analytique*.

Luigi Lagrange
Disegno di Bosio

By introducing a function L = T - V, now called the *Lagrangian* function, where T is the kinetic energy of a system and V is the potential energy, he was able to derive all of *Newton's* equations of motion for any mechanical system using his "calculus of variations." Lagrange is also well known to modern scientists and systems engineers for his "Lagrangian multiplier." He was able to show that the problem of finding a value of x which minimizes the function $f(x)$ subject to an equality constraint of the form $g(x) = 0$, could be reduced to the problem of minimizing the function $f(x) + \lambda g(x)$, with no constraints. The variable λ is the "Lagrangian multiplier." In 1758, he established the Turin Academy of Sciences which was housed in what is now the Egyptian museum in Turin. His fame spread throughout Europe. In 1766, he was appointed director of the Berlin Academy of Science, and in 1797 he became the first professor of mathematics at the *École Polytechnique* in France. It is interesting that while Turin lost a great mathematician to France, it gained one in return, Cauchy, at least for a few years. Cauchy joined the University of Turin as a professor of mathematical physics in 1830 and stayed until 1833, when he was enticed to return to France. The University of Turin hosted a long list of prominent mathematicians at the end of the nineteenth century, including *Vito Volterra* (1860 -1940), a pioneer in the solution of integral equations; *Giuseppe Peano* (1858 - 1932), famous for his axiomatic development of natural numbers (integers); and *Corrado Segre* (1863 - 1924), one of the developers of *differential geometry*. Of course Turin had no monopoly on mathematicians. During this time, mathematicians flourished throughout Italy. To cite a few other famous mathematicians for the time we have *Eugenio Beltrami* (1835 - 1900) in geometry, at the university of Pisa; *Ernesto Cesaro* (1859 - 1907), in analysis, at the University of Naples; *Tullio Levi - Civita* (1873 - 1942), in non-Euclidean geometry, at the University of Padua; and *Giuseppe Vitali* (1875 - 1932), in analysis, at the University of Bologna.

5.3 SCIENTISTS

Yes, there is a difference between a mathematician and a scientist, and the difference was most clearly defined in the sixteenth century by the most famous of all Italian scientist/mathematician *Galileo Galilei*. In fact, *Galileo* is credited with the introduction of the "scientific method." Basically, the scientific method involves the evolution of mathematical models for physical phenomena, *based on experimental data*. The key concept, which *Galileo* introduced, was that of using experimental data to evolve physical theories. In mathematics, the goal is to prove interesting theorems within a system of definitions and postulates. *There is never a need to verify a theorem with experimental data in pure mathematics.*

In our discussion of scientists we will focus on physicists, although important contributions were made by Italians in many other scientific fields, including biology, chemistry, and medicine. Physics is divided into many subspecialties; however, we will focus on three areas in particular, mechanics, electricity, and atomic physics.

Galileo Galilei (1564 - 1642)

Galileo was a philosopher, astronomer, mathematician, but foremost a physicist. He felt very strongly about the need to conduct experiments to test scientific theories, which resulted in constant opposition to his work. This endured during his entire lifetime. He studied philosophy and medicine at the University of Pisa, his native city. When he was 22, he published his first scientific paper, "*La bilancetta*," which described his invention of the hydrostatic balance. Shortly thereafter, he became a professor at the University. It was there that he discovered the law of falling bodies. In his famous experiments of dropping two balls of unequal weight from the

114

Leaning Tower of Pisa, he demonstrated his theory. His successful experiments resulted in a position as professor at the University of Padua in 1592.

During his time at the University of Padua, he became interested in the work of Nicolas Copernicus (1473 - 1543). Copernicus suggested that the sun was the center of the universe and not the earth. This was in direct conflict with the accepted theories of Aristotle and Ptolemys, but agreed with *Galileo's* new natural philosophy based on mathematics. He was not able to prove his theory until he built the first astronomical telescope twenty five years later in 1610. When Galileo announced his discovery, he was met with great opposition. It was even said that his work was contrary to the Scripture and inspired by the Devil. Galileo rebutted by saying that the Scripture should not be taken literally and "it (the Scripture) teaches us how to go to heaven, not how the heavens go." He continued his research for the next several years, but was later denounced by the Holy Inquisition. A prohibition against the Copernican system was declared and Galileo was warned not to defend the doctrine.

Galileo was appointed mathematician and philosopher to the Grand Duke of Tuscany. In 1623 he published *Il Saggiatore* (The Precision Scale) on the philosophy of science. At this same time, he was also working on *Dialogo dei due massimi sistemi del mondo, tolemaico e copernicano*, an indirect attack on the Ptolemaic system. The church finally approved the publication, but his enemies answered by again setting the Holy Inquisition on him. He was forced to read the following apology on his knees:

> *"I, Galileo, son of the late Vicenzo, Florentine, aged seventy years... having been pronounced by the Holy Office to be vehemently suspected of heresy, that is to say, of having*

held and believed that the Sun is the center of the World and immovable and that the Earth is not its center and moves with sincere heart and unfeigned faith, I abjure, curse and detest the aforesaid errors and heresies... and I swear that in the future I will never again say or assert verbally or in writing, anything that might furnish occasion for a similar suspicion regarding me; should I know any heretic or person suspected of heresy, I will denounce him to the Holy Office..."[7]

Galileo was sentenced to house arrest in his villa at *Arcetri* outside of Florence. His most important contribution to physics, *Discorsi Sopra Due Nuove Scienze*, was finished there and smuggled out by a prince of the Medici family. It was published in Holland in 1638. He became blind and then died, still a prisoner, in 1642. In 1737 his remains were moved to Florence and placed in the Church of Santa Croce. It was not until 1893 that the church officially accepted Galileo's views that parts of the Scripture should not be taken literally. Galileo, against tremendous opposition, made some of the greatest contributions to the world of physics and astronomy and completely changed the view of the universe.

Alessandro Volta (1745 - 1827)

Volta, the discoverer of continuous current, was born in Como, Italy which at the time was part of the Austrian Empire. He was born into a noble family, but because of his father's poor money managing skills, his education was taken care of through relatives in the church. Up until the age of seven, his parents were concerned with his slow development and even thought he may become mute.

---

[7] From: The Crime of Galileo, by Giorgio de Santillana, page 312. The University of Chicago Press, 1955.

But, he quickly bloomed into a bright student, intrigued with the physical world around him.

In his mid-teens, he decided to become a physicist despite pressure from relatives, who wanted him to enter the priesthood. At the age of 18, he was conducting his first experiments in electricity. At the age of 24, he published his first scientific paper: *"On the Attractive Force of the Electric Fire,"* and by the age of 30 was named Professor of Physics at the Royal School of Como. It was there that he made his first important discovery: *electrophorous* or "bearer of electricity." This was a significant contribution to science since it was the first device able to produce charges of static electricity repeatedly. During this same time he started experimenting in chemistry. He noticed gasses bubbling in the marshy areas of Lake Maggiore where he liked to fish. He collected the gasses in glass tubes and exploded them with electric sparks. This was a precursor of the spark-fired automobile engine. He also observed what is now called "Charles Law": air at constant pressure expands in the same proportion as the rise in temperature.

In 1782, he became professor at the distinguished University of Padua. There he made his next invention, the *condensing electrophorous*, an instrument that detects electric charge. He combined his electrophorous with a electroscope to make a detector capable of detecting very small quantities of electricity. This lead to the *electrometer*, which measured the force of an electric charge against the force of gravity. He was recognized for his work on the electrometer by being elected as a Fellow of the Royal Society of London in 1791 and by receiving the Copely Medal in 1794.

In 1791 he began experiments on "animal electricity." He was inspired by an article entitled "Forces of Electricity in Their Relation to Muscular Motion," written by a fellow Italian, *Luigi Galvani* (1737 - 1798), Professor of Anatomy at the University of Bologna.

This work lead to his greatest invention, the *electric pile*, which was the first electric battery. His work was admired by Napoleon Bonaparte. *Volta* became a senator and later a count in the Napoleonic empire. When Napoleon was defeated, *Volta* returned quietly to his home in *Canmago*. He died there at the age of 82. In 1881, he was honored by scientists and engineers who decided to name a unit of electromotive force after him. The *Volt* is defined as the difference of electric potential between two points of a conducting wire carrying constant current of 1 ampere, when the power dissipated between those two points is equal to 1 watt. *Volta* was also honored by being put on a 10,000 lire bill. (In the United States only politicians are put on our bills.)

Enrico Fermi (1901 - 1954)

Fermi was born in Rome and, like Galileo, was educated at the University of Pisa. In 1926 he became a professor at the University of Rome. He was awarded the Nobel Prize in Physics in 1938 for his research on quantum theory and atomic structure. Immediately after accepting the Nobel prize, he moved to the United States where he became a professor at Columbia University. At Columbia he supervised the construction of the first nuclear reactor. In 1945 he joined the Institute of Nuclear Studies at the University of Chicago. He is responsible for artificially producing more than 40 radioactive isotopes by neutron bombardment.

In September of 1944, he came to Los Alamos, New Mexico, to work on the atomic bomb. While at Los Alamos National Laboratory, he headed a division, appropriately called the F-Division, of theoreticians and experimentalists. One of his co-workers, another Italian immigrant, was *Emilio Segrè*, who went on to become a group leader at Los Alamos until 1946.

In 1954 he was awarded a $25,000 prize by the Atomic Energy

Commission. This prize was later named the *Enrico Fermi* Award and is given annually to the individual who has contributed most to the development, use, or control of atomic energy. Fermi was also honored in 1955, after his death, by having an atomic element named after him, the fermium (atomic number 100, atomic weight 253, symbol Fm).

5.4 ENGINEERS

Of course, Romans were great engineers. We all know of the roads, aqueducts, and cities built during the times of Imperial Rome (27BC - 476AD). And most people have heard of the engineering interests and accomplishments of *Leonardo da Vinci*. Indeed, many heads of state in Italy at the time tried to employ *Leonardo*, not as an artist, but as an engineer, mainly to build fortifications and weapons of war. Even in the fifteenth century, the defense industry was a major employer of engineers. And, yes, there is a difference between an engineer, a scientist, and a mathematician. Basically, engineers *use* science and mathematics to design devices and systems desired by society. In spite of the fact that the profession of engineering is as old as law and medicine, it was not until relatively recently that schools of engineering were created. The main purpose of the early Italian Universities, and one of the earliest universities in Europe was the University of Bologna founded in 1088, was the training of doctors and lawyers. It was not until seven centuries later that schools were instituted for the training of engineers. One of the early "engineering" schools in Europe was the Royal Artillery School in Turin (*Reale Scuola di Artigliera e Fortificazione*), already mentioned in Section 5.2. This school was founded in 1739 for the training of military engineers by the monarchy of Piedmont. About ten years later, the French founded one of the first "civil" engineering schools in Europe; the "School of Bridges and

Highways." At the present time there was only two "Polytechnics" (Schools specializing in Engineering) in Italy, one in Turin and one in Milano, although now just about every University in Italy has engineering programs.

Galileo Ferraris (1847 - 1897)

Galileo Ferraris was an electrical engineer who discovered the concept of a "rotating magnetic field," which revolutionized the use of electrical power. He showed that one could create a magnetic field which rotates in space, by locating three coils physically 120° apart, while exciting the coils with electrical currents that were electrically 120° out of phase. The rotating magnetic field is the basis for the operation of AC (alternating current) motors, and AC motors were the key to the industrial application of electrical power. The engineer who was credited for discovering the rotating magnetic field in the United States is the famous electrical engineer *Nikola Tesla*, who first proposed the idea in 1881.

Vilfredo Pareto (1848 - 1923)

Pareto was born in Paris of an Italian father and a French mother. His father was a political exile from Genova, at the time controlled by the Piedmontese monarchy, because of his republican sympathies. However, the family returned to Italy in 1858, and *Vilfredo Pareto* completed his engineering studies at the Polytechnic of Turin (*Politecnico di Torino*) in 1869. *Pareto* worked for a number of years as an engineer for the Florence branch of the Rome Railway Company, but his interest shifted over to economics. He applied his analytical engineering training to the study of economics, and in 1896 published a classic book on *mathematical economics* (also referred to as econometrics) entitled *Cours d'Économique Politique*. The book was written in French while he was a professor of Economics at the University of Lausanne in Switzerland. He tried to obtain a teaching position in Italy, but was unsuccessful. In 1893, he received a Chair of Economics at the University of Lausanne and moved permanently to Switzerland. *Pareto* is known world wide by engineers for the concept of optimality he introduced for minimizing more than a single function. The problem is, given a collection of functions $f_1(x)$, $f_2(x)$,..., find a value x which makes *all* the functions "as small as possible." An economic example of a problem of this type, currently called *multiobjective* or *vector optimization*, is where one function is "expenses" and another is the "incident of product defects." Obviously one would like both objectives to be small, but some tradeoff may be required. *Pareto* introduced the concept of non-inferior solutions, which are now popularly called *Pareto optimality solutions.* A solution x* is a non-inferior, or *Pareto optimal*, if there exists no other value of x such that

$$f_i(x) \leq f_i(x^*) \text{ , i = 1, 2, 3....}$$

with strict inequality holding for at least one of the functions.

Pareto's political ideas were popular with the Fascist regime in Italy. Mussolini claims to have taken classes with *Pareto* in Lausanne and called him "the most illustrious of my teachers." What particularly attracted the Fascists was *Pareto's* concept of *elites* ruling a country. Pareto felt that people who reached high positions did so in general because of their abilities, and that they should run the country, rather than politicians selected from masses of people with minimal achievements. Obviously, the Fascists included themselves in with the *elites*. *Pareto* is often associated with Fascism, but it should be recalled that he died well before Fascism reached its heights of power, and in very bad economic times when Fascist ideas were popular with just about all Italians. It is unlikely that *Pareto* would have supported Mussolini as a dictator, given his aversion to any kind of absolute rule.

Guglielmo Marconi (1874 - 1937)

Marconi, the father of broadcasting, was born in *Bologna* to a Italian father and Irish mother. *Marconi* did not attend public school but was tutored on the family estate. He never obtained a formal degree, but studied math and physics passionately. Even at an early age he showed great interest in electricity. In 1894, he learned of the work of Hertz who successfully radiated electromagnetic waves, and that planted the seed for Marconi's great idea of the wireless telegraph. He was later quoted as saying (in recalling his thoughts at that time), "It seemed to me that if the radiation could be increased, developed and controlled it would be possible to signal across space for considerable distances. My chief trouble was the idea was so elementary, so simple in logic, that it seemed difficult to believe no one else had thought of putting it into practice. I argued, there must be more mature scientists who had followed the same line of thought and arrived at almost similar conclusions. From the first idea was so real to me that I did not realize that to others the theory might appear quite fantastic."

In the late 1890s, he began experiments at the family estate *Villa Grifone* in *Pontecchio* with financial assistance from his father. In 1895 he successfully transmitted a signal from one mile away by means of a directional antenna. He spent the rest of his life improving his wireless transmission system. He patented it in 1897 and formed the Marconi Wireless Telegraph Co. Ltd in London. Initially, Italy did not recognize the significance of Marconi's work and refused to assist him financially, therefore, *Marconi* went to England to continue his work; however, he always remained loyal to Italy. Being brought up by an Irish mother, he was fluent in English. In 1899, he transmitted across the English Channel between England and France and in 1901 successfully transmitted across the Atlantic Ocean between Poldhu in Cornwall, England, and Saint John's in

Newfoundland, Canada. The Italian and English Navies adopted *Marconi's* system and soon ships were able to send distress signals to shore. *Marconi's* system was used aboard the Titanic and *Marconi* is credited with saving the lives of the 712 survivors.

There were many legal battles over the Marconi patents. Marconi did not actually discover the "wireless," but he put together a team that made it practical. He was the first to admit that the road to the wireless was paved by many scientists before him, and that he only made the final adjustments to make it practical. However, most of the engineers and scientists of the time credit *Marconi* with the invention and felt it appropriate to call the wireless the "Marconi wireless." His portrait and some of his equipment is depicted on a 2,000 lire bill. He received the Nobel Prize in Physics in 1909 and was in charge of the Italian wireless service during World War I. He spent his last years experimenting with shortwaves and microwaves. *Marconi's* invention changed the world by linking the entire globe through wireless communication.

5.5 NOTES AND REFERENCES

More information on many of the Italian mathematicians and scientists discussed in this chapter may be found in Kramer's two volumes, *The Nature and Growth of Modern Mathematics, Volumes 1 and 2*. Saccheri's text , *Euclides Vindicatus,* has been translated into English (See Halsted in the References section).

Many books have been written about, and by, Pareto, e.g. Bucolo's *The Other Pareto*; Freund's *Pareto*; and Pareto's own classic volume, *Manual of Political Economy*.

A collection of papers on the life and works of Riccati may be found in Bittanti's edited volume, *Count Riccati and the Early Days of the Riccati Equation*.

A detailed account of Lagrange's life and accomplishments may be found in Burzio's, *Lagrange* (in Italian).

For more information on Maria Gaetana Agnesi see Osen's, *Women in Mathematics*.

The life of Marconi and his development of the wireless communication is chronicled in Dunlap's *Marconi - The Man and His Wireless*. A summary of Volta's contributions may be found in Bordeau's, *Volts to Hertz, The Rise of Electricity*.

CHAPTER 6. Italian Culture Through Popular Songs

6.1 INTRODUCTION

One of the best ways to learn the culture of any country is through its popular songs. Popular songs help you learn the language, especially the spoken language. They help you learn the history of a country, its eating habits, its value system, its geography, etc. Of course, songs from opera could accomplish many of these same goals, and, as everyone knows, Italy is famous for its operas. However it is a bit intimidating for the average person to sing along with *Pavarotti*, and opera, when "belted" out by an opera singer is difficult to understand even for the native speaker. So we have elected to focus on popular songs.

Since there was no official Italian language before the unification of Italy in 1861, one can expect that many popular "Italian" songs are actually songs in one dialect or another, and indeed this is the case. But the dialect that dominates popular songs in Italy is Neapolitan. Many of the most beautiful "Italian" songs come from Naples, songs like *O Sole Mio*, *Santa Lucia*, *Vieni Sul Mar*, *Duorme Carmè*, *Funiculì-Funiculà*, *Torna a Surriento*, *Parlami d'Amore Mariù*, *Oi Marì*, *O'Paese d'O Sole*, *Marechiare*, etc. In the sequel we have collected songs in Italian, and in the Italian "dialects" of Neapolitan, Piedmontese, and Sicilian. We have focused on songs that are commercially available on audio cassettes or CDs. The relevant cassettes and CDs are identified in the *Notes and References* section at the end of this chapter. After each song we include a list of key vocabulary words. Words and phrases are translated in the order they appear in the songs.

The subject matter of Italian popular songs varies enormously, however four themes do standout.

• Songs about *Mamma* (Mom).
• Songs about *Maria* (Mary)
•Songs about *amore* (love) and *matrimonio* (marriage).
• Songs about one's *paese* (hometown).

It should be noted that the words of popular songs are not standardized, so that the words on any particular cassette or CD may vary from those listed here.

6.2 SONGS IN ITALIAN

The songs we have included in this section deal with a variety of themes, e.g. *Mamma*, *Maria*, *amore*, *paese*, etc., but they are all written in standard Italian.

♦ ***Chitarra Romana***. Chitarra Romana means Roman guitar. This is a famous Roman love song. It is a sad song about a loved one who no longer comes to the balcony (*balcone*) to greet her lover. Almost every home in Italy has a balcony. The balcony was at one time a center for social life. Television is keeping most people indoors these days.

Chitarra Romana
Di Lazzaro – Bruno

1.
Sotto un manto di stelle,
Roma bella mi appare.
Solitario è il mio cuore,
disilluso d'amor,
vuol nell'ombra cantar.
Una muta fontana al balcone lassù ...
O chitarra romana,
accompagnami tu!

2.
Suona, suona, mia chitarra,
lascia piangere il mio cuore!
Senza casa e senza amore,
mi rimani solo tu!
Se la voce è un po' velata,
accompagnami in sordina ...
La mia bella Fornarina
al balcone non c'è più!

3.

Lungotevere dorme
mentre il fiume cammina.
Io lo seguo perché
mi trascina con sé
e travolge il mio cuor.
Vedo un'ombra lontana,
e una stella lassù ...
O chitarra romana,
accompagnami tu!

4.

Se la voce è un po' velata,
accompagnami in sordina ...
La mia bella Fornarina
al balcone non c'è più!
O chitarra romana,
accompagnami tu!

Vocabulary

Sotto un manto di stelle - Beneath a canopy of stars
Roma bella mi appare - Beautiful Rome appears to me
Solitario il mio cuore - Lonely my heart
disilluso d'amor - disappointed in love
vuol nell'ombra cantar - (my heart) wants to sing in the shadow (*vuol*, short for *vuole*, and *cantar*, short for *cantare*)
Una muta fontana - a silent fountain
al balcone lassù - and a balcony above
O chitarra romana - Roman guitar
accompagnami tu - (you) accompany me

Suona - Play**mia chitarra** - my guitar
lascia piangere il mio curoe - let my heart cry (*lascia* from the verb *lasciare* - to let)
Senza casa - Without a home
e senza amore - and without love
mi rimani solo tu - only you are left for me
Se la voce è - If my voice is
un po' velata - a bit muffed
in sordina - softly
La mia bella Fornarina - my beautiful Fornarina
al balcone non c'è più - is no longer on her balcony

♦ *L'Italiano*. "Let me sing, I'm an Italian (*Lasciatemi cantare, sono un italiano*)." This is a song about modern Italy. "With a car radio always in the right hand (*Coll' auto radio sempre nella mano destra*)." You cannot leave your car radio in a car in Italy. It almost surely will be stolen. So you see many Italians walking around with their auto radios in hand. American culture now dominates the young people in large Italian cities. Posters with American themes are everywhere. "Too much American on all the posters (*Con troppa America sui manifesti*)." There is also a certain sadness in the look of some young people, perhaps reflecting concern about an uncertain future. "Hello Italy, hello Maria, with your eyes full of sadness (*Buongiorno Italia, buongiorno Maria, con gli occhi pieni di malinconia*). Hello God, you know I exist too (*Buongiorno Dio, sai che ci sono anch'io*)."

L'Italiano
Minellono-S. Cutugno(1983)

1.
Lasciatemi cantare, con la chitarra in mano,
Lasciatemi cantare, sono un italiano.

2.
Buongiorno Italia, gli spaghetti al dente.
Un partigiano come presidente.
Coll' auto radio sempre nella mano destra.
Un canarino sopra la finestra.

3.
Buongiorno Italia con i tuoi artisti.
Con troppa America sui manifesti.

Con le canzoni con amore, con il cuore.
Con le donne, sempre meno suore.

4.
Buongiorno Italia, buongiorno Maria,
con gli occhi pieni di malinconia.
Buongiorno Dio, sai che ci sono anch'io.

5.
Lasciatemi cantare, con la chitarra in mano,
Lasciatemi cantare, una canzone piano piano.
Lasciatemi cantare, perche ne sono fiero.
Sono un italiano, un italiano vero.

6.
Buongiorno Italia, che non si spaventa,
con la crema da barba, alla menta.
Con un vestito gessato sul blu,
e la moviola la domenica in tivù.

7.
Buongiorno Italia, con il caffe' ristretto.
Le calze nuove nel primo cassetto.
Con la bandiera in tintoria,
e una seicento giù di carrozzeria

Repeat 4 and 5

Vocabulary

Lasciatemi cantare - Let me sing
con la chitarra in mano - with
the guitar in hand
sono un italiano - I`m an Italian

131

(*sono*, from the verb *essere* - to be)

gli spaghetti al dente - spaghetti lightly cooked

Un partigiano come presidente - a resistance fighter as president

Coll' auto radio - with the car radio

sempre - always

nella mano destra - in the right hand

Un canarino - a canary

sopra la finestra - at the window

i tuoi artisti - your artists

sui manifesti - on posters

Con le canzoni - with songs

con amore - with love

con il cuore - with heart

Con le donne - With women

sempre meno suore - always fewer nuns

gli occhi - eyes

pieni di malinconia - full of sadness

Dio- God

sai che - you know that

ci sono anch'io - I exist too

canzone - song

piano piano - very softly

perché - because

ne sono fiero - I'm proud of it

con la crema da barba - with the shaving cream

alla menta - mint flavored

un vestito - a suit

gessato - plastered

sul blu - blue tinted

con il caffè ristreto - with straight coffee

Le calze nuove - The new socks

nel primo cassetto - in the top draw

Con la bandiere in tintoria - with the flag at the dry cleaner

e una seicento - a six hundred (Fiat car)

giù di carrozzeria - in bad condition

♦ *Mamma*. This is obviously a "Mamma" song. Mothers are extra special in Italy. Italians love their families, but most of all they love their mothers. Many Italians had to leave their mothers to find work and a better life. For an Italian, the joy of being able to return to one's mother is almost beyond description. This classical song probably comes as close to describing this event as any song can. "Mom, I am so happy, because I am returning to you (*Mamma son tanto felice, perché ritorno da te*). My song tells you (*La mia canzone ti dice*), that for me this is a most beautiful day (*ch'è il più bel giorno per me*)! Mom, my song flies only to you (*Mamma, solo per te la mia canzone vola*)! you will be with me (*Sarai con me*), you will never again be lonely (*tu non sarai più sola*)!"

Mamma
Cesare Andrea Bixio – Bixo Cherubini (1943)

1.
Mamma, son tanto felice
perché ritorno da te.
La mia canzone ti dice
ch'è il più bel giorno per me!
Mamma, son tanto felice
Viver lontano, perché?

2.
Mamma ...
Solo per te la mia canzone vola!
Mamma ...
Sarai con me, tu non sarai più sola!

133

3.

Quanto ti voglio bene!

Queste parole d'amore,

che ti sospira il mio cuore,

forse non s'usano più.

Mamma ...

Ma, la canzone mia più bella sei tu!

Sei tu, la vita,

e per la vita non ti lascio mai più!

4.

Sento la mano tua stanca

cerca i miei riccioli d'or.

Sento la voce ti manca

la ninna nanna d'allor.

Oggi la testa tua bianca

io voglio stringere al cuor!

Repeat 2, 3

Mamma, mai più!

Vocabulary

son - I am (*sono*, from the verb *essere* - to be)

tanto felice - so happy

ritorno - I am returning

da te - to you

La mia canzone - my song

ti dice -tells you (*dice*, from the verb *dire* - to say)

ch'è - that it is (*è*, from the verb *essere* - to be)

il più bel giorno - the most beautiful day

per me - for me

Viver - to live (*vivere*)

lontano - far away

perché - why

Solo - only

per te - for you

vola - flies (from the verb *volare* - to fly)

Sarai con me - you will be with me (*sarai*, from the verb essere - to be)
sola - lonely
Quanto - How much
ti voglio bene - I love you
Queste parole - these words
d'amore - of love*che ti sospira il mio cuore* - that my heart sighs to you (*sospira*, from the verb *sospirare* - to sigh)
forse - maybe
non s'usano più - are not used anymore (*usano*, from the verb *usare* - to use)
Ma, la canzone più bella sei tu - But, you are my most beautiful song (*sei*, from the verb *essere* - to be)
la vita - life

non ti lascio mai più - I will never leave you again (*lascio*, from the verb *lasciare* - to leave)
Sento - I feel
la mano tua stanca - your tired hand (*mano*)
cerca - is looking for
i miei riccioli d'or - my golden curls
Sento la voce ti manca, la ninna nanna d'allor - I hear (*sento*) that you can't sing the old lullaby (*ninna nanna*)
Oggi - today
la testa tua bianca - your white head of hair
io voglio - I want (*voglio*, from the verb *volere* - to want)
stringere al cuor - to hug to my heart (*cuor*)

♦ *Mi Scappa la Pipì, Papà.* This is a modern Italian children's song about a boy who has to make *pipì* at all the wrong times. With our Anglo-Saxon hang ups with the body and bodily functions, it is unlikely that a song of this type would ever have been as popular in the United States as it was in Italy a few years ago. "I have to make peepee, daddy (*Mi scappa la pipi, papà*). I really can't hold it anymore (*non ne posso proprio più*), I'm going to do it right here (*Io la faccio qui*)." He gets the urge at the wrong moments (sound familiar?), while watching a movie (*cìnema*), attending a wedding (matrimonio), and at a soccer stadium (*stadio*).

Mi Scappa la Pipì, Papà

1.
Con i nostri chiar di luna, quando al cinema si va.
Il bambino mio fa festa, e un po' anche suo papà.
ma nel buio, sul più bello, lui mi dice così:

2.
Mi scappa la pipì, mi scappa la pipì, mi scappa la pipì, papà.
Mi scappa la pipì, mi scappa la pipì, mi scappa la pipì, papà.
Mi scappa la pipì, mi scappa la pipì, mi scappa la pipì, papà.
Non ne posso proprio più, io la faccio qui!

3.
Invitati a un matrimonio, invitati siamo qua.
Io, mia moglie, ed il bambino, con gli sposi sempre là.
Ma allo scambio dell' anello, lui mi dice così.
Repeat 2

4.

Allo stadio c'è fermento, con mio figlio sempre qua.
Ho giocato la schedina, la mia vita cambierà.
Ma al momento del rigore, lui mi dice così:
Repeat 2

5.

Ma no, ma non è possibile,...
Non ne posso proprio più, io la faccio qui!

Vocabulary

Con i nostri chiar di luna - With these bright moon-shining nights
quando al cinema - when to the movies
si va - we go (from the verb *andare*)
Il bambino mio - My boy
fa festa - is happy (literally, "is having a feast")
e un po' anche suo papà - and a little bit also his father (is happy, that is)
nel buio - in the dark
sul più bello - at the best moment (literally, "on the most beautiful")
lui mi dice così - he says
Invitati - Guests
un matrimonio - a wedding
siamo qua - we are here (from

the verb *essere*)
mia moglie - my wife
gli sposi - the couple
sempre là - still there
allo scambio dell' anello - at the exchange of the ring
stadio - stadium (by default a stadium in Italy is a soccer stadium)
c'è fermento - there is excitement
con mio figlio sempre qua - with my son always here
Ho giocato la schedina - I played the soccer lottery
la mia vita - my life
cambierà - will change
Ma al momento del rigore - but at the penalty shot (11 meters from the goal).

137

♦ *Parlami d'Amore, Mariù*. Though perhaps not so obvious, this is a *Maria* song. There are so many ways to say Mary in Italian, e.g. *Mariù*, *Marì*, *Mariuccia*, *Mariella*, *Marietta*, etc. Every region of Italy has at least one *Maria* song, but this one is probably the most well known of all of them. In section 4.3 we listed a Piedmontese *Maria* song, *Dlà dal Pont*, and in the next section you will find a classic Neapolitan *Maria* song *Maria, Marì*. The refrain starts, "Speak to me of love, Mariu (*Parlami d'Amore, Mariù*)." It then goes on "You are my whole life (*Tutta la mia vita, sei tu*). Your beautiful eyes shine (*Gli occhi tuoi belli brillano*), they flash like dreamy flames (*fiamme di sogno scintillano*)! Tell me this is no illusion (*Dimmi che illusione non è*), tell me that you are all mine (*dimmi che sei tutta per me*)! Here near your heart, I will suffer no more (*Qui sul tuo cuor non soffro più*)!"

Parlami d'Amore, Mariù
Ennio Neri – Cesare Andrea Bixio

1.
Come sei bella, più bella stasera, Mariù!
Splende un sorriso di stella negli
occhi tuoi blu!
Anche se avverso il destino domani sarà,
oggi ti sono vicino, perché sospirar?
Non pensar!

2.
Parlami d'amore, Mariù!
Tutta la mia vita sei tu!

138

3.

Gli occhi tuoi belli brillano
fiamme di sogno scintillano!
Dimmi che illusione non è;
Dimmi che sei tutta per me!
Qui sul tuo cuor non soffro più:
Parlami d'amore, Mariù!

Repeat 3

Vocabulary

Come sei bella - How beautiful you are (*sei*, from the verb *essere* - to be)

stasera - tonight

Splende un sorriso - A smile shines (*splende*, from the verb *splendere* - to shine)

di stella - like a star

negli occhi tuoi blu - in your blue eyes (*occhi* - eyes)

Anche - even

se avverso - if adverse

il destino - destiny (the future)

domani - tomorrow

sarà will be (*sarà*, future of the verb *essere* - to be)

oggi - today

ti sono vicino - I am near you (at your side)

perché - why

sospirar - sigh

Non pensar - don't worry

(literally, don't think about it)

Parlami! - speak to me! (from the verb *parlare* - to speak)

d'amore - of love

Tutta la mia vita - my whole life

sei tu - you are (*sei*, from the verb *essere* - to be)

Gli occhi tuoi belli - Your beautiful eyes

brillano - shine

fiamme - flames

di sogno - of a dream

scintillano - sparkle

Dimmi - Tell me (from the verb *dire* - to say)

che illusione non è - that this is no illusion (*è* - from the verb *essere* - to be)

che sei tutta per me - you are all mine (*sei* - you are, from the verb *essere* - to be)

Qui - here

139

sul tuo cuor - by your heart
non soffro più - I will suffer no more (*soffro* - I suffer, from the verb *soffrire* - to suffer)

♦ *Piemontesi*. This is a recent (1991) paese song about the Italian state of Piedmont and its people. There is a lot of sentiment in Italy at the present time, especially in northern Italy, for more state autonomy. This song sings the praises of Piedmont and its people (Piemontesi). If the Lega Nord[8] has its way this could become a "national" anthem. The refrain goes "People of Piedmont, of long ago (Piemontesi d'una volta). People of Piedmont, without age (Piemontesi senza età)." The song then describes the Piedmontese who lived a "hard and labored life (vita dura e travaja - in Piedmontese)." It is often said the Piedmontese are courteous, but two faced (Piemontesi falsi e cortesi). But they see themselves as serious, hard-working people. Garibaldi and the king of Piedmont, Vittorio Emanuele II, often disputed, hence many Piedmontese felt Garibaldi hurt Piedmont in some of his actions. Thus the line: We who "Garibaldi harmed"! (Noi che, "Garibaldi ha fatto male"!). Of course no real song about Piedmont could end without some mention of polenta and vino rosso.

Piemontesi
Mauro Panattoni – Francesca Ferraresi (1991)

1.
Noi che siamo nati nella nebbia
gente di montagna e di pianura.
Noi che siamo chiusi e un po' scontrosi.
Noi che a volte questa vita "è dura."
Noi che amiamo il vino buono e rosso.

---

8   Political party advocating strong state autonomy.

2.

Noi che stiamo bene anche con niente.
Noi che dicon "falsi e cortesi",
ma che in fondo siamo brava gente.
Noi che abbiamo fatto anche l'Italia.
Noi, gente famosa senza storia.

3.

Noi che, "Garibaldi ha fatto male"
ma che in fondo ognuno poi è uguale.
Noi che lavoriamo senza gloria.
Noi che "mi son fatto io da solo".
Noi nelle risaie e nei cortili.

4.

Noi "un buon bicchiere dopo il coro".
Noi che abbiamo intorno le montagne.
Noi che abbiamo fatto il "partigian".
Noi che raccogliamo le castagne,
e che non sappiamo stare con le mani sempre in mano.

5.

Noi,
Piemontesi di una volta.
Piemontesi senza età.
Piemontesi di una volta.
"Vita dura e travajà".

6.

Noi che abbiamo visto i grattacieli.
Noi che ormai parliamo americano.
Noi che "mamma, dammi cento lire".

Noi che non scordiamo l'italiano.

7.
Noi che forse torneremo un giorno.
Noi che invece non siamo partiti.
Noi la Russia sotto verdi prati
noi che non siamo più ritornati.

8.
Noi che i nostri figli non capiamo.
noi che ragioniamo all'antica.
Noi che, "i nostri vecchi erano sacri,"
e capiamo solo la fatica.

9.
Noi che profumiamo di bucato.
Noi che, "prima cosa è la famiglia."
Noi che sorridiamo al brigadiere,
per poter sposare nostra figlia.

10.
Noi che abbiamo intorno le campagne.
Noi "polenta e lait, cheur au man."
Noi la sera insieme intorno al fuoco,
con le rughe dei cent'anni
 e lo sguardo un po' lontano.
Repeat 5 several times

Vocabulary

Noi - we
che siamo nati - that were born

(*siamo nati* from *essere nati* - to be born)

nella nebbia - in the fog
gente - people
di montagna - of the mountains
di pianura - of the plains
che siamo chiusi - who don't
speak too much (*siamo*, from the
verb essere - to be)
un po' scontrosi - a bit peevish
a volte - sometimes
questa vita - (this) life
è - is (from the verb *essere* - to
be)
dura - hard
che amiamo - who love
(*amiamo*, from the verb *amare* -
to love)
il vino buono e rosso - good red
wine
che stiamo bene - who are okay
(*stiamo*, from the verb *essere* - to
be)
anche con niente - even with
nothing
che dicon "falsi e cortesi" -
whom people call "two-faced and
courteous"
ma - but
che in fondo - in the final
analysis
siam brava gente - we are good
people
Noi che abbiamo fatto - who
have made
anche l'Italia - even Italy
gente famosa - famous people

senza storia - without a history
ha fatto male - made a mistake
ognuno - everyone
poi - then
uguale - equal
che lavoriamo - who work
(*lavoriamo*, from the verb
lavorare - to work)
senza gloria - without glory
mi son fatto io da solo - a self
made man
nelle risaie - in the rice fields
nei cortili - in the court yards
un buon bicchiere - a good glass
(of wine, of course)
dopo il coro - after a chorus
Noi che abbiamo intorno - who
have around us
le montagne - the mountains
il "partigian" - the partisan
che raccogliamo - who pick
le castagne - the chestnuts
che non sappiamo stare - who
do not know how to stay
(*sappiamo*, from the verb *sapere*
- to know)
con le mani sempre in mano -
sitting on our hands (literally,
"with our hands in hand")
grattacieli - sky scrapers
che ormai parliamo - who at this
point speak (*parliamo*, from the
verb *parlare* - to speak)
americano - English (literally,
American)

mamma, dammi cento Lire -
Mom, give me a hundred Lire
che non scordiamo - who do not
forget (*scordiamo*, from the verb
scordare)
l'italiano - Italian (language)
che forse torneremo - who
maybe will return (*torneremo*,
from the verb *tornare* - to return)
un giorno - one day
che invece - who on the contrary
non siamo partiti - have not left
(*partiti*, past participle of the
verb *partire* - to leave)
sotto - under
verdi prati - green fields
che non siamo più ritornati -
who never have returned
(*ritornati*, past participle of
ritornare - to return)
i nostri figli - our children
non capiamo - we do not
understand (*capiamo*, from the
verb *capire* - to understand)
i nostri vecchi erano sacri - our
old people were sacred
capiamo solo la fatica - we

understand only hard work
che profumiamo di bucato - who
have a fresh smell
prima cosa è la famiglia - the
family comes first
che sorridiamo - who smile
al brigadiere - at the "chief of
police"
per poter sposare - so that we
can marry
nostra figlia - our daughter
*che abbiamo intorno le
campagne* - who are surrounded
by farms
polenta e lait - Piedmontese corn
meal dish (*polenta*) and milk
(*lait*, in Piedmontese)
cheur - heart (*cuore*, in Italian)
la sera - evening
insieme - together
intorno al fuoco - around the
fireplace
con le rughe dei cent'anni -
lines one-hundred years old
e lo sguardo un po' lontano -
and a bit of a far-away look

♦ *Vivere.* This is a love song? Maybe, if one can sing about falling out-of-love. "What a magnificent day it is today (*Oggi che magnifica giornata*), what a day of happiness (*che giornata di felicità*)! My beautiful woman left me (*La mia bella donna se n'è andata*), she finally left me in peace (*m'ha lasciato alfine in libertà*)." The refrain goes, "To live without sadness (*Vivere senza malinconia*)! To live without anymore jealousy (*Vivere senza più gelosia*)!" How great it is to fall out-of-love! Why? "Because life is beautiful (*Perché la vita è bella*), and I want to live it ever more (*e la voglio vivere sempre più*)!"

Vivere
Cesare Andrea Bixio

1.
Oggi che magnifica giornata,
che giornata di felicità!
La mia bella donna se n'è andata,
m'ha lasciato alfine in libertà.
Son padron ancor della mia vita
e goder la, voglio sempre più.
Ella m'ha giurato nel partir
che non sarebbe ritornata mai più!

2.
Vivere senza malinconia!
Vivere senza più gelosia!
Senza rimpianti,
senza mai più conoscere cos'è l'amore
Cogliere il più bel fiore,
goder la vita e far tacere il cuore.

146

Ridere sempre così giocondo,
ridere delle follie del mondo,
vivere finché c'è gioventù
perché la vita è bella
e la voglio vivere sempre più1

3.
Spesso la commedia dell'amore
la tua donna recitar ti fa.
Tu diventi allora il primo attore
e ripeti quello che vorrà.
Sul terz'atto scende già la tela,
finalmente torna la realtà,
e la tua commedia dell'amor
in una farsa trasformata sarà!

Repeat 2

4.
Vivere pur se al cuore
ritorna un attimo di nostalgia...
Io non ho più rancore,
e ringrazio chi me l'ha portata via...
Vivere finché c'è gioventù,
perché la vita è bella
e la voglio vivere sempre più!

Vocabulary

Oggi che magnifica giornata -
What a magnificent day it is
today

che giornata - what a day
di felicità - of happiness
La mia bella donna - My

147

beautiful woman

se n'è andata - left me (*andata*, past participle of *andare* - to go)

m'ha lasciato - she finally left me

in libertà - in peace (free)

Son padron ancor - I am the master again (*son*, short for *sono*, from the verb *essere* - to be)

della mia vita - of my life

e goder la, voglio sempre più - and enjoy it, I want to evermore

Ella m'ha giurato - She swore to me

nel partir - in parting (*partir*, short for *partire* - to part)

che non sarebbe ritornata - that she would not return

mai più - ever again

Vivere - To live

senza - without

malinconia - sadness

senza più - without anymore

gelosia - jealousy

senza mai più - without any more

rimpianti - regrets

conoscere - knowing

cos'è l'amore - what love is

Cogliere - To gather

il più bel - the most beautiful

fiore - flower

goder - enjoy

la vita - life

e far tacere - and quite

il cuore - the heart

Ridere - To laugh

sempre - always

così giocondo - so joyously

delle follie del mondo - of the follies of the world

finché - as long as

c'è - there is (*è* from the verb *essere* - to be)

gioventù - youth

perché - because

la vita - life

è bella - is beautiful

e la voglio vivere - and I want to live it (*voglio*, from the verb *volere* - to want)

sempre più - evermore

Spesso - Often

la commedia - play (drama)

dell'amore - of love

la tua donna - your woman

recitar ti fa - makes you recite (*recitar,* short for *recitare* - to recite)

Tu diventi - You become

il primo attore - the main actor

e ripeti - and you repeat

quello che vorrà - whatever she wants (*vorrà*, future tense of *volere* - to want)

Sul terz'atto - At act three

scende giù la tela - the curtain descends

finalmente - finally

torna la realtà - reality returns

(*torna*, from the verb *tornare* - to return)
e la tua commedia dell'amor - and your drama of love
in una farsa trasformata sarà - will be transformed into a farce
pur se al cuore - even if in your heart
ritorna - returns

un attimo - a moment
di nostalgia - of nostalgia
Io non ho più rancore - I have no more bitterness
e ringrazio - and I thank
chi me l'ha portata via - who took her away from me (*portata*, past participle for *portare* - to take)

♦ *Uno Per Tutte.* One for all. One fellow, and all the girls, *Claudia, Paola, Laura,* and *Giulia.* "I think of them, and I see cloudless skies" (*Vi penso, e vedo cieli senza nuvole*). But there is a problem, its only a dream. "Then I open my eyes, and realize that there is no one, there is no one by my side" (*Poi apro gli occhi, allor mi accorgo che, non c'è non c'è nessuna accanto a me*).

Uno Per Tutte
T. Renis - Mogol – A. Testa

1.

*Sei quasi fatta per me, dipinta per me, **Claudia**.*
*Però confesso che tu, mi piaci di più, **Paola**.*
Di tutte, tutto mi va, oh la, la, la sempre.
Non so decidermi mai, mi trovo per ciò nei guai.

2.

Vi penso, e vedo cieli senza nuvole,
e mille mandolini mi accarezzano.
Poi apro gli occhi, allor mi accorgo che,
non c'è, non c'è nessuno accanto a me.

3.

*Innamorato di te, desidero te, **Laura**.*
*Non sono bello, però, che colpa ne ho, **Giulia**.*
Ho sulla bocca per voi, oh la la, la baci.
Ed io li dedico a chi per prima dirà di sì.

4.

Repeat 2 and 3.

Repeat "*Ed io li dedico a chi, per prima dira di sì*" three times

Vocabulary

Sei quasi fatta per me - You are almost made just for me

dipinta per me - painted for me

Però confesso che tu, mi piaci di più - But I confess, I like you more

Di tutte - With all

tutto mi va - everything is great

sempre - always

Non so decidermi mai - I can never decide

mi trovo per ciò - so I find myself

nei guai - in trouble

e mille mandolini

m'accarezzano - and a thousand mandolins caress me

Innamorato di te - In love with you

desidero te - I desire you

Non sono bello - I'm not good looking

però, che colpa ne ho - but, it is not my fault

Ho sulla bocca per voi - I have on my lips for you

baci - kisses

Ed io li dedico - And I dedicate them

a chi - to whoever

per prima dirà di sì - first says yes

151

6.3 SONGS IN THE NEAPOLITAN DIALECT

As noted in the introduction, some of the most beautiful Italian popular songs are from Naples. In fact probably more than 90% of all the songs that Americans think of as being "Italian" are in reality songs from Naples, sung not in Italian, but in the Neapolitan dialect, songs like *Santa Lucia, Funiculì-Funiculà, 'O Sole Mio, Maria-Marì, Torna a Surriento, 'O Paese d' 'o Sole*, etc., etc. Naples is really the cradle of "Italian" song, and the Golden Age of Neapolitan music, which had its origins in the *Villanelle* of the 17th century, was the period from about 1830 to 1930. It all started with the first *Piedigrotta* music festival in 1835. *Piedigrotta* was an annual music festival held every 7- 8 September, where new Neapolitan songs were first presented to the public. The hit of 1835 was Sacco's, *Te Voglio Bene Assaje* (I Love You So Much). They say that for a long time it was the only song you would hear in the streets of Naples. During the Fascist era, dialects were discouraged and not many new Neapolitan songs appeared. But, in the fifties there was a rebirth of Neapolitan songs, songs like *Luna Rossa, Anema e Core, Malafemmena, Guaglione, Aummo-Aummo*, etc. The *Piedigrotta* music festival lasted until 1954. It was replaced by the *il Festival della Canzone Napoletana* which was performed at the *Mediterraneo Theatre*. This Neapolitan music festival lasted until 1970, when purely Neapolitan music festivals went out of fashion.

One word that appears in many Neapolitan songs is   *scetate* (wake up!). Apparently falling asleep while being serenaded is a problem in Naples. A rare Neapolitan song that councils going to sleep, rather than waking up is the song *Carmela*, which says *"Duorme Carmè. 'O cchiù bello d' 'a vita è durmì* (Go to sleep Carmela. The most beautiful thing in life is to sleep)."

A few points here on the Neapolitan language may help in understanding the words of these songs. More on the grammar of the

152

language may be found in Appendix III. First of all, Neapolitan is pronounced essentially the same as Italian, with a few exceptions. One very noticeable exception is the way the letter "s" is pronounced in certain words. For example in Neapolitan, the "s" in *scullata* (low cut) sounds like the "sh" in the English word "shoot." In Italian, it would sound like the letter "s" in the English word "sea." Another big difference in Neapolitan versus Italian, is that final "o" and final "e" sound like "e" in the English word "the." So that the Neapolitan neighborhood of *Pusilleco*, that appears in so many classical Neapolitan songs, sounds like it should be spelled "*Pusilleche*" in Italian. Also it may help you to recognize Neapolitan words if you are aware of some letter changes that occur between Neapolitan and Italian. For example:

Italian		**Neapolitan**
b→v	*bocca* (mouth)	*vocca*
	bacio (kiss)	*vaso*
g→j	*giocare* (to play)	*juca'*
	giornata (day)	*jurnata*
q→c	*qua* (here)	*ccà*
	questo (this)	*chisto*
p→ch	*più* (more)	*cchiù*
	piango (I cry)	*chiagno*

♦ *A Marechiare.* *Marechiare* (*Marechiaro*, in Italian) is the name of a section of Naples that borders the bay. The words were written by one of Naples' most famous poet and song writter, *Salvatore Di Giacomo.* It is about a girl, *Carulì,* and the window (*fenesta*) of her apartment that faces the bay of Naples. *A Marechiare ce sta 'na fenesta* (At Marechiaro there is a window). It is said that when *Di Giacomo* wrote the song he had never seen this famous window. But, now there is a house in Marchiaro with a window facing the bay, and a plaque next to the window commenorating this famous song and its composer. This site is a must-see for any lover of Neapolitan music.

A Marechiare
Salvatore Di Giacomo – Francesco Paolo Tosti (1885)

1.
Quanno sponta la luna a Marechiare
pure li pisce nce fanno all'ammore,
se revotano ll'onne de lu mare,
pe' la priezza cagneno culore.
Quanno sponta la luna a Marechiare.

2.
A Marechiare ce sta 'na fenesta,
la passiona mia nce tuzzulea,
nu carofano addora int' a 'na testa,
Passa ll'acqua pe' sotto e murmulea.
A Marchiare ce sta 'na fenesta...

3.
Chi dice ca li stelle so' lucente
nun sape st'uocchie ca tu tiene 'nfronte,

sti doie stelle li ssaccio io sulamente,
dint'a lu core ne tengo li pponte.
Chi dice ca li stelle so' lucente?

4.
Scetate, Carulì, ca ll'aria è doce!
Quanno maie tanto tiempo aggio aspettato?
P'accumpagnà li suone cu' la voce,
stasera 'na chitarra aggio purtata.
Scetate, Carulì, ca ll'aria è doce!

Vocabulary

Quanno sponta la luna – When the moon comes up
pure – even (*anche*, in Italian)
li pisce – the fish
nce fanno all'ammore – romance each other
pe' la priezza – for the joy of it
cagneno culore – the change color
la passiona mia – my passion
nce tuzzulea – nudges me
nu carofano – a carnation (flower)
addora – perfumes
int' a 'na testa – in a vase (*testa*, *vaso* in Italian)
passa ll'acqua – water (the sea) passes
pe'sotto – underneath (the

window)
e murmulea – and whispers
Chi dice – Some say
ca li stelle so' lucente – that the stars are brilliant
nun sape – does not know
st'uocchie ca tu tiene 'nfronte – these eyes of yours
sti doie stelle – these two stars
li ssaccio io sulamente – only I know
dint'a lu core – in my heart
ne tengo li pponte – I feel their piercing
Scetate – Wake up
ca ll'aria è doce – because the air is sweet
Quanno maie tanto tiempo – How very long a time

155

aggio aspettato – I've waited for you
P'accumpagnà – to accompany
li suone – the sounds
cu' la voce – with a voice

stasera - tonight
'na chitarra – a guitar
aggio purtata – I have taken (with me)

♦ **'A Tazza 'e Café.** (*La Tazza di Caffè* in Italian and The Cup of Coffee in English) This song, written by an ex-waiter, *Giuseppe Capaldo* in 1918, was inspired by the aloof behavior of a bar cashier by the name of *Brigeta* (in Neapolitan). Like a cup of coffee, *Brigeta* seems bitter (*amare*) on top, but sweet as sugar (*zucchero*) at the bottom. As a matter of fact, the colder she gets the more exquisite (*squisita*) she becomes, like the pleasure of drinking a cup of iced coffee (*caffè granita*). *Capaldo* is also very famous for two other songs he wrote, *Ll'arte d' 'o Sole* and *Comme Facette Mammeta.* Both of these songs are included in the CD by *Renzo Arbore*, "*Pecchè nun ce ne jammo in America.*" (See Section 6.6)

'A Tazza 'e Café
Giuseppe Capaldo – Vittorio Fassone (1918)

1.
Vurria sapè pecchè si me vedite
facite sempe 'a faccia amariggiata.
Ma vuie quanto cchiù brutta ve facite,
cchiù bella all'uocchie mieje ve presentata.
I' mo nun saccio si ve n'accurgite?

2.
Ma cu sti mode, oje Brigeta,
tazza 'e café parite.
Sotto tenite 'o zzucchero
e 'ncoppa amare site.

3.
Ma i' tanto ch'aggia avutà
E tanto ch'aggia girà.
C' 'o ddoce 'e soto 'a tazza

fin'a mmocca m'adda arrivà

4.
Cchiu tiempo passa, cchiù v'arraffreddate
mmece 'e ve riscaldà "Caffè squisito"
'O bello è ca si pure ve gelate.
Site 'a delizia d' 'o caffè granite.
Facenno cuncurrenza 'a limunata.

5.
Repeat 2 and 3.

6.
Vuje site 'a mamma de' rrepassatore?
E i', bellezza mia, figlio 'e cartare.
Si vuje ve divertite a cagnà core.
I' faccio 'e ccarte pe' senza dènare,
bella pareglia fosseme a ffa' ammore?

7.
Repeat 2.

Vocabulary

Vurria sapè pecchè – I would like to know why
si me vedite – when you see me
facite sempe – you always make
'a faccia amariggiata – a sour face
vuie – you (*voi*, in Italian)
cchiù – more (*più*, in Italian)

ve facite – you appear
all'uocchie mieje – in my eyes
I' – I (*Io*, in Italian)\
mo – now (*addesso*, in Italian)
nun saccio – I don't know
si ve n'accurgite – if you realize it
cu sti mode – with this behavoir

tazza 'e café parite – you appear like a cup of coffee
Sotto tenite 'o zzucchero – on the bottom sugar
e 'ncoppa amare site – and on top, (you are) bitter
E tanto ch'aggia girà - and I stirred and stirred
C' 'o ddoce 'e soto 'a tazza – Until that the sweetness (*ddoce*) at the bottom of the cup
fin'a mmocca m'adda arrivà – came to the top
Cchiu tiempo passa – The more time goes by
chhiùu v'arraffreddate – the colder you get
mmece – instead of (*invece*, in Italian)
'e ve riscaldà – heating yourself up again
ca si pure ve gelate – even if you freeze
Site 'a delizia – you would be the pleasure
d' 'o caffè granite – of coffee on crushed ice
Facenno cuncurrenza – surpassing
'a limunata – lemon ice
Vuje site – You are
'a mamma de' rrepassatore – (an expression for someone who makes fun of people)
figlio 'e cartare – (an expression for someone who can get things done, literally, son of someone who writes legal papers)
ve divertite – you amuse yourself
a cagnà core – in changing loved ones (literally, changes heart)
I' faccio 'e ccarte – I will write up papers
pe' senza dènare – without paying anything
bella pareglia – nice couple
fosseme – we would be
a ffa' ammore – as lovers

♦ *Aummo, Aummo.* This relatively modern Neapolitan song (1954) may be found on the CD, *Napoli, Due Punti e a Capo*, with music played by the *Renzo Arbore* orchestra. *Renzo Arbore* is well known for his efforts to revive songs in the Neapolitan dialect. Although a modern song, it deals with an age old Italian problem for lovers, that is how to get past parents (*genitori*) to see each other. The girl is *Catarì*, short for *Catarina*, and the boy (nameless) is trying to sneak up to see *Catarì, aummo, aummo* (Neapolitan way of saying quietly, secretly). In the fifth stanza, the boy lays out his plans to get to Catarì, in case the door is closed. He has to prepare a snack for the family dog (*ce vò adduobbeco p'è cane*), and he has to prepare a ladder to climb up (*ce vò 'a scala pe' saglì*).

Aummo, Aummo
L. Cioffi – G. Cioffi (1954)
1.

Catarì,
Tu nun ghiesce maie d' 'a casa,
pecchè maie te fanno ascì!
Catarì,
stò murenno pe' st' ammore,
nun me fido cchiù e suffrì!

2.
Catarì,
ce ll'hé a dì a sti ggenitore,
mò l' avessero 'a capì!

3.
Catarì,
nun te pozzo vasà,

160

i' me sento 'e murì!

4.

Quacche notte, zittu, zitto,
chianu, chiano, a pied' 'e chiummo,
aummo, aummo,
saglio 'ncoppo, quatto, quatto,
mazzecanno scevingummo,
aummo, aummo.
Nun m'appiccio 'a sicaretta,
ca sinò se vede 'o fummo,
aummo, aummo,
si ce 'ncoccia quaccheduno,
ch' ammuina pò vvenì!

5.

Catarì,
e si trovo 'a porta 'nchiusa,
saie che faccio pe' trasì?
Catarì,
tengo pronto tutt' 'o piano,
pe' ffa chello che vogl' i'!
Catarì,
ce vò adduobbeco p' 'e cane,
ce vò 'a scala pe saglì!

6.

Catarì,
t'aggio afforza vasà!
Nun me fido 'e suffrì!

7. Repeat 4 then,

161

Catarì, Catarì

8. Repeat 2.

9. Repeat 6, then
aummo, aummo.

Vocabulary

tu nun ghiesce maie d' 'a casa -
you never leave the house
pecchè maie te fanno ascì -
because they (the parents) never
let you out
stò murenno pe' st' ammore -
I'm dying of this love
nun me fido cchiù e suffrì - I
can't take the pain anymore
ce ll'hé a dì a sti ggenitore - you
must tell your parents (*genitore*,
in Italian)
mò l' avessero 'a capì - it's time
they understood me
nun te pozzo vasà - I can't kiss
you
i' me sento 'e murì - I feel I'm
going to die
Quacche notte - One night
zittu - quietly
chianu - slowly
a pied' 'e chiummo - with lead
feet (an idiomatic expression
meaning, to walk very quietly, on
tip toes)

saglio 'ncoppo - I climb up a bit
mazzecanno scevingummo –
chewing gum
Nun m'appiccio 'a sicaretta - I
don't light my cigarette
ca sinò se vede 'o fummo -
otherwise you will see the smoke
si ce 'ncoccia quaccheduno - If I
run into anyone by surprise
ch' ammuina pò vvenì - what
chaos (*ammuina*, in the
Neapolitan dialect) can result
e si trovo 'a porta 'nchiusa - and
if I find the door closed
saie che faccio pe' trasì - do you
know what I will do to enter
(*trasi*, in Neapolitan, *entrare*, in
Italian)
tengo pronto tutt' 'o piano - I
have a complete plan
pe' ffa chello che voglì - to do
what I have to do
ce vò adduobbeco p' 'e cane - I
need a snack (*adduobbeco*) for
the dog

162

ce vò 'a scala pe saglì - I need a
ladder to climb up
t'aggio afforza vasà - I need to
kiss (*vasà*, in Neapolitan,
baciare, in Italian) you

Naples

163

♦ **_Guaglione._** *Guaglione* in the Neapolitan dialect means "little kid." This is a pre-puberty love song (only in Italy!). Written in 1956, this is one of the songs of the post World War II Neapolitan musical renaissance. The best advice the "little kid" gets is to *Curre 'mbraccio addù mammà* (Go run back to your mother's arms). It is too early for love!

Guaglione
Nisa – G. Fanciulli (1956)

1.
Curre 'mbraccio addù mammà,
nu' fa 'o scemo piccerì,
dille tutta 'a verità
ca mammà te pò capi! ...

2.
Stai sempe cca, 'mpuntato cca 'mmiez a 'sta via,
nu' mange cchiù, nu' duorme cchiù, che pecundria!
Uè, picceri, che vene a di 'sta gelusia?
Tu vuò suffrì, tu vuò murrì ... chi t' o fa fà suffrì

3.
Repeat 1.

4.
E passe e spasse
sotto a 'stu balcone,
ma tu sì guaglione!!
Tu nu' cunusce 'e femmene,
si' ancora accussì giovane!
Tu sì guaglione! ...

Che te mise 'ncapa? Va a giucà 'o pallone!
Che vonno dì 'sti llacreme?
Vattè, nu' mme fa ridere!

5.
Repeat 1.

6.
Nun 'e pittà, nun alliscià 'sti mustaccielle
nu' cerca a te, nu' sò pe' te chille uocchie belle.
Nun 'a penzà, va a pazzià cu 'e guagliuncelle,
nu' t'avvelì, c'è tiempo oi nì, pe' te 'nguaià!

7. Repeat 1, 4,

Vocabulary

Curre - run
'mbraccio - in the arms of
addù mammà - your mother
'o scem o - stupid one
piccerì - little one
'mpuntato cca - stuck here
'mmiez a 'sta via - in the middle of this street
che pecundria – (*che tristezza*, in Italian) now sad
che vene a di? - What does it mean?
'sta gelusia - this jealousy
chi t' o fa fà - what do I have to do with you
Tu nu' cunusce 'e femmene - You don't know about women
Che te mise 'ncapa - What did you put in your head
Va a giucà - Go play
Che vonno - What good
'sti llacreme - these tears
Vattè - Go away
nu' me fa ridere - don't make me laugh
Nun 'e pittà - Don't paint
nun alliscià - shine
'sti mustaccielle - this little mustache
Nun 'a penzà - Don't think of her
oi nì - in the future
pe' te 'nguaià - to get into trouble

165

♦ *L'Hai Voluto Te!* This is a falling out-of-love song. In Italy there are probably as many falling out-of-love songs, as falling in-love songs. But Americans prefer the Italian falling in-love songs, so songs of this type are rarely heard in the United States. The title translates roughly into, "That's the way you wanted it." It is about this fellow who gets a dear-John note (*biglietto*) from his girl friend. He responds by saying, "Well then (*E allora*). With the blonde and the brunette (*Con la bionda e la nera*), every evening (*ogni sera, ogni sera*), I'm going strolling (*Me ne vado a passeggià*). In your face (*alla faccia tua*), in your face (*alla faccia tua*)." There is a classic Italian hand gesture that goes with *alla faccia tua*. The hand, palm down and fingers toward the face, is flicked out from the chin. You are likely to see this gesture at least once in every Italian movie. The music is by *G. Cioffi*, who in the late thirties wrote the music to many popular Neapolitan "love" songs. The version of this song which appears in the CD *Renzo Arbore - L'orchestra Italiana* is a modern version of the song, and at the end you can hear some Neapolitan "rap."

L'Hai Voluto Te!
G. Pisano – G. Cioffi (1938)

1.
Si me vide 'e suspirà
che te po mpurtà,
non sospiro mai per te
penso solo a me.

2.
M'hai mandato un bel biglietto,
nel biglietto c'era scritto:

166

i' me so' scucciato 'e te'
nun ne voglio più sapé

3.
E allora,
con la bionda e con la nera
ogni sera ... ogni sera,
me ne vado a passeggià.
Alla faccia tua
Alla faccia tua.

4.
Con la bionda e con la nera
me ne vado a passeggià.

5.
Embé, embé
l'hai voluto te
Essì, essì
t'aggia fà murì!

6.
L'hai voluto te
essì ... essì
t'aggia fa murì!
Alla faccia tua
Alla faccia tua.

7.
Con la bionda e con la nera
me ne vado a passeggia.
Embé, embé

Essì, essì
t'aggia fà murì!

Vocabulary

Si me vide 'e suspirà - If you see me sigh

che te po mpurtà - what does it matter to you

non sospiro mai per te - I never sigh for you

penso solo a me - I'm thinking only of myself

M'hai mandato - You sent me

un bel biglietto - a nice note

nel biglietto c'era scritto - In the note there was written

i' me so' scucciato 'e te' - I am bored of you

nun ne voglio più sapé - I don't want to know anymore about it

E allora - Well, then

Con la bionda e con la nera - With the blond and with the brunette

ogni sera - every evening

me ne vado a passeggià - I'm going strolling

Alla faccia tua - In your face

Embé - Well then (*ebbene*, in Italian)

t'aggia fà murì - I have already killed you

essì - yes

♦ **Maria, Marì.** This is probable the *mamma* of all *Maria* songs. Written in 1899, with words by *V. Russo* and music by *E. Di Capua*, this is another of those world famous Italian songs from Naples. The lover in this case loses so much sleep trying to see his *Marì*, that he dreams of resting in her arms. The refrain goes, "Oh Mary, Oh Mary, how much sleep I have lost over you (*Oj Marì, Oj Marì, quanta suonno ca perdo pe' te*)! Let me sleep (*Famm' addurmi*), in your embrace just for awhile (*abbracciato nu poco cu te*)!"

Maria, Marì
Vicenzo Russo – Eduardo Di Capua (1899)

1.
Aràpete fenesta,
famm'affacctà a Maria,
ca stongo mmiez' 'a via
speruto p' 'a vedè.

2.
Nun trovo n'ora 'e pace;
'a nott' 'a faccio juorno
sempe pe' sta ccà attuorno,
speranno 'e ce parlà!

3.
Oj, Marì, oj Marì,
quanta suonno ca perdo pe' te!
Famm'addurmì,
abbracciato nu poco cu te!
Repeat 3

4.
Pare ca già s'arape
na senga 'e fenestella.
Maria c' 'a manella
nu segno a me me fa!

5.
Sona, chitarra mia!
Maria s'è scetata.
Na bella serenata,
facimmela sentì.

Repeat 3 twice

Vocabulary

Aràpete fenesta - Open window
famm'affaccià a Maria - let me
see Mary
ca stongo mmiez' 'a via -
because I am in the middle of the
street
speruto p' 'a vedè - hoping to see
her
Nun trovo n'ora 'e pace - I can't
find a moment of peace
'a nott' 'a faccio juorno - I make
night into day (day: *jurno* in
Neapolitan, *giorno* in Italian)
sempe pe' sta ccà attuorno -
always staying around here (here:
ccà in Neapolitan, *qui* in Italian)
speranno 'e ce parlà - hoping to

be able to speak to her
Oj, Marì - Oh Mary
quanta suonno ca perdo pe' te -
how much sleep I'm losing over
you
Famm'addurmì - Let me sleep
(sleep: *addurmì* in Neapolitan,
dormire in Italian)
abbracciato nu poco cu te - in
your embrace just for awhile
Pare ca già s'arape - It looks
like it is opening now
na senga 'e fenestella - a gleam
through a little window
Maria c' 'a manella - Marie with
her little hand
nu segno a me me fa - signals to

170

me

Sona, chitarra mia - play my guitar

Maria s'è scetata - Mary has awaken (awaken: *scetata* in Neapolitan, *svegliare* in Italian)

Na bella serenata - a beautiful serenade

facimmela sentì - let me hear it

♦ **'O Paese d' 'O Sole.** This is a song about the joy a Neapolitan feels when he/she finally is able to come back to their hometown, Naples. The song starts, "Today I am so happy (*Ogge sto tanto allero*), that I nearly started crying for the joy of it (*ca quase quase me mettesse a chiagnere pe' sta felicità*). But is it true or is it not true (*Ma è overo o nun è overo*), that I have returned to Naples (*ca so' turnato a Napule*)?" The refrain is a burst of praise for the sun and the sea of Naples, "This is the home of the sun (*Chist'è 'o paese d' o' sole*), this is the home of the sea (*chist'è 'o paese d' 'o mare*)." This song was written in 1925 with words and music by *L. Bovio* and *V. D'Annibale*.

'O Paese d' 'O Sole
Libero Bovio – Vincenzo D'Annibale (1925)

1.
Ogge sto tanto allero ca quase quase,
me mettesse a chiagnere pe' sta felicità.
Ma è overo o nun è overo,
ca so' turnato a Napule?
Ma è overo ca sto ccà.
'O treno steva ancora 'int' 'a stazione
quanno aggio 'ntiso 'e primme manduline.

2.
Chist'è 'o paese d' 'o sole,
chist'è 'o paese d' 'o mare,
chist'è 'o paese addò tutt'e parole,
so' doce e so' amare,
so' sempe parole d'ammore.

3.
Tutto, tutto è destino. Comme putevo
fà furtuna all'estero s'io voglio campà a ccà?
Mettite 'nfrisco 'o vino,
tanto ne voglio vevere
ca m'aggia 'mbriacà...
Dint' 'a 'sti quatto mura j' sto cuntento:
mamma me sta vicino, e Nenna canta:

Repeat 2

Vocabulary

Ogge sto tanto allero - Today I am so happy (*allero, allero* - happy, in Italian)
ca quase quase me mettesse a chiagnere - that I nearly started crying
pe' sta felicità - for the joy of it
Ma è overo o nun è overo - But is it true or is it not true
ca so' turnato a Napule - that I have returned to Naples (*che sono ritornato a Napoli*, in Italian)
Ma è overo ca sto ccà - But is it really true that I am here
'O treno steva ancora 'int' 'a stazione - The train was still in the station
quanno aggio 'ntiso 'e primme manduline - when I heard the first mandolin

Chist'è 'o paese d' 'o sole - this is the home of the sun (*Questo è il paese del sole*, in Italian)
d' 'o mare - of the sea (*del mare*, in Italian)
chist'è 'o paese addò tutt'e parole - this is the land where all the words
so' doce e so' amare - are sweet and are bitter
so' sempe parole d'ammore - are always words of love
Tutto, tutto è destino - Everything, everything is destiny
Comme putevo fà furtuna all'estero - How could I make my fortune abroad
s'io voglio campà a ccà - if I want to live here (*se voglio campare qui*, in Italian)
Mettite 'nfrisco 'o vino - pour

173

me a cool glass of wine
tanto ne voglio vevere - how
much I want to drink one (*vevere*
in Neapolitan, *bevere* in Italian)
ca m'aggia 'mbriacà - that I
have to get drunk
Dint' 'a 'sti quatto mura - In
these four walls

j' sto cuntento - I am happy (*io
sono contento*, in Italian)
mamma me sta vicino - Mom is
by my side
e Nenna canta - and the little girl
sings (*Nenna* in Neapolitan,
fanciulla in Italian)

♦ **'O Sole Mio.** This is perhaps the most well known popular Italian song in the world, written in 1898 with words by *G. Capurro* and music by *E. Di Capua*. *'O sole mio* means "my sun," and the song starts, "What a beautiful thing (*Che bella cosa*) is a day in the sun (*è na jurnata 'e sole*)."

'O Sole Mio
Giovanni Capurro – Eduardo Di Capua (1898)

1.
Che bella cosa è 'na jurnata 'e sole,
n'aria serena doppo è 'na tempesta!
Pe' ll'aria fresca pare già na festa...
Che bella cosa è 'na jurnata 'e sole.

2.
Ma n'atu sole
cchiù bello, oj ne',
'o sole mio
sta 'nfronte a te!

3.
'O sole, 'o sole mio,
sta 'nfronte a te!
Sta 'nfronte a te!

4.
Quanno fa notte e 'o sole se ne scenne,
me vene quasi 'na malincunia;
sotto 'a fenesta toja restarrìa
quanno fa notte e 'o sole se ne scenne.

Repeat 3

Vocabulary

Che bella cosa - What a beautiful thing
è 'na jurnata - is a day (*è un giorno*, in Italian)
'e sole - in the sun
n'aria serena - a calm air
doppo è 'na tempesta - after a storm
Pe' ll'aria fresca - the clean air
pare già na festa - feels like a holiday
Ma n'atu sole - But another sun
cchiù bello - how beautiful (*che bello*, in Italian)
oj ne' - oh girl (*ne': nenna* in Neapolitan, *fanciulla* in Italian)
sta 'nfronte a te - faces you
Quanno fa notte - when it is night time
e 'o sole se ne scenne - and the sun sets
me vene quasi 'na malincunia - I almost get sad
sotto 'a fenesta - under the window
toja restarrìa - I would stay here

♦ *Reginella.* This is a song from the golden age of Neapolitan music, with words and music by the famous Neapolitan song writer, *Libero Bovio.* *Reginella* means "little queen", and when the song was written in 1917, the Italian monarchy was in full bloom. It is not a happy love song. The lovers have broken up and now he says "*ma, 'e vvote tu, distrattamente pienze a me* (but, occasionally, in a casual way, think of me)!"

Reginella
Libero Bovio – Gaetano Lana (1917)

1.
Te sì fatta 'na veste scullata,
'nu cappiello cu 'e nastre e cu 'e rrose,
stive 'mmiezo a tre o quatto sciantose,
e parlave francese: è accussì?
Fuie l'atriere ca t'aggio 'ncuntrata?
Fuie l'atriere, a Tuledo, gnorsì ...

2.
T'aggio vuluto bene a tte!
Tu m'è vuluto bene a me!
Mo nun 'nce amammo cchiù,
ma, 'e vvote, tu,
distrattamente pienze a me!

3.
Reginè, quanno stive cu mmico
nun magnave ca pane e cerase;
nuje campàvamo 'e vase- e che vvase!-
tu cantave e chiagnive pe' mme

177

E 'o cardillo cantava cu ttico:
"Reginella 'o vo' bene a 'stu Rrè"!

4.
Mo nun 'nce amammo cchiù,
ma, 'e vvote tu
distrattamente parle 'e me!

5.
Repeat 2.

Vocabulary

Te sì fatta - You made yourself
'na veste scullata - a low cut dress
'nu cappiello - a hat
cu 'e nastre - with ribbons
stive 'mmiezo a - you were in the middle of
sciantose - singers
è accussì? - Right?
Fuie l'atriere - It was yesterday
ca t'aggio 'ncuntrata - that I had met you
Tuledo - A major street in Naples (Toledo)
gnorsì - yes sir
T'aggio vuluto bene a tte! - I loved you!
Tu m'è vuluto bene a me! - You loved me!

Mo - now
nun 'nce amammo - we don't love each other
cchiù - anymore
ma, 'e vvote - but sometimes
distrattamente - causually
pienze a me - think of me
quanno stive - when you were
cu mmico - with me
nun magnave ca - you only ate
pane e cerase - bread and cherries
nuje campàvamo - were survived
'e vase - on kisses
chiagnive pe' mme - cried for me
'o cardillo - the goldfinch
cantava cu ttico - sang with you
'o vo' bene - love
a 'stu Rrè - this king

178

♦ *Santa Lucia Luntana*. This song was written in 1919 (words and music by *E. A. Mario*). It is the "other" *Santa Lucia* song. The one more people are likely to know goes:

> *Sul mare luccica,*
> *l'astro d'argento,*
> *placida è l'onda*
> *prospero il vento.*
> *Venite all'agile,*
> *barchetta mia.*
> *Santa Lucia! Santa Lucia!*

Santa Lucia is a Neapolitan neighborhood, and this *Santa Lucia* song is about someone who has to leave his home town. "*Santa Lucia,* how sad it is to be far away from you (*Santa Lucia, luntano 'a te, quanta malincunia*)."

Santa Lucia Luntana
E. A. Mario (1919)

> *1.*
> *Partono 'e bastimente,*
> *pe' terre assaje luntane.*
> *Càntano a buordo: sò napulitane.*
> *Càntano pe' tramente,*
> *'o golfo già scumpare,*
> *e 'a luna, 'a miezo 'o mare,*
> *nu poco 'e Napule lle fa vedé.*

179

2.

Santa Lucia, luntano 'a te,
quanta malincunia!
Se gira 'o munno sano,
se va a cercà fortuna,
ma quanno sponta 'a luna,
luntano 'a Napule nun se po' sta!

3.

Santa Lucia, tu tiene sulo nu poco 'e mare,
ma cchiù luntana staje, chiù bella pare.
È 'o canto d''e Ssirene,
ca tesse ancora 'e rrezze!
Core nun vo' ricchezze:
si è nato a Napule, ce vo' murì!
Repeat 2

Vocabulary

Partono 'e bastimente - The ships are leaving

pe' terre assaje luntane - for far away lands

Càntano a buordo - They are singing on-board (the ship)

so napulitane - I am Neapolitan

pe' tramente - while

o' golfo - the bay (of Naples)

già scumpare - is already disappearing

e 'a luna - and the moon

'a miezo 'o mare - in the middle of the sea

nu poco 'e Napule lle fa vedé - Lets them see a bit of Naples

luntano - far away

'a te - from you

quanta malincunia - how sad it is

Se gira 'o munno sano - If I travel around the world safely

se va a cercà fortuna - If I go looking for a fortune

ma quanno sponta 'a luna - but when the moon breaks out

luntano 'a Napule - far from Naples

180

nun se po' sta - one cannot stay
tu tiene sulo nu poco 'e mare - you have just a small part of the sea
ma cchiù luntana staje - but the more far away one is
chiù bella pare - the more beautiful you seem
È 'o canto d''e Ssirene - It is at the song of the Siren
ca tesse ancora 'e rrezze - who still weaves nets (fishing nets: *rrezze* in Neapolitan, *reti* in Italian)
Core - The heart
nun vo' ricchezze - does not want riches
si è nato a Napule - if you are born in Naples
ce vo' murì - there you want to die

♦ *Te Voglio Bene Assaje.* This is perhaps the most famous of all Neapolitan songs. The words were written by *Raffaele Sacco* in 1835 (also often listed as 1839), and there is some controversy about who wrote the music. Some say *Fillippo Campanella* (whom we cite below) and others say *Gaetano Donizetti*. It is one of the songs that initiated the *Piedigrotta Music Festival*, and was performed so often that many Neapolitans finally became sick of hearing it. The refrain of this song goes, *I' te voglio bene assaje, e tu non pienz' a me* (I love you so much, and you don't even think of me). A reporter of that time was so tired of this song that he wrote the following words to the music in his paper:

> Goodbye my beautiful Naples.
> I'm going far away from you.
> Why such a strange thought,
> you may ask me, why?
> Because that song now
> makes me nauseous.
> "I love you so much,
> and you don't even think of me."

Te Voglio Bene Assje
Raffaele Sacco – Fillipo Campanella (1835)

1.
Pecché quanno me vide
te 'ngrife comm' 'a gatto?
Nennè, che t'aggio fatto
ca no mme può vedé?
Io t'aggio amato tanto,
si t'amo tu lo saje.

182

2.

I' te voglio bene assaje
e tu non pienz' a me!

3.

La notte tutte dormeno,
e io che buo' dormì!
Penzanno a nenna mia
me sent'ascevolì!
Li quarte d'ora sonano
a uno, a ddoje, a tre.

Repeat 2

4.

Recordate lu juorno
ca stive a me becino
e te scorreano 'nzino
le llacreme accossì.
Diciste a me: "Nun chiagnere
ca tu lo mio sarraje"
Repeat 2

Vocabulary

quanno me vide – when you see me
te 'ngrife – you get angry
comm' 'a gatto – like a cat
Nennè – Girl (*Bambina*, in Italian)

che t'aggio fatto – what did I do to you
ca no mme può vedé – that you can't stand me (*che non mi puoi vedere*, in Italian)
t'aggio amato tanto – I loved

183

you so much
tu lo saje – you know
io che buo' dormì – how can I
sleep
me sent'ascevolì – I feel myself
going down (*mi sento venire
meno*, in Italian)
Li quarte d'ora sonano – The
quarter hour rings
ddoje - two (*due*, in Italian)
lu juorno – the day (*il giorno*, in
Italian)

ca stive a me becino – that you
were by my side
te scorreano 'nzino – they fell
in your lap
le llacreme – my tears
accossì – like this (*così*, in
Italian)
Diciste a me – You said to me
Nun chiagnere – Don't cry (*Non
piangere*, in Italian)
ca tu lo mio sarraje – because
you will be mine

♦ *Torna a Surriento*. *Surriento* (*Sorrento*, in Italian) is a city on the bay of Naples. It is a mixed "*amore/paese*" song. A loved one is to leave the city. The refrain goes, "Don't leave me (*Ma nun me lassà*), don't torment me this way (*nun darme stu turmiento*). Come back to Sorrento (*Torna a Surriento*), let me live (*famme campà*)." *Torna a Surriento* was written in 1904, with words by *G. B. DeCurtis* and music by *E. DeCurtis*, two of Italy's most famous song writers. Actually, there is a story that this was not really a love song. It is said that it was written to entice the popular postmaster of Sorrento to return to the city to straighten out the postal mess at the time.

Torna a Surriento
Giambattista DeCurtis – Ernesto DeCurtis (1904)

1.
Vide 'o mare quant'è bello!
Spira tantu sentimento,
comme tu a chi tiene mente,
ca scetato 'o faje sunnà.

2.
Guarda, guà chistu ciardino;
siente, sie' sti sciure arance:
nu profumo accussì fino
dinto 'o core se ne va.

3.
E tu dice: "J' parto, addio!".
T'alluntane da stu core.
Da la terra de l'ammore.
Tiene 'o core 'e nun turnà?

4.

Ma nun me lassà,
nun darme stu turmiento!
Torna a Surriento,
famme campà!

5.

Vide 'o mare de Surriento
che tesoro tene 'nfunno;
chi ha girato tutto 'o munno
nun l'ha vista comm'a ccà.

6.

Guarda attuorno sti Sserene,
ca te guardano 'ncantate
e te vonno tantu bene ...
Te vulessero vasà.

Repeat 3 and 4

Vocabulary

Vide 'o mare - look at the sea
quant'è bello - how beautiful it is
Spira tantu sentimento - It
radiates so much sentiment
comme tu - like you
a chi tiene mente - whom I am
thinking of
ca scetato – who awake
'o faje sunnà - makes me dream
Guarda - Look
guà - here

chistu ciardino - this garden
(*questo giardino*, in Italian)
siente - smell
sie' sti sciure arance - these
orange blossoms
nu profumo - a smell
accussì fino - so fine
dinto 'o core se ne va - which
(the smell) enters the heart
E tu dice - And you say
J' parto - I am leaving (*Io parto,*

in Italian)
addio - goodbye
T'alluntane da stu core - Far
away from this here heart
Da la terra de l'ammore - From
the land of love
Tiene 'o core - Take my heart
'e nun turnà - and don't come
back
nun me lassà - don't leave me
nun darme stu turmiento - don't
torment me this way
Torna a Surriento - Come back
to Sorrento
famme campà - let me live
che tesoro tene 'nfunno - what a
treasure you have in the final
analysis (*nfunno* is *al fondo* in
Italian and translates to "in the
final analysis" in English)
chi ha girato tutto 'o munno -
anyone who has travelled around
the world (*munno* is *mondo* in
Italian)
nun l'ha vista comm'a ccà -
hasn't seen anything like this
Guarda attuorno sti Sserene -
Look around at the sirens
ca te guardano 'ncantate - that
are looking at you with
fascination
e te vonno tantu bene - and who
love you so much (*te vonno tantu
bene* is *ti vogliono tanto bene* in
Italian)
Te vulessero vasà - They ask to
be kissed (*vasà* is *baciare* in
Italian)

6.4 SONGS IN THE PIEDMONTESE DIALECT

The reader may want to refer to section 4.2 for the pronounciation of Piedmontese words. Probably the most important thing to note with respect to pronounciation is that the Piedmontese "ò" is pronounced like the Italian "o", but that the Piedmontese "o" without an accent is pronounced like the Italian "u." More details on the Piedmontese dialect may be found in Appendix II.

Unlike Neapolitan songs that have become famous throughout the world, most Piedmontese songs never left Italy, actually never left Piedmont. Nevertheless, songs from Piedmont and songs from Naples have many common themes, for example, romantic love and love of the "hometown." These themes are illustrated by some of the songs in this section, e.g. *Pocionin* (romantic love) and *La Lun-a 'd Moncalé* (love of the hometown). However, there is an emphasis on food and wine in Piedmontese folk songs that is not found in most other regions of Italy. This is illustrated by the songs *Polenta* and *Marieme, Veuj Marieme* (which is sort of a love song, but the bottom line is about drinking *Barbera* and *Grignolino,* classic red wines of Piedmont).

The lyrics listed in this section were, for the most part, transcribed from cassetts and CDs. Unfortunately, these items contain no information on the authors of the songs or the year they were written. Unlike Neapolitan music, Piedmontese music is not well documented.

♦ *La Lun-a 'd Moncalé*. *Moncalé* is Piedmontese for *Moncalieri*, a small suburb of Turin, on one of the hills just east of the *Po* river. It is a pretty little town, once a very popular place for young people from Turin to go to meet and dance. The song starts, "The sun breaks through (*Sponta 'l sol*), and the moon too (*e la lun-a*), and the moon of *Moncalé* (*e la lun-a 'd Moncalé*). Shining on the girls (*a fà ciair a le fije*), going dancing at night (*a la sèira, andé a balé*)." The heroine of this song is a young bride, *Rosa*. After *Maria*, *Rosa* is probably the most popular girls name in Italy, and just like *Maria* there are many ways to say *Rosa*, e.g. *Rosetta*, *Rosina*, and *Rosella*.

La Lun-a 'd Moncalé

1.
Sponta 'l sol, e la lun-a,
e la lun-a a Moncalé,
a fà ciair a le fije,
a la sèira andé a balé.
Rosa, Rosetta, sposa diletta
le tue pupille mi fanno innamorar.

2.
Sponta 'l sol, e la lun-a
brila an cel a Moncalé
për fà ciair a le cobie,
për peui feje inamoré.
Rosa, Rosina, sposa divina
le tue carezze mi sanno consolar.

3.
Da Turin le totin-e

as na ven-o a Moncalé

e se 'n cel a-i é la lun-a

faran tuti inamoré.

Rosa, Rosella, sposa mia bella,

le tue parole, mi sanno incatenar.

Vocabulary

Sponta 'l sol - The sun breaks through

la lun-a - the moon

a fà ciair - Lighting up

a le fije - at the girls (f*ije*, in Italian *ragazze* - girls)

la sèira - the evening (*seira*, in Italian, *serra*)

andé - go

a balé - dancing

sposa - bride

diletta - dear

le tue pupille - your eyes

mi fanno innamorar - make me fall in love

fà ciair - to light up

le cobie - the couples

për peui feje inamoré – to then make them fall in love

tue carezze - your caresses

mi sanno consolar - console me

Da Turin - from Turin

le totin-e - the girls (another way to say *fije*- girls)

as na ven-o - come

e se 'n cel a-i é la lun-a - and if in the sky there is the moon

faran tuti inamoré - make them all fall in love

sposa mia bella - my beautiful bride

le tue parole - your words

mi sanno incatenar - know how to enchant me

♦ *La Polenta.* This is a satirical ode to a dish once eaten by the poor people of Piedmont three times a day, seven days a week. This song was commonly sung in the old Italian taverns (*Osterie*), just to let off stem about having to eat *polenta* all the time. The refrain goes, "*Salve polenta, piatto da re* (Hail polenta, the king's dish). *I tuoi fedeli s'inchinano ai tuoi pié* (Your faithful fans, bow at your feet)." *Polenta* is a corn meal mush cooked by stirring corn meal slowly into a pot of boiling water, while the mixture is kept hot enough to be popping bubbles all the time. As the song goes (in Piedmontese), "*Fé la giré, sauté, polé, polé, polenta* (Stir it, let it pop, pole-, pole-, polenta)." Of course no one could afford to buy meat to go with the *polenta*, so they would cook whatever small birds they could catch, that's right "*la polenta con j'osej* (polenta with birds)."

As the economic situation in Piedmont improved, the consumption of *polenta* decreased. Now it is considered a rare treat eaten on special occasions, and has become a fairly chic Italian dish in the rest of the world.

La Polenta

1.
Un bel di tra l'Oglio e il Brenta
vien al mondo, vien al mondo la polenta.
E la polenta, era il cibo degli dei.
la polenta con j'osej,
e con j'osej, e con j'osej

2.
Salve polenta, piatto da re!
I tuoi fedeli s'inchinano ai tuoi pié.
Salve polenta piatto da re!
Fela giré, sauté, polé

fela giré, sauté, polé
fela giré, sauté, polé, polé, polen
fela giré, sauté, polé
fela giré, sauté, polé
fela giré, sauté, polé, polé, polenta.

3.

Tra le ali di un tacchino,
viene al mondo, viene al mondo polentino, il
polentino.
Tra le ali d'un cappone, vien al mondo un
polentone,
il polentone, il polentone, il polentone, il
polentone.

4.
Repeat 2.

5.

Come manna del deserto
era buona, era buona e saporita e ben condita.
L'han mangiata i senatori,
l'han trovata molta buona
e molto buona, e molto buona, e molto buona.

6.
Repeat 2.

7.

Polenta, polentin, polentorum,
benedictum, benedictorum,
noi cantoma ancor!

8.

Repeat 2.

Vocabulary

Un bel di - One fine day

tra l'Oglio e il Brenta - between
Oglio and Brenta (two small
rivers in northern Italy)

vien al mondo - is born

era il cibo - it was the food

degli dei - of the gods

con j'osej - with cooked birds
(Piedmontese)

Salve polenta - Hail polenta

Tra le ali - Between the wings

di un tacchino - of a turkey

il polentino - the little polenta

d'un cappone - of a capon

il polentone - the big polenta

Come manna - Like food from
god

del deserto - in the desert

era buona - it was good
(Piedmontese)

e saporita - and savory

e ben condita - and well cooked

L'han mangiata - They ate it
(Piedmontese)

i senatori - the senators
(Remember Turin was the first
capital of Italy.)

l'han trovata - they found it
(Piedmontese)

molta buona - very good

noi cantoma ancor - we keep on
singing (Piedmontese)

♦ *Marieme, Veuj Marieme.* "Married, I want to get married (*Marieme, veuj marieme*)." Getting maried is a traumatic event in any culture. But it was especially so at one time in the small villages in Piedmont. One needed and wanted a wife, but with few candidates to choose from and no possibility of divorce, it was a very scary proposition. "I want to get married (*veuj marieme*), whatever it costs (*ch'a costa lòn ch'a costa*)." But then "To have a beautiful wife (*avèj na fomna bela*), is a real big problem (*a l'é na gran disperassion*)." Obviously, it is hard to keep a beautiful woman down on the farm. Even "tying her up is not enough (*a basta nen gropela*)." And anyway, "she only creates problems (*fa mach giré ij boton*)." Then there are problems with a blonde wife (*na fomna bionda*), a big wife (*na fomna granda*), a rich wife (*na fomna rica*), a crazy wife (*na fomna fòla*), and a red-headed wife (*na fomna rossa*). The final decision is to marry a bakers daughter (*na panatera*). "As long as there is something to drink (*basta mach ch'a sia da bèive*), from evening to morning (*da la sèira a la matin*). Of course in Piedmont "to drink" means red wine, e.g. *Barbera* and *G*rignolino.

Marieme, Veuj Marieme

1.
Marieme veuj marieme, veuj deje na mariolà,
ch'a costa lòn ch'a costa, ch'a costa lòn ch'a costa.
Marieme veuj marieme, veuj deje na mariolà,
ch'a costa lòn ch'a costa, basta mach che sìa marià.

2.
Avèj na fomna bela, a l'é na gran disperassion,
a basta nen gropela, a basta nen gropela.
Avèj na fomna bela, a l'é na gran disperassion,

a basta nen gropela, e at fà mach giré ij boton.

3.

*Avèj na fomna **bionda**, a l'é na gran disperassion,*
ij tò amis a-j fan la ronda, ij tò amis a-j fan la
ronda.
Avèj na fomna bionda, a l'e na gran disperassion,
ij tò amis a-j fan la ronda, e at fà mach giré ij boton.

4.

*Avèj na fomna **granda**, a l'é na gran disperassion,*
përchè chila comanda, përchè chila comanda.
Avèj na fomna granda, a l'é na gran disperassion.
Perche chi la comanda? E a fa mach giré ij boton.

5.

*Avèj na fomna **rica**, a l'é na gran disperassion,*
ij còrn an testa 't fica, ij còrn an testa 't fica.
Avèj na fomna rica, a l'é na gran disperassion,
ij còrn an testa 't fica, e at fà mach giré ij boton.

6.

*Avèj na fomna **fòla**, a l'é na gran disperassion,*
a deurm a pansa mòla, a deurm a pansa mòla.
Avèj na fomna fòla, a l'é na gran disperassion,
a deurm a pansa mòla, e at fà mach giré ij boton.

7.

*Avèj na fomna **rossa**, a l'é na gran disperassion,*
la testa a smija na cossa, la testa a smija na cossa.
Avèj na fomna rossa, a l'é na gran disperassion,
la testa a smija na cossa, e at fà mach giré ij boton.

8.

*Veuj pijé na **panatera**, ch'a fasa ij biciolan,*
ch'a-j fasa 'nt na manera, ch'a-j fasa 'nt na manera.
Veuj pijé na panatera, ch'a fasa ij biciolan.
Ch'a-j fasa 'nt na manera, ch'a-j ëstago drit an man.

9.

*E bote, mese bote, **barbera e grignolin**,*
basta ch'a-i sìa da bèive, basta ch'a-i sìa da bèive.
*E bote e mese bote, **barbera e grignolin**,*
basta ch'a i sìa da bèive, da la sèira a la matin.

Repeat 1, Repeat 2.

Vocabulary

veuj deje na mariolà - I want to have a wedding
ch'a costa lòn ch'a costa - whatever it costs
Avèj - to have (*avere*, in Italian)
na fomna - a wife (*moglie*, in Italian)
bela - beautiful
a l'é - is (*è*, in Italian)
na gran disperassion - a real big
a basta nen - it is not enough
gropela - tie her up
at fà mach giré ij boton - she only makes trouble (This is an idiomatic expression. *Giré* means "turn" and *boton* means "buttons." In Italian on would say, *fa solamente girare le scatole*.)
ij tò amis - your friends
a-j fan la ronda – line up behind her
granda - big
chi la comanda - who will give her orders
rica - rich
ij còrn - the horns
an testa - on the head
' t fica - poke you
fòla - crazy

196

a deurm a pansa mòla - she sleeps on her stomach
na fomna rossa - a red-headed wife
na cossa - a pumpkin
la testa a smija na cossa - her head looks like a pumpkin
Veuj pijé - I want to take (marry)
na panatera - a baker's daughter
ch'a-j fasa - who makes
biciolan - a type of Piedmontese bread stick

ch'a-j ëstago - that stay
drit - upright
an man - in your hand
bote - half bottles
barbera - *barbera* wine
grignolin - *gringnolino* wine
basta ch'a-i sìa da bèive - as long as there is something to drink
sèira - evening
matin - morning

Piedmontese Girl Spinning (see following song)

197

♦ *Mia Mama Veul Che Fila.* This is an old Piedmontese *Mamma*-type song. It was written at a time when cloth was spun at home, and Mamma had to push the girls to get the spinning done. "My mother wants me to do some spinning (*Mia mama veul che fila*)." But the girl has a reason for each day of the week for why she is not able to do the spinning. "On Mondays, I look for lice (*Mi ël lunes, sercò le poless*). On Tuesdays I have to play cards (*Mi ël martes gieugo le carte*).,*" and so on, with nested repetitions.

Mia Mama Veul Che Fila

1.

La mia mama a veul che fila 'l lùn-es.

2.

Mì, ël lùn-es masso le pùless,
un pò 'd sossi, un pò 'd solà.
La mìa mama,
fé da sin-a e da disné
la mìa mama a veul che fila,
mi I peuss pa filé.

3.

Mìa mama a veul che fila 'l màrtes.

4.

Mi, ël màrtes I leso le carte.
Repeat 2

5.

La mìa mama a veul che fila 'l mèrcol.

6.

Mi, ël mèrcol vado da Berto
Repeat 4

7.

Mìa Mama a veul che fila 'l giòbia.

8.

Mì ël giòbia lustro la lòbia
Repeat 6

9.

Mìa mama a veul che fila 'l vënner.

10.

Mi, ël vënner, I cheujo la sënner.
Repeat 8

11.

Mìa mama a veul che fila 'l saba.

12.

Mi, ël saba I speto la paga.
Repeat 10

13.

Mìa mama a veul che fila 'd festa.

14.

Mi la testa perdo la testa.
Repeat 12

Vocabulary

La mìa mama a veul che fila – My mother wants me to do some spinning

ël lùn-es – on Monday (*lunedì*, in Italian)

masso – I kill (*uccido*, in Italian)

le pùless – lice (*pidocchi*, in Italian)

un pò 'd sossì – a little bit of this (*un poco di questo*, in Italian)

un pò 'd solà – a little bit of that (*un poco di quello*, in Italian)

fé da sin-a – Make dinner

e da disné – and lunch (*pranzo*, in Italian)

mi I peuss pa – I can't (*non posso*, in Italian)

filé – spin (*filare*, in Italian)

màrtes – Tuesday (*martedi*, in Italian)

leso le carte – I read the papers

mèrcol – Wednesday (*mercoledi*, in Italian)

vadò da Berto – I go to Albert's

giòbia – Thursday (*giovedi*, in Italian)

I lustro la lòbia – I shine the (wooden) balcony

vënner – Friday (*venerdi*, in Italian)

cheujo la sënner – I sweep the ashes (*spazzo la cenere*, in Italian)

saba – Saturday (*sabato*, in Italian)

I speto la paga – I wait to get paid

festa – Sunday (*domenica*, in Italian)

perdo la vesta – I put on my dress (*metto la vesta*, in Italian)

♦ *Pocionin.* Unlike *Mariem, Veuj Marieme,* this is an upbeat Piedmontese song about marriage. From the reference to *ël Valentin,* it obviously takes place in Turin. *Ël Valentin* is a park in Turin that borders the *Po* river. It was one of the most popular places in Turin for young people to meet. Apparently cities, with large numbers of possible mates, are more conducive to generating happy marriage songs than small villages. There is no doubt about this potential mate. "Little sweetheart (*Pocionin*)." "She is good, wise, and so beautiful (*L'é brava, giudissiosa, e tanto bela*)." "The day I asked her to marry me (*Ël di ch'I l'hai ciamaijé da sposela*), she answered me with a beautiful kiss (*l'a dame për rispòta 'n bel basin*)." Of course they marry, and when she tells him he is going to be a daddy, he says "Sweetheart, I will then have two loves (*pocionin, mi l'avrai doi amor*), I will have another flower to put next to you (*mi l'avrai 'n autra fior da butete davsin*). There will be in my house a madonna and a child (*A-I sara 'nt la mia ca na madona e 'n bambin*)."

Pocionin
De Magistris – Clerici

1.
L'é pròpi 'n pocionin cola morfela
ch'a ven con mi la sèira al Valentin.
L'é brava, giudissiosa e tanto bela,
l'é l'àngel dël mè cheur e mi I-j veuj bin.
Ël di ch'I l'hai ciamaje dë sposela,
l'ha dame për rispòsta 'n bel basin.

2.
Pocionin, 't ses na reusa d'amor,
la pì bela dle fior, dël pì bel dij giardin.

Pocionin, mi veuj dette 'l mè cheur,
it saras mè boneur, mi it veuj sempre davzin.
Vivo mach për avèj sta fortun-a,
për podèj vive sempre con ti.

3.

Pocionin, l'é gentil la toa vos,
ël tò sguard delissios, ël tò fé birichin.
Pocionin, it ses na perla dël cel,
mi veuj dette 'l pì bel ël pì doss dij basin.

4.

Godoma 'd nòst amor tuta la blëssa,
e soma doi colomb an-namorà.
Jér sèira 'nt un moment ëd tenerëssa,
guardandme 'nt j'euj, con soa vos ëdlicà,
fasend un bel soris e na carëssa,
l'ha dime con passion: it ses papà.

5.

Pocionin, l'era 'l sègn dël mè avnì,
d'avèj n'àngel con ti, për covrilo 'd basin.

6.

Pocionin, mi l'avrai doi amor,
mi I l'avrai n'autra fior da butete davzin.
L'é 'l tò amor ch'am andòra la vita.
It ses la còsa pì sacra për mi.

7.

Pocionin, tò regal a l'é 'l pì bel,
ch'I spetèissa dal cel, che ciamèissa al destin.

Pocionin, it l'has fame papà,
a-i sarà 'nt la mìa ca, na madòna e 'n bambin.

8.
Pocionin, l'era 'l sègn dël mè avnì,
d'avèj n'àngel con ti për covrilo 'd basin.
Repeat 6 and 7

Vocabulary

pocionin – little sweetheart
(*tesorucia*, in Italian)
cola morfela – that pixie
ch'a ven – who comes
con mi – with me
la sèira – evenings
tanto bela – so beautiful
mè cheur – my heart
mi I-j veuj bin – I love her
Ël di – The day
l'hai ciamaje – I asked her
l'ha dame – she gave me
basin – kiss (*bacio*, in Italian)
reusa – rose
la pì bela – the most beautiful
fior – flower
veuj dete – I want to give you
it saras – you will be (*tu sarai*, in Italian)
davzin – near
mach – only (*solamente*, in Italian)
për avèj – to have

për podèj – to be able to
la toa vos – your voice
tò fé birichin – your naughty behavior
cel – sky (*cielo*, in Italian)
euj – eyes (*occhi*, in Italian)
dël mè avni – of my future
con ti – with you
për covrilo – to cover him
mi I l'avrai – I will have (*io avro*, in Italian)
për mi – for me
ch'I spetèissa – that I could expect
al destin – from destiny
it l'has fame papà – you made me a daddy
a-i sarà – there will be (*ci sara*, in Italian)
la mìa ca – my house
na madòna – a madonna
'n bambin – a chil

203

6.5 SONGS IN THE SICILIAN DIALECT

There is a certain "bitterness" in many Sicilian folk songs. Perhaps it is because of the 2,500 years of domination by foreigners, or the poverty the island has suffered over the past 100 years (resulting in the mass emigration that occurred at the turn of this century to the United States). There appears to be a lot of truth in the title of LaFay's article which appeared in the National Geographic magazine about Sicily, "Sicily, where all the songs are sad." Even the famous Sicilian author *Giuseppe Tomasi di Lampedusa*, writes about how even a gay Piedmontese song, *La Bella Gigugin* (popular during the *Risorgimento* period) is transferred into a "sad" song. He writes, describing Sicilians going to vote for a plebiscite on unification with the kingdom of *Vittorio Emanuele II*, "they sang a few verses of *La Bella Gigugin* transformed into a kind of Arab wail, a fate to which any gay time sung in Sicily is bound to succumb." Even when the melody appears gay, the song is sad. An example of this is the classic Sicilian song *Vitti Na Crozza* (I Saw a Skull), which is about dying, and dying without an honorable funeral. Another classic Sicilian folk song is *Ciuri, Ciuri* (*Fiori, Fiori* in Italian and *Flowers, Flowers* in English). This also has a gay bouncing melody, but its about love turned sour. One line goes "Every night I will pass by you, to spite you eternally (*Tutti li notti passu c'avanti, ppi fariti dispettu eternamenti*, in Sicilian)." Of course not all Sicilian folk songs are sad. To illustrate the point, we have included another classic song, a "*Mamma*" song, which is very gay, entitled *Mamma, Ciccio Mi Tocca* (Mom, Ciccio is Teasing Me).

204

♦ *Ciuri, Ciuri.* This is a classical Sicilian folk song. *Ciuri* means flowers in Sicilian (*Fiori* in Italian) and is pronounced like *sciuri*. It is another falling-out-of-love song, like *Vivere* in section 6.2. The refrain goes, "Flowers, flowers, flowers all year around (*Ciuri, ciuri, ciuri di tuttu l'annu*), the love you gave me I'm sending back (*l'amuri ca mi dasti ti lu tornu*)."

Ciuri, Ciuri
Molino – Pastura

1.
Ciuri, ciuri,
ciuri di tuttu l'annu
l'amuri ca mi dasti
ti lu tornu!
Ciuri, ciuri,
ciuri di tuttu l'annu
l'amuri ca mi dasti
ti lu tornu!

2.
Ciuri di ruvittàri e spini santi,
se tu passar, cantar mi senti,
non cantu nè p'amuri nè p'amanti
per cchi mi passi mancu pi la menti.

3.
Repeat 1

4.
Ciuri di rosi russi a lu sbucciàri,

205

amàra a l'omu ca fimmini cridi,
amàra a cu si fà supra 'nniàri!
Lustru di paradisu no ni vidi!

5.
Repeat 1

6.
Ciuri di gersuminu abbrancicanti,
missa dormiri cantu allegramenti.
Tutti li notti li passu c'avanti
ppi fariti dispettu eternamenti.

7.
Repeat 1

8.
Tutti li notti li passu c'avanti
ppi fariti dispettu eternamenti

9.
Repeat 1

Vocabulary

Ciuri – Flowers (*Fiori*, in Italian)
di tuttu l'annu – all year around
l'amuri ca mi dasti – the love
you gave (*l'amore che m'hai
dato*, in Italian)
ti lu tornu – I am sending back
di ruvittàri - of bramble bushes
spini santi - holy thorns

se tu passar, cantar mi senti – if
you pass by, you hear me singing
non cantu – I do not sing
nè p'amuri - not for love
nè p'amanti - nor for lovers
*per cchi mi passi mancu pi la
menti* - whom I am not even
thinking of

206

di rosi russi – of red roses (*di rose rosse*, in Italian)

a lu sbucciàri – about to blossom

amàra a l'omu ca fimmini cridi – woe to the man who trusts women (*guai all'uomo che alle donne crede*, in Italian)

amàra a cu si fà supra 'nniàri – woe to be he who lets himself be dominated (*guai a chi si fa dominare*, in Italian)

lustru di paradisu no ni vidi – the light of heaven he will not see (*luce di Paradiso non ne vede*, in Italian)

Ciuri di gersuminu abbrancicanti – Climbing Jasimen (*gersuminu*) flowers

missa dormiri – when I go to sleep

cantu allegramenti – I sing happily

Tutti li notti – every night (*Tutte le notti*, in Italian)

li passu c'avanti – I pass here in front of you (*le passo qui davanti*, in Italian)

ppi fariti dispettu – to spite you (*per fare a te dispetto*, in Italian)

eternamenti – eternally

♦ *Mamma, Ciccio Mi Tocca.* Traditionally, Sicilians were more puritanical than the purest Puritan. A girl had to have permission from her mother even to look at a boy. Of course, in the end something more than "looking" could occur. This classical Sicilian folk song is about getting mom's permission to tease, to hug, and to kiss. *Ciccio* is a nickname for *Francesco,* and *Ciccio mi tocca* literally means *Francesco* is "touching me," but idiomatically means *Francesco* is "teasing me." The song goes, "Oh mom, oh mom Ciccio is teasing me (*Oh mamma, oh mamma, c'è Ciccio ca mi tocca*), what should I do (*chi mi consighi tu*)?" Mom answers, "Oh daughter, oh daughter if your heart is beating (*Oh figghia, oh figghia se lo tu cori batti*), your love is strong, so it's okay with me (*è forti lo tu amuri e pregiudizi non cci nè*)." Oh boy, there's the green light! "So Ciccio, go ahead and tease me (*Allur Ciccio, toccami*), mom says yes (*la mamma dissi si*). Tease me Ciccio, now that mom is not here (*toccami Ciccio, che mamman non c'è*)." Editorial note: At this point *tocca* may have lost its idiomatic meaning.

Mamma, Ciccio Mi Tocca

1.
Oh mamma, oh mamma, c'è Ciccio cà mi tocca.
Chi mi consigghi tu, chi mi consigghi tu.
Oh figghia, oh figghia si lu to cori batti,
è forti lu to amuri, e pregiudizi non cci n'è.
Allura, Ciccio toccami, la mamma dissi si.
Tocca la manu, toccala, si tu la vo tuccari!
Toccami, Ciccio toccami, non t'ha affruntari no!
Mamma Ciccio mi tocca. Toccami Ciccio che mamma nun c'è!

2.

Oh mamma, oh mamma c'è Ciccio cà mi stringi.
Lu lassu fari si, lu lassu fari no?
Oh figghia, oh figghia, diccillu à lu to cori.
Ti dissi lassa fari, nun mi dumannari chiù.
Allura Ciccio stringimi, la mamma ha dittu si!
Bellu, allu pettu stringimi, stringimi acussi!
Stringimi Ciccio, stringimi, nun t'affruntari no!
Mamma Ciccio mi stringi. Stringimi Ciccio ca
fari si pò!

3.

Oh mamma, oh mamma, c'è Ciccio cà mi vasa.
L'hai a vasari si, l'hai a vasari no?
Oh figghia, oh figghia si lu to cori canta,

4.

la mamma chiù non cunta, à responsabili sì tu.
Allura Ciccio vasami, la mamma dissi sì!
Tocca la vucca, vasami, vasami da acussì!
Vasami Ciccio, vasami, nun t'affruntari no!
Mamma Ciccio mi vasa. Vasami Ciccio cà fari si
pò.

Repeat 4

5.

Mamma Ciccio mi stringi. Stringimi cà si pò!
Mamma Ciccio mi tocca. Toccami ...

Vocabulary

c'è Ciccio cà mi tocca – Ciccio is "teasing me" (mi stuzzica, in Italian)

figghia – daughter (figlia, in Italian)

cori – heart

lu to amuri – your love (il tuo amore, in Italian)

si tu la vo tuccari – if you want to "tease her"

Toccami - tease me

non t'affruntari – don't be bashful

c'è Ciccio cà mi stringi – There's Ciccio who is hugging me

Lu lassu fari – should I let him do it (lo lascio fare, in Italian)

diccillu à lu to cori – ask your heart (literally "tell it to your heart")

Ti dissi lassa fari – (if your heart) tells you to go ahead

nun mi dumannari chiù – don't ask me anymore (non mi domandare più, in Italian)

Allura Ciccio stringimi! – So Ciccio hug me!

La mamma ha dittu si – mom says yes

Bellu – handsome

allu pettu stringimi – hug me to your chest

stringimi acussi – hug me this way

Ciccio mi vasa – Ciccio is kissing me (Ciccio mi bacia, in Italian)

L'hai a vasari – should I kiss him (lo devo dar un bacio, in Italian)

si lu to cori canta – if your hear sings

la mamma chiù non conta – your mother doesn't matter anymore

à responsabili sì tu – you are the responsible one (la resposabile sei tu, in Italian)

Allura Ciccio vasami! – So Ciccio, kiss me!

Tocca la vucca – touch my mouth

vasami da acussì – kiss me like this

210

♦ *Ortigia in Blues.* This is a modern Sicilian song about an old part of the city of *Siracusa* called *Ortigia*. When originally colonized by the Greeks circa 400 b.c., *Ortigia* was "just a spit (*solo uno sputo*) of an island ," as stated in the opening line of the song. Latter it was joined by bridges to the main island of Sicily. Every building, every rock, every street in *Ortigia* is pregnant with its history of over 2500 years. Where the sun shines new life is born, but "In the dark places, Ortigia cries the blues (*Unn'è scuru, Ortigia, chianci 'n blues*)."

Ortigia in Blues
Liddo Schiavo – Antonyo Canyno (1992)

1.
È sulu nu sputu,
na macchia di terra ammenzu o mari.
Ma quanta genti fici sunnari,
quannu addumò di torti culuri.

2.
Nu barcuneddu abbrancica nu muru,
e ciunciulia cu na cannalata morta.
La vecchia petra splenni comu oru.

3.
Torti vaneddi tagghianu lu suli,
e unni arriva nasci vita nova.
Unn'è scuru, lu scogghiu, chianci'n blues.

4.
L'aria é 'mpastata di scirrocu.
Bagnati stradi specchianu la luna,

ca scivulannu cadi dintra o mari.
Repeat 4

5.
E li lampiuni allonganu li codda
dannu luci a'n ponti addurmisciuto.
Unn'è scuru, Ortigia, chianci 'n blues.

Vocabulary

È sulu nu sputu – it is only a spit (of an island)
na macchia di terra – a spot of earth
ammenzu o mari – in the middle of the sea (*in mezzo al mare*, in Italian)
Ma quanta genti fici sunnari – but how many people it made dream
quannu addumò di torti culuri – when it lights up with strong colors (*quando si accese di forti tinte,*in Italian)
Nu barcuneddu – a little balcony (*un balconcino*, in Italian)
abbrancica nu muru – climbs up a wall (*si arrampica su un muro*, in Italian)
e ciunciulia cu – and chatters with (*e chiacchiera con*, in Italian)
na cannalata morta – a dead rain pipe (*una grondaia morta*, in Italian)

La vecchia petra splenni comu oru – The old rock shines like gold (*La vecchia pietra splende come oro*, in Italian)
Torti vaneddi tagghianu lu suli – Intricate little streets cut off the sun (*Intricate stradine tagliano il sole*, in Italian)
e unni arriva – and where it (the sun) arrives (*e dove arriva*, in Italian)
nasci vita nova – new life is born
Unn'è scuru – where it is dark (*Dov'è buio*, in Italian)
lu scogghiu – the island (*l'isola*, in Italian)
chianci'n blues – cries the blues (*piange un blues*, in Italian)
L'aria é 'mpastata di scirrocu – The air is pregnant with sirocco winds
bagnati stradi specchianu la luna – wet streets reflect the

212

moon
ca scivulannu cadi dintra o mari
– that gliding (the moon) falls
into the sea
E li lampiuni allonganu li codda
– and the street lamps stretch
their necks (*E I lampioni
allungano il collo*, in Italian)

*dannu luci a'n ponti
addurmisciuto* – give light to a
sleeping bridge (*danno luce ad
un ponte addormentato*, in
Italian)
*Unn'è scuru, Ortigia, chianci 'n
blues* – Where it is dark, Ortigia,
cries the blues

♦ *Vitti Na Crozza.* This is one of those "sad" Sicilian songs, although you could never tell by the beat of the music. The plucking of the *marranzano* (Jews' harp) is often used to accompany Sicilian music, and it is used here to maintain a lively beat to a sad story about dying without a decent funeral. An old man sees a skull on a pile of rocks (in some versions a cannon, *cannuni* in Sicilian). He speaks to the skull, and the skull answers, "I died without the church bells ringing (*Murivi senza toccu di campani*)." That is,"I died without a proper funeral." Probably the most poignant line in the song is the line "Now that I have arrived at the age of eighty (*Ora ca su arrivatu a uttant 'anni*), I call for life and death answers me (*chiamu la vita, e morti m'arrispunni*)."

Vitti Na Crozza

1.
Lla, lla, lla, leru – Tirù.
Lla, lla, lla, leru – Tirù.
Lla, lla, lla, leru – Tirù.
Lla, lla, lla.

2.
Vitti 'na crozza supra nu cantuni.
Fui curiusu e ci vosi spiari.
Idda m'arrispunni con gran duluri:
"Murivi senza toccu di campani!"

Repeat 1 twice

3.
Si nni eru, si nni eru li mè anni,

214

Si nni eru, si nni eru 'n sacciu a unni!
Ora ca su arrivatu a uttant 'anni,
chiamu la vita e morti m'arrespunni.

Repeat 1 twice

4.
Cunzàtimi, cunzàtimi lu lettu,
ca di li vermi su' mangiantu tuttu.
Se non lu scuntotar non è piccatu.
Lu scuntu ali 'atru mundu a sanguliu tu.

5.

Repeat 1 twice

Vocabulary

Vitti – I saw
'na crozza – a skull (*teschio*, in Italian)
cantuni – a pile of rocks
Fui curiusu – I was curious
ci vosi spiari – I wanted to question it
Idda – It
m'arrispunni – answered me
con gran duluri – with great pain
Murivi – I died
senza toccu di campani – without ringing bells (meaning without a proper funeral)
Si nni eru – they are gone (*Se ne*

sono andati, in Italian)
'n sacciu a unni – I don't know where
Ora ca su arrivatu a uttant 'anni – Now that I have reached eighty
chiamu la vita – I call for life
morti m'arrespunni – death answers me
Cunzàtimi – arrange
lu lettu – the bed
ca – because
di li vermi – from the worms
su' mangiantu tuttu – I'm all eaten up

6.6 NOTES AND REFERENCES

Neapolitan songs are the best documented of all songs in Italian dialects. This is because for so many years (1830 – 1930), Neapolitan music dominated popular music coming from all other parts of Italy. Words for Neapolitan songs were written by famous poets, like *Salvatore di Giacomo* (1860 – 1934), and the music was written by famous musicians, like *Francesco Paolo Tosti* (1846-1916). Songs in dialects like Piedmontese and Sicilian never became very popular outside of their local regions. It was not until the 1930's that popular songs written in the official Italian language started becoming popular throughout Italy and elsewhere. A person who played a key role in popularizing Italian songs, sung in Italian, was the song writer and musician *Cesare Andrea Bixio*. Two of his most famous songs *Mamma and Parlami d'Amore, Mariù* may be found in Section 6.2. The singer *Carlo ButI* made these songs famous, not only in Italy, but also in America, with all its Italian immigrants. Of course, radio helped expand popular songs beyond local regions. Since the common language was official Italian, it was logical that as communications improved, more songs would be written in Italian.

In the 1990's the orchestra leader *Renzo Arbore* produced a series of CDs, *Napoli-Punto e a Capo, Napoli-Due Punti e a Capo*, and *Napoli-Punto Esclamativo* where classic Neapolitan songs are played with a modern beat. Arbore recently produced another *CD Pecchè Nun Ce Ne Jammo in America?* (Why Don't We Go To America?), which in addition to the lead song with the above title, contains a number of Neapolitan songs presented in section 6.3.

The history of popular Neapolitan music is traced in detail in Paliotti's, *Storice della Canzone Napolitana*. The edited volume of Luca Torre (See References) contains a good collection of Neapolitan songs for the period 1200-1930. Translations of many

216

Neapolitan songs into Italian may be found in the text of Imperiali and Recalcati, *La Canzone Napolitana*. The three volume CD, *Napolitana di Roberto Murolo – Antologia Cronologica della Canzone Partenopea*, contains Neapolitan songs from 1200 to 1960, performed by *Roberto Murolo*, son of the famous song writer *Ernesto Murolo* (1876 – 1939). These CDs include booklets with translations of Neapolitan songs into Italian, and comments on each song (138 songs total). One can listen to many of the songs *Carlo Buti* sang in the 1930's and 1940's on the CD *Carlo Buti-Greatest Hits*.

The songs listed in sections 6.2 – 6.5 may all be found in the following recordings.

•*Mamma, Luciano Pavarotti* (CD, 411 959-2)

> London Records
> Division of Polygram Records, Inc.
> 810 Seventh Ave
> New York, NY 10019

Songs: *Mamma, Parlami d'amore Mariù, Vivere, Chitarra Romana*

•*The Music of Italy* (CD, WLD 009)

> Tring International PLC
> Licensed from the Long Island Music Company Limited

Songs: *L'italiano, Parlami d'amore Mariù, O Sole Mio, 'O paese d'o sole, Santa Lucia Luntana*

•*All the Best From Italy, Vol II* (Cassette, CLUC 076)

> Distributed by:
> Distribution Madacy Inc.
> P.O. Box 50
> Town of Mount Royal, Quebec, Canada H3P 3C7

Song: *Mi scappa la pipi papa*

•*Le Piu Belle Canzoni Piemontesi, Mario Piovano* (Cassette, NK 33108)

      RCA, SPA

      Rome, Italy

Songs: *Mia mama veul che fila, Ciao Turin, La luna 'd Moncale, Marieme veuj marieme, Pocionin*

•*Canta Piemonte, 1991* (Cassette, PMP-MC 13043)

      Distributed by:

      CANTERO Edizioni Musicale e Disco grafiche

      Via Duca d'Aosta, 63

      14100 Asti, Italy

Song: *Piemontesi*

•*Vecchi Canti d'Osteria* (Cassette, 205)

      Distributed by:

      Piemonte in Bancarella

      Corso Siccardi, 4

      10122 Torino, Italy

      Song: *La Polenta*

•*Gipo A So Piemont – Vol 2* (CD, CDP 576)

      Fonit – Cetra

      Via Bertola, 34

      Torino, Italy

      Songs: *Dla Dal Pont, Porta Pila*

•*Souvenir di Sicilia* (Cassette, SEA 0284)

      Distributed by:

      Sea Musica

      Via S. Maria di Betlem, 31

      Catania, Italy

Songs: *Vitti Na Crozza, Ciuri-Ciuri, Mamma Ciccio Mi Tocca*

•*Syracusante, Antonyo Canyno* (CD, STR 1092)
> Warner Music Italia, SPA
> Siracusa, Italy
> Song: *Ortigia in Blues*

•*Renzo Arbore – L'Orchestra Italiana (Famose Canzoni Napoletane)* (CD, 74321-36092-2)
> BMG Music
> New York, New York
> 75 Rockefeller Plaza
> New York, NY 10019
> Songs: *Aummo-Aummo, Guaglione, Maria-Marì, Torna a Surriento, Reginella, 'O Sole Mio*

•*Renzo Arbore – L'Orchestra Italiana (Due Punti e a Capo)* (CD, 61676-2)
> Elektra Entertainment
> Time Warner Company
> 75 Rokefeller Plaza
> New York, NY 10019
> Songs: *L'Hai Voluto Te, Torna a Surriento, Aummo-Aummo*

•*Renzo Arbore – L'Orchestra Italiana – Pecche Nun Ce Ne Jammo in America?* (CD, TCDMRL 430222 7432143022)
> Distributed by:
> Local BMG Company A
> BMG Entertainment
> Song: *Te Voglio Bene Assaje, Guaglione, Reginella*

•*Papaveri e Papere (Vol. 1)* (CD, Drive 613)

Discomagic S.P.A.
via Mecenate, 78/A
20138 Milano, Italy
Song: *Uno Per Tutte*

•*Napoletana di* **Roberto Murolo** – *Antologia Cronologica della Canzone Partenopea, Volumes I, II, II* (CD, 74321391442)

Distributed by:
Local BMC Company A
BMG Entertainment
Songs: *Te Voglio Bene Assaje, Maria-Marì, O' Sole Mio, Reginella 'A Tazza 'e Café, Santa Lucia Luntana, Torna a Surriento*

•*Carlo Buti – Greatest Hits* (CD, RMCD 4131)

Distributed by:
Replay Music
Songs: *Chittara Romana, Mamma*

CHAPTER 7. A Tale of Two Italies: Piedmont and Sicily

7.1 INTRODUCTION

The title of this chapter is inspired by Dicken's *A Tale of Two Cities*. Piedmont and Sicily are two regions of Italy, which are so different, like Dicken's Paris and London. Piedmont is a land-locked region of northern Italy, capped by the Alps. Sicily is an island off the coast of southern Italy, with a major volcano, *Etna*, but no mountain ranges. The racial stock of the two regions is radically different. The original people in Piedmont were the Ligurians (Taurini tribe), then came the Celts, Goths, Lombards, and Franks. The original people in Sicily were the Siculi and Sicani tribes, then came the Phoenicians, Greeks, Vandals, and Arabs. The dialect of Piedmont and Sicily are mutually incomprehensible. Finally their political history is the history of two totally different countries. From 1000 AD on, Piedmont was essentially ruled by one dynastic family, the House of Savoy. The Savoys originally came from an area just south of lake Geneva, and for many years their main capital was in the French city of Chambery. But in 1562 *Emanuele Filiberto*, a Savoy duke moved the capital from Chambery to Turin, and the Savoy dynasty took on a decidedly Italian bent. *Emanuele Filiberto* also switched the official court language from French to Italian in 1562. On the other hand, Sicily was always a "country" ruled by foreigners, the French, the Spanish, the Austrians, yes and even the Piemontese.

But amazingly enough, these two different "countries" were "united" four separate times in their history. Our tale is that of the four "unifications" of Piedmont and Sicily. The first time under the Romans, circa 200 BC, the second time under the emperor Frederick II, circa 1220 AD, the third time under the House of Savoy in 1713, and the fourth time under a unified Italy in 1861.

7.2 THE FIRST UNIFICATION: THE ROMAN EMPIRE

The pre-Roman populations of Piedmont and Sicily were of entirely different origins. Piedmont was first settled by Celtics and Ligurian tribes. One particular Ligurian tribe, the *Taurini*, founded a village on the Po river which they called *Taurasia*. In 221 BC, when the Romans first arrived, they reached *Taurasia* and called the city *Taurinorum*. When Hannibal crossed the Alps in 218 BC, the city put up resistance but was defeated and destroyed. By 150 BC the Romans again established their rule in Piedmont, then part of what was called *Cisalpine Gaul*. In 49 BC, the Taurinian city by the Po was officially recognized by the Romans and given the name *Julia Taurinorum*. By the time of Ceasar Augustus, the Piedmont region officially became part of a Roman region, called *Transpadana*, and the city *Julia Taurinorum* was renamed *Julia Augusta Taurinorum* (now the city of Turin, or in Italian *Torino*).

In contrast, the first known people in Sicily were the native tribes called *Siculi* in eastern Sicily, and *Sicani I*, in western Sicily. About 800 BC the Phoenicians arrived in Sicily. The Phoenicians established the city of Carthage in northern Africa just south of Sicily. The Greeks also started to settle in Sicily about the eighth century BC. They established cities they called Messene (*Messina*), Katane (*Catania*), Syracuse (*Siracusa*), Panormos (*Palermo*), etc. In those days when a Greek father told his son, "go west young man," he meant Sicily and southern Italy. For many years the Carthagians and the Greeks shared the island, with the Carthagians in the western part and the Greeks in the eastern part. The Greeks called Sicily *Trinacria*, because of its three-sided triangular appearance. By 241 BC, the Romans had decisively defeated the Carthagians and they then made Sicily a Roman province. For about 500 years Piedmont and Sicily were part of the same country, "the Roman Empire," with one official language, Latin, and one ruler, the Roman emperor. The collapse of the Roman Empire in 476, marked the end of the first Piedmont-Sicily unification. But if one visits Piedmont or Sicily, one can still see many signs of the common Roman heritage, city gates, Roman villas, temples, and amphitheaters. In Turin, one can see an old Roman gate, now called *Porta Palatina* and a nearby Roman amphitheater. The city of Agrigento in Sicily is famous for its many Greek and Roman temples. In the town of *Piazza Armerina* in Sicily, one can visit a well-preserved Roman villa, originally constructed in the third century AD.

7.3 THE SECOND UNIFICATION: FREDERICK II.

After the collapse of the Roman Empire, Germanic tribes poured into Italy, the Lombards (569 AD) into Piedmont and northern Italy, and the Vandals (451 AD) in Sicily and southern Italy. The Greek Byzantine Empire then reconquered most of Italy, and from 663 – 668 the city of Syracuse in Sicily was the empire's capital. In 774 the Franks, under Charlemagne (*Carlo Magno*), invaded the Piedmont area and created the marquisates of Turin (*Torino*), Ivrea, and Monferrat (*Monferrato*). In 800 AD, Charlemagne was crowned as the first Holy Roman Emperor, and ruled over most of northern and central Italy. Meanwhile in 827 AD, Arabs invaded Sicily and made Palermo their capital on the island. Moslem Arabs then ruled Sicily for about 200 years, establishing Palermo as one of the most advanced cities in the Mediterranean.

About the year 1060, a Norman by the name of Guiscard invaded Sicily. Guiscard was one of the sons of Tancred de Hauteville, a warrior-adventurer from French Normandy. In 1091, Roger (*Ruggero*), another son of Tancred, defeated the last of the Moslems in the city of Noto, and for the next 100 years the Normans ruled Sicily. In 1130 Roger II, acquired most of southern Italy and declared Sicily and his land in southern Italy the "Kingdom of Sicily." Roger II made his capital Palermo. His court in Palermo was one of the most advanced in all of Europe. He was very tolerant of all the people who lived in the city, Greeks, Black Africans, Latins, Persians, Lombards, Jews, etc., and he encouraged scholarly activities of all types. A book on the geography of the world was written by the Arab Al'Idrisi with encouragement of Roger II, and became known, especially in the Arab world, as the "Book of King Roger." The Norman palace in Palermo still exists, and is one of the most interesting places to visit even today. At about the same period of time, another "French" dynasty was being initiated in the Piedmont area by a warrior-adventurer called Humbert the Whitehanded (*Umberto Biancamano*). Originally from an area in France just south of Lake Geneva, now the French department called Savoy, *Umberto* extended his regime across the Alps into Piedmont when his son *Oddone* married *Adelaide di Susa*. This was the start of the Savoy Dynasty in Piedmont, which was to become the reigning monarchy of a United Italy, and last until the end of World War II. In 1235, the Savoy Count *Amedeo* IV conquered the city of Turin. The House of Savoy then ruled a region that straddled both sides of the Alps, with dual capital cities, one in France, Chambery, and one in Italy, Turin. However on the Italian side the House of Savoy had many competitors, most notably the Marquisate of Monferrat (*Monferrato*) and the Marquisate of *Saluzzo*. Meanwhile in Sicily, Frederick (*Federico*) II, crowned Holy Roman Emperor in 1220, was consolidating his rule over various parts of the Italian peninsula, including the Piedmont region. Frederick II was the grandson of Frederick I (*Barbarossa*), from the Hohenstaufen dynasty of Swabia (Germany), and the grandson of Roger II, on his mother's side. It was under Frederick II that we saw the second unification of Piedmont and Sicily, although of all the unifications this one was probably the weakest of all. Frederick II ruled his

224

empire from Palermo. His court in Palermo was considered the most illustrious of all the courts of the time. Indeed he was commonly called *Stupor Mundi* (Wonder of the World). He encouraged the study of all the arts and sciences, and the development of a Sicilian dialect, which was to achieve great prominence in the development of the Italian language. His court language was latter referred to as "the Sicilian School" (*Scuola Siciliana*). (It is interesting to note that at about this same time, the Piedmontese dialect was developing into a written language through the various courts in Torino, Monferrat, Saluzzo, etc. In 1224, Frederick II founded the University of Naples, one of the early universities in Europe, after Bologna (1088), and Padua (1222). Like his grandfather, he was at odds with the Popes in Rome, who feared a Holy Roman Emperor with complete control of the Italian Peninsula. When Frederick II decided, in the 1230's, that the Muslims in Sicily had to be deported, he sent them to the city of *Lucera* in Apulia, largely to spite the Catholic pontifs. We will identify Frederick II's reign as Holy Roman Emperor from 1215 – 1250 as the second Piedmontese – Sicilian unification, although as previously noted it was not a strong unification. The court languages in Palermo and Torino were different, and the control Frederick II exercised over the Piedmontese feudalities was at best nominal. The bastard son of Frederick II, Manfred, married a Savoy princess, but the links between Piedmont and Sicily of this period were destroyed on Decemer 13, 1250 when Frederick II died, and Manfred was defeated by Charles of Anjou (France) in 1266. One can visit the tombs of Roger II and Frederick II in the famous cathedral of Palermo.

7.4 THE THIRD UNIFICATION: THE HOUSE OF SAVOY.

After the defeat of Manfred in 1266, the French ruled Sicily and southern Italy, under Charles of Anjou, until the Sicilian Vespers of

1282, when the Sicilians rebelled against their French rulers. See section 1.5 for more details on the Sicilian-Vesper incident. After the Sicilian Vespers, the House of Aragon (Spanish), under Peter III, took control of Sicily and remained in power on the island until 1412. From 1412 to 1713, Sicily was ruled by Viceroys from Spain. The three hundred year Spanish rule in Sicily was not a happy time for most of the people. The Spanish were in Sicily to exploit the island, not to colonize it. The Spanish Viceroys allowed the local Sicilian Barons to rule over the people at will, and in the interior of the island there was no law and order. Indeed many say that this period of time helped plant the seeds of the Mafia in Sicily.

In Piedmont, a long string of "Amedeos" (Savoy Counts) ruled during the period 1200 – 1500. Most notable of the Amedeos were Amedeo VI (1334 – 1383) known as the Green Count (*Conte Verde*); Amedeo VII (1383 – 1418) known as the Red Count (*Conte Rosso*); Amedeo VIII (1418 – 1451) and Amedeo IX (1465 – 1472). In 1381, Amedeo VI mediated a truce between Venice and Genova, which brought the House of Savoy into prominence with respect to the rest of the Italian peninsula. Amedeo VI was called the "Green Count" because of the colors he wore at tournaments. In Turin, there is a copper statue of the Green Count (Amedeo VI), which interestingly enough is green due to the oxidation of the copper statue material. In 1405 Amedeo VII founded the University of Turin, which boasts as one of its most illustrious graduates (1506) the famous Dutch scholar Erasmus. Amedeo VIII became the first Duke of Savoy (promotion from Count), and in 1439 was elected Pope at the council of Basel. Amedeo IX consolidated the power of the House of Savoy in the Piedmont area, but for many years after his death, the French dominated Piedmont. However, in 1562, the Savoy Duke, *Emanuele Filiberto*, recaptured Torino with the help of the Spanish, and established the city as the capital of his dukedom.

He made Dante's Italian the official court language, and fortified the city with the construction of a military complex called the *Cittadella*. The façade of the Cittadella still stands in Turin, and is a popular tourist attraction. It now houses a famous artillery museum. One can also see a statue of *Emanuele Filiberto* in the famous *Piazza San Carlo* in Turin. In spite of the fortification of Turin, the French returned to dominate Piedmont, until 1706 when the Savoy Duke, Vittorio Amedeo II was able, with the help of the Austrian, to oust the French from Turin. With the treaty of Utrecht in 1713, Vittorio Amedeo II, was awarded the island of Sicily, and became the first Savoy king, as King of Sicily. The House of Savoy ruled Sicily from 1713 to 1720, and this we identify as the third unification of Piedmont and Sicily. Vittorio Amedeo II spent the first year of his reign as king in Sicily. He tried to find ways to improve the economy of Sicily, and bring order into the interior of the island. His efforts at reform were not always appreciated, especially by the Sicilian Barons who had been allowed to have their own way under the Spanish Viceroys. It did not help matters when a serious famine occurred right after he returned to Turin. When something goes really bad, Sicilians still say to this day, *pari ca ci passò casa Savoia* (it looks like the House of Savoy has been here). This third unification was terminated in 1720 when *Vittorio Amedeo II* was forced to switch the island of Sicily for the island of Sardinia. Vittorio Amedeo II then became king of Sardinia, and the House of Savoy ruled Sardinia from Turin up to 1792, when Napoleon forced the royal Savoy family into exile in Sardinia.

7.5 THE FOURTH UNIFICATION: GARIBALDI.

After the Piedmontese left Sicily in 1720, the island was ruled by Austria until 1734. From 1734 until 1860 the island was ruled by a succession of Bourbon monarchs. The Bourbon dynasty was originally French, but then a branch developed in Italy. A short survey of Italian Bourbon rule in Sicily is given below.

ITALIAN BOURBON RULE

• 1734 – 1759 Charles IV. King of the two Sicilies (Sicily and Naples)

• 1759 – 1806 Ferdinand IV. King of Naples (Sicily ruled by Spanish Monarchy)

• 1806 – 1815 Ferdinand IV becomes Ferdinand III, King of Sicily

• 1816 – 1825 Ferdinand III becomes Ferdinand I, King of the two Sicilies

• 1825 – 1830 Frances I. King of the two Sicilies

• 1830 – 1859 Ferdinand II. King of the two Sicilies

• 1859 – 1860 Francis II. King of the two Sicilies

The Italian Bourbons made Naples their capital, and during most of their reign, Sicily was essentially a neglected "province." Meanwhile in Piedmont, the Marquisate of Monferrato was absorbed by the House of Savoy in 1713, and by the treaty of Aix-La-Chapelle, the House of Savoy gained the seaport of Nice (*Nizza*) in 1748. While Sicily was being governed from Naples, Piedmont was developing an indigenous monarchy, centered in Turin, with a strong military tradition. However with the French Revolution and the invasion of Italy by Napoleon everything changed. In 1798, *Carlo Emanuele* IV, the reigning Savoy monarch was exiled by Napoleon to Sardinia, and Ferdinand I abandoned Naples and fled to Palermo. After the defeat of Napoleon, all the monarchies of Italy were restored, but the Austrians became the dominant power on the peninsula. In 1848 *Carlo Alberto*, of the House of Savoy, declared war on Austria, but was defeated at Novara, and then abdicated to his son *Vittorio Emanuele* II. In 1859 Vittorio Emanuele II, with the help of the French, finally defeated the Austrians and annexed *Lombardia* to his kingdom. The price the House of Savoy had to pay for cooperation from the French, was the loss of Savoy territory north of the Alps, and the seaport of Nice. Momentum then built up for the unification of the Italian peninsula, and in May of 1860, Garibaldi landed in Marsala to free Sicily from Bourbon rule. Garibaldi defeated the Bourbon army and in October of 1860 he held a plebiscite in Sicily for formation of a union with a united Italy under King *Vittorio Emanuele* II. Sicilians voted 99.5% in favor of the union, and the fourth and final unification of Piedmont and Sicily was initiated. March 7, 1861, the Piedmontese monarch *Vittorio Emanuele* II was proclaimed "king of Italy." Piedmont and Sicily were then officially part of one nation, with a common language (Tuscan dialect), and a common government. In 1946 Sicily was declared an autonomous region, but the unification of Italy persisted.

7.6 NOTES AND REFERENCES.

A very complete history of Sicily from 800 AD on, is given in Smith's two volume work, *A History of Sicily*. The November 1994 issue of the National Geographic includes an excellent article on the migration of the Greeks to Italy and Sicily, between the eighth and third centuries BC. See also the March 1976 article of National Geographic on Sicily, which covers the entire span of Sicilian history. Many books have been written about Frederick II. See, for example Abulafia's book cited in the References section. A very complete chronicle of Piedmont and the House of Savoy may be found in Cognasso's *Storia di Torino* or Oliva's *I Savoia*, both written in Italian. Unfortunately there are few histories of Piedmont available in English. Pollack's book Turin 1564 – 1680, is in

English, but it covers only a limited period of time. However it is a period of time that was very critical in the development of the House of Savoy in Piedmont. During the years 1564 – 1680, the city of Turin expanded from the original small Roman city of Taurinaorium to the capital city of the Piedmontese monarchy. Another text in English which deals a limited period of Piedmontese history is Eugene Cox's, *The Green Count of Savoy.* It covers the rule of Amedeo VI (the Green count) during the fourteenth century.

The Bourbon dynasty in Italy is chronicled in a number of books, e.g. Acton's *The Bourbon's of Naples* (in English) and Colletta's *Storia del Reame di Napoli* (in Italian).

CHAPTER 8. An Italian "West Side Story"

8.1 INTRODUCTION

In this chapter, the first author will relate his early childhood experiences growing up in the Central Park West district of Manhattan, New York. So for the rest of this chapter, the "I" will mean Peter Dorato. The title of this chapter was inspired by the famous movie/play "West Side Story", a musical about love and life in a mixed Anglo/Spanish area of Manhattan's upper west side. My story is less about love, at least romantic love, and more about life. In particular, about life amongst first and second generation Italians, more specifically Piedmontese immigrants, trying to make a new life in America.

8.2 THE BEGINNINGS

It all started when *Eufrosina Dorato* (Aunt Rosie) came to New York after marrying *Pierin Garda* (Uncle Pete) in her home town of *Villadeati* in the *Monferrato* section of Piedmont. She was my father's (*Fioretto Dorato*) sister, and she was anxious to leave her rather severe father, my grandfather *Gaspare Dorato*. They settled in what was called the "Hell's Kitchen" district of Manhattan, roughly the area between 30th Street and 60th Street, and 7th Avenue and 10th Avenue. My father also found grandpa *Gaspare* impossible to live with, so when his sister, *Eufrosina,* invited him to join her in New York he did not hesitate to leave. Actually the *Dorato* family was relatively well off in *Villadeati*. They owned many of vineyards where grapes for wines from *Monferrato* were grown; including *Barbera del Monferrato*, *Grignolino*, *Freisa*, etc. But in addition to problems with his father, my father had an older brother *Giuseppe Dorato*, and with the *primogenito* (first born) culture of the time, his older brother was likely to inherit all the land. That was another reason to leave, a reason common to many Italian immigrants to America, and in 1924 he did just that. My father found a job as a cook in New York City, and after saving some money, he decided it was time to get married. Naturally, he thought of marrying a Piedmontese girl, since his limited English and relative poverty were two large obstacles to marrying an American. So in 1931, he returned to *Villadeati* to look for a wife. Fortunately for him there was a very attractive young girl, *Rosina Lachello* (my mother), who was extremely anxious to leave *Villadeati*. She dreaded the idea of having to live in a small farming community (population of about 450) for the rest of her life as the wife of a grape farmer. So they married on July 16th, 1931 and then sailed to America on the *S.S. Roma*. They settled in an apartment at 416 West 45th Street, full of immigrants from Piedmont and other parts of Italy. My father was a cook for the nursing staff at Columbia Presbyterian Medical Center, located on Broadway, between 165th and 168th Streets, and my mother went to work as a dressmaker in the garment district. She had been trained as a dressmaker in *Villadeati*. She ended up working in the New York garment industry for over forty years. Her last boss was Bill Blass, the famous dress designer. When she retired, he let her have the sewing machine she had used at work as a retirement gift. On December 17, 1932, I was born at Columbia Presbyterian Medical Center. Because my father worked there as a cook, there were no medical expenses. I do not think we would have had any money to pay them anyway. Just before my birth, my father's younger brother *Pietro Dorato* died in a motorcycle accident. *Pietro* had been one of the first in *Villadeati* to show any interest in higher education. At the time of his death, he was preparing for the entrance exams for the University in *Torino*. He was a very quiet, but popular person in *Villadeati*, and his death came as a sad shock

Rosina and Fioretto Dorato, New York, 1931

to everyone, including my parents in America. It was natural then
for them to think of naming me after him. When my father was

asked for a name to put on my birth certificate he said little *Pietro*, i.e. *Pierino*, and that was my legal name until I had it changed to Peter many years later. Many of my friends and relatives still call me *Pierino*, especially in Italy.

Right after I was born my mother returned to work, and I was taken care of by a baby sitter during the day. But the baby sitter would keep me in the house all day, and my mother was unhappy about the situation so she started looking for a more "capable" sitter. While pushing me in my carriage in Central Park, my mother overheard some women, with young babies, talking in *Piedmontese*. One particular woman, *Maria,* had a daughter (Josephine) who was about my age. Maria indicated her interest in taking care of me while my mother worked. The problem was that *Maria* lived up on West 67th Street, and getting back and forth between 67th Street and 45th Street was a problem. So in 1935 we moved to 67th Street. This then starts this "West-Side" story.

8.3 THE NEIGHBORHOOD

We lived on the top floor (5th floor) of a walk-up apartment house in a poor "immigrant" block, West 67th Street between Amsterdam Avenue and Eleventh Avenue, in a section of Manhattan referred to as the "Central Park West" district. Central Park West was the street that ran north-south just west of Central Park, and the section between about 60th Street and 100th Street west of Central Park West defined the rough boundaries of the district. It was the area just north of the "Hell's Kitchen" district we had come from. The top floor of a walk-up apartment house was generally the cheapest to rent, and that probably explains why we always lived on the top floor. But it did have other advantages, mainly its easy access to the roof. The roof was a social gathering place, especially at night after a warm summer day, as you may remember from the roof scenes in the movie, *West Side Story*. As children we were allowed to play there. It had its dangers, but it was safer than letting us run around in the streets. Of course, one disadvantage was the long climb up to the fifth floor. But maybe this was also an advantage, it kept us healthy. Two other favorite playing areas were the court yard at the center of the apartment complex, and the backyard at the back end of the apartment complex. I can still hear my mother yelling, in Piedmontese, from the window, "*Ven su, a l'è ora 'd mangé* (Come up, it's time to eat)." From the backyard you could see all the iron fire-escapes, which almost everyone used as little garden areas to grow herbs and tomatoes. From 67th Street and Amsterdam Avenue we also had the advantage of being just a few blocks from Central Park, with all its hills and playgrounds, not to mention the lake and zoo. What a paradise Central Park was for us! Near our apartment house we had a barber shop and grocery store, both Italian of course. On our block we also had the Catholic Church, Saint Matthews, which all the catholics in the neighborhood attended. There was always at least one mass in Italian, actually Latin, with an Italian sermon, each Sunday. I remember attending catechism classes there, and ultimately receiving my first Holy Communion in 1943. Religious ceremonies were very important to our family, As was the case for most Italian immigrant families. West of 11th Avenue we had railroad yards and west of the yards the Hudson river. What an insurmountable barrier the Hudson river seemed at the time, like the classic *New Yorker* magazine cover that showed 10th Avenue, the Hudson river, and then a thin stripe that was the rest of the world, up to China and Russia. There was an empty lot on the north side of our block, that served as the neighborhood playground, and one short block east of us was Broadway, with all its stores and movie houses. A few blocks north was the public elementary school, P.S. 94, which I attended until we moved in 1943, and on Central Park West, between 63rd and 64th street was the *Society for Ethical Culture* and the *Ethical Culture School* where I attended preschool with *Josephine*. This society founded the first free kindergarten in New York City, and was a famous institution for its experiments in advanced educational methods. There were many Italians on our block, some Irish and Hispanics, and a few Afro-American and Jewish people. In those days, almost every block was segregated, one way or another. Apartment houses were further "segregated." The one we lived in was mostly Piedmontese. I only aquired Jewish friends when we moved to Washington Heights in upper Manhattan in 1943, and non-Piedmontese Italian friends when we moved to Jackson Heights in Queens in 1951. Serious non-white friendships developed for me only after I was married and we had moved to Huntington, Long Island in 1963. Within our apartment house, it was like a village in Piedmont. We keep our doors open almost all the time, so that the children could go from one apartment to the other to play. Each apartment was like a house in the village. Everywhere we heard only Piedmontese. I grew up bilingual in that neighborhood, having learned Piedmontese and broken English from my parents. Like most Italian immigrants we spoke a dialect at home, not proper Italian, even though both of my parents were literate in Italian. Consequently, I became quite fluent in Piedmontese. However, after I married in 1956 and left my parents, I stopped speaking Piedmontese. I can still understand it when spoken, and with some recent studies I have learned a bit of the grammar. I remember a few of the Piedmontese expressions my parents used when we lived on 67th street, most of them having to do with eating, e.g. *a l'è ora 'd mangé* (it's time to eat), *mangia e sta cito* (eat and keep quite), *mangia tut, neh* (eat everything, okay), *fà ël brav* (be good), *adess va a gieughe* (now go play)! The thing I remember saying most in Piedmontese is *am scapa da pissé* (I have to make peepee).

236

One of the most important people in the neighborhood was the iceman. I remember he was Italian, but not Piedmontese, and his name was "Joe." I also remember that from the time I could carry a tray of water, it was my job to empty the water from the icebox after the ice melted. I also remember how tired Joe looked after reaching our floor lugging our chunk of ice up five flights of stairs. We always left him a good tip.

8.4 FAMILY AND FRIENDS

We did not have much family in America. Aunt Rosie and Uncle Pete and their son *Ildo* were about it, except for a few very distant cousins scattered here and there. Most of our family was still in Piedmont. My mother had two sisters, *Evelina* and *Ondina* living in Torino and a brother, *Memore,* and parents *Nonno Evasio* and *Nonna Pierina* living in *Villadeati*. *Memore* ultimately moved to *Torino* and died of a heart attack when he was 55. My father's parents, *Nonno Gasprin* and *Nonna Marietta,* together with a brother *Giuseppe* also lived in *Villadeati*. *Giuseppe* was executed by the Germans on October 9, 1944 together with ten other men from *Villadeati* in reprisal for the shooting of a German soldier near the village. In the summer of 1938, we returned to visit *Villadeati* and our relatives. As a six year old, I remember the trip only vaguely. We sailed out on the S.S. *Rex* and returned on the *S. S. Conti di Savoia*. I remember the port of *Genoa*, where we landed, and the village on a hill that was *Villadeati*. I do not remember everyone who came to greet us in *Genoa*, but I do remember *Nonno Evasio* was there. When I was confirmed I was given the middle name *Evasio*. I was then *Pierino Evasio Dorato*. I kept using *Evasio* for a long time, until after college, but eventually dropped it. At the *Doratos* in *Villadeati*, I remember the barn with all the animals being just a door away from the dining room where we ate. This was the first time I had seen my grandparents, *grand* (grandfather) and *granda* (grandmother), as they say in Piedmontese, and it was also the last time, except for my grandmother *Pierina*. My next trip to Italy was after the war in 1950 and by then they all had died, except *Pierina*, who sadly died just a few weeks before my next visit to *Villadeati* in 1962. I felt I had missed something without grandparents, but I did not realize how much until I became a grandparent myself. Anyway, we made the most of the little family we had in America. Aunt Rosie and Uncle Pete moved to Queens, but we often visited each other and had huge meals with such Piemontese standards as *agnolòt alla piemontèisa* (Piedmontese ravioli), *polenta e cunij* (polenta and rabbit), *bagna cauda* (heated oil-garlic-anchovy sauce for dipping vegetables), *buji con bagnet verd* (boiled meats with a parsley-anchovy sauce), *gnòch* (potato dumplings, *gnocchi* in Italian), etc. At our house my mother did the cooking for guests. Although my father was a cook, he always worked in American type restaurants and was not as adept as mother in preparing *Piedmontese* meals. On occasion he did prepare steaks with a butter-garlic sauce, a dish we eat to this day. At Uncle Pete and Aunt Rosie's (or as my parents would say in *Piedmontese, barba Pierin e magna Frusin-a*) it was Uncle Pete who did the cooking. He was a waiter by profession, but a great cook.

On 67th Street we had many close *Piedmontese* friends, that were essentially family to us. There was *Maria* (from *Ivrea*) whom we have already mentioned, her husband *Stevo* (from *Bollengo*), and their daughter Josephine; *Ines* and *Charlie* (both from *Albiano*), and their son Alfred; and *Catherin* and *Tony* (I don't remember where in Piedmont they came from) and their daughter *Rita*, etc. All the children were about my age and we were all like cousins. We also had close friends that did not live on 67th Street, e.g. *Tina* and *Remigio* (from *Casale*) and their children *Vilma* and *Armando*; and

Front: Josephine and Pierino
Back: Maria and Rosina
1937

Fioretto and Pierino
South Beach, 1939

Armando and Vilma, 1938

L. to R.: Dolores, Pierino
Josephine, Alfred
1938

Jolanda and *Tony* (from *Milano*), and their daughter *Armanda*. Both these families lived on Bleeker Street in the "Little Italy" section of

239

Greenwich Village, on a block between 6th Avenue and MacDougal Avenue. I believe my parents had first met them when they were all living in the "Hell's Kitchen" district together. One big difference between *Vilma, Armando*, and *Armanda* and my friends on 67th Street was that they spoke Italian with their parents, and not Piedmontese. Actually, we as children generally spoke English to each other, and Piedmontese only with our parents and their friends. But Bleeker Street was a much more Italian block than 67th Street. The majority of the people on Bleeker Street were Italian, from all parts of Italy. One almost had to speak correct Italian. Also, Bleeker Street was full of food carts in the street, something we did not have on 67th Street.

A few years after we arrived on 67th Street, *Maria* decided to go to work, and my mother had to find someone else to take care of me. After some searching she found a young housewife on 67th Street, *Mildred*, who was from *Calabria*, and whose husband was from Spain. *Mildred* had a daughter *Dolores*, again about my age. Because their mothers took care of me for so long, both Josephine and Dolores became more than just "cousins" to me, they became more like sisters. It is interesting to note how many of the Piedmontese who lived on 67th Street had only one child, at a time when most other Italians in America were having large families. This was probably the case, because we were in the midst of the depression, and jobs were difficult to find, and northern Italians tended to be very conservative about their economic situation. My mother often told me later in life how worried my father was about losing her income if she had to stay home to take care of a "large" (more than one child) family.

Prior to starting school at P.S. 94, all my friends were Piedmontese. However, at P.S. 94, which had a very ethnically mixed population, I met a Jewish boy by the name of *Fred*. He became one of my best school friends. He lived in one of the expensive apartments on Central Park West. I visited his apartment once, and was amazed to see how different it was from where we lived. I lost contact with Fred, but I did learn that he had gone on to become a doctor.

8.5 REST AND RECREATION

I did not see my father much during the week, since he was a cook on a night shift. He had few hobbies, outside of making wine, but on the weekends he would take me for long walks to Central Park to visit the zoo, to go rowing on the lake, etc. His English was limited. He "read" the *New York Daily News*, because it had so many photographs and so few words. I liked it also, because of all the cartoons. My father did not smile or joke easily. His experience in trench warfare in World War I had a lasting affect throughout his life. The Dorato side of the family also had a reputation of being on the "serious" side. My mother was just the opposite. From what I hear of my grandfather *Evasio*, this was also a inherited trait. When I went to Central Park with my mother it was always with a group of her friends and a group of my friends. We did not visit anything, they talked and we played. My father and I would also regularly go the local "Newsreel" theater, which was on Broadway, just a few blocks north of us. He went for the news, and I went for the cartoons. At home we listened to a radio station that broadcasted in Italian. My mother loved to listen to Italian songs, a trait I inherited. I remember one singer in particular, *Carlo Buti*, and one radio ad for cigarettes, *Parode* cigarettes, *più le fumi più le godi* (the more you smoke them, the more you enjoy them).

With the little money my parents saved, they used it to get away from 67th Street during the summer. One favorite place to go was

South Beach on Staten Island (now under the Verazzano Bridge). We went with friends from both 67th Street and Bleeker Street. I remember being at South Beach often with *Josephine*, *Vilma*, and *Armando*. All the families would rent tiny rooms with a central common kitchen area in houses near the beach. Of course, everyone (sometimes as much as four families in one house) was Piedmontese.

Another popular place for us to spend summers was Torrington, Connecticut. There was a little Piedmontese community there, and in particular, my mother had a distant cousin, that I called *magna Lena*, living there. I called her husband *barba Pete*, although they were not really aunt and uncle. They had a daughter, *Norma*, and a son, *Dino,* who were a bit older than me. Norma helped take care of me, because my parents would usually leave me in Torrington for awhile and return to the City to work. I would spend most of the summer in Torrington, so I made some good friends there also, in particular *Rose* and *Barbara* who lived on the same block on Oak Avenue. It is interesting how many of my good friends were girls. But I did have a lot of more casual friends on 67th Street that were boys, and we played boy's games. On 67th Street, games meant *stickball* and *handball*. We played both with the same kind of ball, one made of soft rubber about the size of a baseball, which was called a "spaldeen." Handball was played in the empty lot that served as a playground, and stickball was played in the street, with essentially the same rules as baseball. Both were very inexpensive sports, the balls were very cheap, and the stick was generally a sawed-off discarded broom. Sports like tennis and skiing were unknown to us. We could have played soccer. It was a popular sport in Italy. But at the time soccer was totally un-American. Like all immigrants from Europe, the young second generation wanted to play only "American" games.

8.6 POSTSCRIPT

In 1943, when I was 11 years old, we moved away from 67th Street, up to Washington Heights in upper Manhattan. It was probably a very good move for me, since 67th Street was becoming a very tough neighborhood and I was reaching the age when it was easy to get into trouble (maybe if we had stayed, this West Side story would have a sad ending, like the movie). We moved to 182nd Street, between Saint Nicholas Avenue and Wadsworth Avenue, 616 West 182nd Street to be precise. This was a very mixed neighborhood, but just a few blocks south was a mostly Jewish area. I went to a public school that was just across the street from our apartment house (walk-up 5th floor apartment, of course). I made a number of Jewish friends at school, most notable perhaps was *Donny*, and many of us went on to Brooklyn Technical High School together. I remember playing in a basketball league at the Young Mens Hebrew Association (YMHA) just opposite the George Washington Bridge. Brooklyn Tech High was about one-hour subway ride from 182nd Street, and I remember all the hours I spent on the New York City subways during my high school days. We moved from Washington Heights in 1951 to a two family house in Jackson Height, Queens (35-39 93rd Street). My parents had purchased the house and we had *Tina*, *Remigio*, *Vilma*, and *Armando* from Blecker Street renting the lower part of the house. We lived there while I was an engineering student at the City College of New York, another one-hour subway trip each way. At City College I became good friends with *Charlie* and *Henry*, engineering students and Italian-Americans like myself, but not from Piedmont. *Charlie* and *Henry's* families had come from Sicily. I discovered another Italian world with them. After obtaining my B.S. in Electrical Engineering in December of 1955, I went to Columbia University to start an M.S. degree program. My parents, who had only completed the fourth grade in Italy, wondered

243

why I had to keep going to school. Was I being left back? Someone at work explained to my mother that going to graduate school was not being "left back." In June of 1956, I received my M.S. degree from Columbia and a few days later I married a young French girl, *Madeleine*, who was taking care of a child of a rich family that lived (guess where?) on Central Park West. My mother had a long list of Piedmontese girls I should marry, but after I explained that the Piedmontese royal House of Savoy had strong French roots, she felt a lot better. After we were married, my wife and I moved to an apartment house nearby my parents. While we lived there our children Christopher, Alexander, and Sylviawere born. My mother then became known as *Nonni* (short for *Nonnina*, which translates to Granny in English) and my father as *Nonno* (Grandpa in English). After getting my M.S. degree I became an instructor in Electrical Engineering at City College of New York for one year. I then decided to go on for a Ph.D. at the Polytechnic Institute of Brooklyn (now Polytechnic University). I finished my Ph.D. at Poly in 1961 and stayed on as a faculty member until 1972. In 1963 we moved to Huntington, Long Island (36 Trainer Court) where our last child, Veronica was born. There were no Piedmontese that we knew in Huntington, and my Italian roots were vanishing into the "twilight of ethnicity", to quote the title of Alba's book on Italian Americans. In 1972, we moved to Colorado Springs, where I taught Electrical Engineering at the Colorado Springs campus of the University of Colorado. My parents retired and stayed in Jackson Heights. Then in 1976, I accepted the position of department chairman at the University of New Mexico in Albuquerque. In 1978, my father passed away and my mother came out to live with us in Albuquerque. She rekindled my interest in Italy and Italians, and in 1991 I took a one-year sabbatical at the *Politecnico di Torino*, in Turin, Italy. After the sabbatical I became very interested in Italian culture, and that brings us essentially up to the present time.

When I look back at my "West Side" days, I realize that I was really pretty lucky. My parents worked hard, like all the parents I knew on 67th Street, and although there were many things they never had, for example an automobile, we had enough food to eat, clothes to wear, and lots of friends.

All my friends finished high school, and most went on to college. *Armando* received a Ph.D. at Columbia University and went on to teaching history at Rhode Island College. His dissertation was published as a book (*The Critics of the Italian Parliamentary System, 1860 – 1915*) in 1992. For most of us, I think I can say our west-side stories had happy endings, even if things Piedmontese have become only memories.

In 1960 they started tearing down the old apartment houses on 67th Street, to start construction on new expensive high-rise apartments. Just south of 67th Street, the construction of Lincoln Center for the Performing Arts was started, at about the same time.

July 29, 1997, my mother died, and one of our last "physical" links to Piedmont was severed. Our Piedmontese-American family is now down to the children of my first cousin *Ildo*, *Tommy* and *Caroline*. In Italy, I still have my two aunts, *Evelina* and *Ondina*, and first cousins, *Beppe*, *Elsa*, *Fausto*, *Piera*, *Piero*, and *Rosa*. Actually, we see each other more now than we did in the 67th Street days, since I travel often to Italy and Europe for technical conferences.

8.7 NOTES AND REFERENCES

A very complete description of various districts in New York City can be found in *The WPA Guide to New York City*. This guide contains detailed maps of all the districts, including the district Central Park West (page 277) which we have described in this chapter. There are many books that describe the Italian-immigrant experience in the United States. One in particular, *Italian-American Folklore*, is co-authored by a Piedmontese-American, *Frances Malpezzi*. *Malpezzi* discusses a wide range of topics including customs, recreation and games, music, food, etc. experienced by immigrants from all parts of Italy. An excellent collection of papers on the issues associated with first and second generation Italians in America is Luisa Del Giudice's *Studies in Italian American Folklore*.

Puzo's *Fortunate Pilgrim* deals with an immigrant family from southern Italy that lived on a block like 67th Street, but in the Hell's Kitchen district of Manhattan. On the other hand, Chay's book *Pilgrim's Pride* is a story of a Piedmontese immigrant family, but one that settled in a mining community in southern Colorado. Finally the process of assimilation, common to all immigrant groups in America is well described in Richard Alba's *Into the Twilight of Ethnicity*. Alba's basic thesis is that after three generations, almost all cultural links to the old country are lost. See the Reference section for more information on these books.

APPENDIX I. Elements of Italian Grammar

1. NOUNS, ARTICLES, AND ADJECTIVES

In Italian, like most languages other than English, nouns and articles have genders. The general rule is that masculine nouns end in *o* and feminine nouns in *a* in the singular, and *I* and *e* respectively, in the plural. Associated articles are listed below:

Articles

Masculine	**Feminine**
il – the (singular)	*la* – the (singular)
I – the (plural)	*le* – the (plural)
uno, un – a (singular)	*una* – a (singular)

Examples:

il libro – the book	*un libro* – a book	*le case* – the houses
I libri – the books	*la casa* – the house	*una casa* – a house

Unfortunately there are exceptions to the above rules. For example:

> *la mano* – the hand (feminine noun ending in *o*)
> *il problema* – the problem (masculine noun ending in *a*)
> *il cantante* – the singer (masculine noun ending in *e*)
> *la nipote* – the niece (feminine noun ending in *e*)
> *le labbra* – the lips (plural noun ending in *a*).

In any case the gender of a noun is always defined by the article, so it is important to learn the article that goes with every noun. There are some other complications in the use of articles, for example in front of masculine nouns starting with a vowel, *x*, *z*, *gn*, *ps*, or *s*, *il* becomes *lo* (*gli* in the plural*)*. In addition, *lo* and *la* before vowels become *l'*. For example:

>*lo zio* – the uncle
>*gli zii* – the uncles
>*lo stato* – the state
>*lo psicologo* – the psychologist
>*l'anno* – the year
>*l'ora* – the hour

Italians use articles much more than we do in English. For example, one would say, *vado visitare la Maria* (I am going to visit "the" Mary).

Adjectives, words that modify nouns, in Italian must agree in gender and number with the nouns they modify. For example:

>*Il nuovo libro* – the new book
>*la bella ragazza* – the beautiful girl
>*I nuovi libri* – the new books
>*le belle ragazze* – the beautiful girls
>*il libro chiuso* – the closed book
>*le porte aperte* – the open doors
>*I libri aperti* – the open books.

2. PERSONAL SUBJECT PRONOUNS

English is one of the few languages that does not distinguish between the **polite** form of speech, used to address someone one does not know well, or someone of high position, and the **familiar** form of speech, used to address family and close friends. In the pronouns listed below we will use the notation (pol.) and (fam.) to distinguish these two cases. The "incorrect" use of these two forms might raise some eyebrows between Italians, but "errors" of this type by foreigners are generally tolerated. Italians usually appreciate any attempt to speak their language. In the table below, we summarize Italian subject pronouns, that is pronouns that form the **subject** of a sentence.

Subject Pronouns

Singular	Plural
io – I	*noi* – we
tu – you (fam.)	*voi* – you (fam.)
Lei – you (pol.)	*Loro* – you (pol.)
lui – he	*loro, essi* – they (masculine)
lei – she	*loro, esse* – they (feminine)
esso – it (masculine)	
essa – it (feminine)	

In formal writings, *egli* is used for *lui*, and *ella* for *lei*. Note something rather strange, the same word (except with a capital letter) is used for **you** (pol.) and **she**. This is a real peculiarity of Italian. One of the few languages that has the same usage is German where "Sie" means "you" (pol.), and "sie" means "she." This peculiarity is not found in any of the other romance languages. A common explanation of this is that all the terms associated with royalty had a feminine ending (e.g. *il duca* – the duke, *la signoria* – royalty). Thus the polite form of "you" evolved into "she." Most of the Italian dialects, the languages spoken amongst common people, do not use this formal form of "you." In any case it is important to note that in conjugating verbs, the form *Lei* is conjugated the same as *lui* and *lei*.

3. SOME IMPORTANT IRREGULAR VERBS – PRESENT TENSE

In Italian, all verbs, regular or irregular, have one of three endings,

-*are*, -*ere*, -*ire*, e.g. *fare* (to do), *avere* (to have), *dire* (to say). Most –*are* verbs have "regular" conjugations, while most –*ere* verbs are irregular. In this section we present the conjugation, in the present tense, of four very common but irregular verbs, *fare, avere, essere,* and *dire*. Regular verbs are conjugated by removing the above endings and adding appropriate endings to the resulting stems. For irregular verbs all parts of the verb are changed in irregular ways. We start with irregular verbs rather then regular verbs, because these verbs are used so often. Note that we have placed a parenthesis around the subject pronoun in the listings below. This is because in Italian the subject pronoun is normally omitted. This is possible because the ending for each conjugation uniquely implies the appropriate pronoun. This is another peculiarity of Italian.

Fare – to do/to make

Singular	Plural
(io) faccio. – I do	*(noi) facciamo.* – We do
(tu) fai. – You (fam.) do	*(voi) fate.* – You (fam.) do
(Lei) fa. – You (pol.) do	*(Loro) fanno.* – You (pol.) do
(lui, lei) fa. – He, she does	*(loro) fanno.* – They do

avere – to have

(io) ho. – I have	*(noi) abbiamo.* – We have
(tu) hai. – You (fam.) have	*(voi) avete.* – You (fam.) have
(Lei) ha. – You (pol.) have	*(Loro) hanno.* – You (pol.) have
(lui, lei) ha. – He, she has	*(loro) hanno.* – They have

essere – to be

(io) sono. – I am	*(noi) siamo.* – We are
(tu) sei. – You (fam.) are	*(voi) siete.* – You (fam.) are
(Lei) è. – You (pol.) are	*(Loro) sono.* – You (pol.) are
(lui, lei) è. – He, she is	*(loro) sono.* – They are

dire – to say

(io) dico. – I say	*(noi) diciamo.* – We say
(tu) dici. – You (fam.) say	*(voi) dite.* – You (fam.) say
(Lei) dice. – You (pol.) say	*(Loro) dicono.* – You (pol.) say
(lui, lei) dice. – He, she says	*(loro) dicono.* – They say

The table below compares the conjugation of the verb *essere* (to be) with two other romance languages, French and Spanish.

Italian – *essere*	French – **être**	Spanish – **ser**
(io) sono – I am	je suis	yo soy
(tu) sei – you (fam.) are	tu es	tú eres
(Lei) è. – you (pol.) are	vous êtes	usted es
(lui, lei) è. – he, she is	il, elle est	él, ella es
(noi) siamo. – we are	nous sommes	nosotros somos
(voi) siete.-you (fam.) are	-------	vosotros sois
(Loro) sono.-you (pol.) are	vous etes	ustedes son
(loro) sono. – they are	ils, elles sont	ellos, ellas son

Note that "you" familiar/plural does not exist in French. Also note

251

that "you" polite/singular in French and Spanish is not "she."
Finally, note that *loro* in Italian is used for both the masculine and feminine.

4. REGULAR VERBS – PRESENT TENSE

The conjugation of regular verbs is simplified by the fact that the stem (part of the verb which remains after *–are*, *-ere*, and *–ire* are removed) is invariant, and endings follow the same rule for each conjugation. The conjugation of *–are*, *-ere*, and *–ire* verbs are often referred to as the first, second, and third conjugation. We illustrate below the three regular conjugations with verbs *amare* (to love), *vivere* (to live), and *capire* (to understand).

Amare	*vivere*	*capire*
(io) amo. – I love	*vivo.* – I live	*capisco.* – I understand
(tu) ami. – you (fam.) love	*vivi.* – you (fam.) live	*capisci.* – you (fam.) understand
(Lei, lui, lei) ama. – you (pol.), he, she loves	*vive.* – you (pol.), he, she lives	*capisce.* – you (pol.), he, she understand
(noi) amiamo. – we love	*viviamo.* – we live	*capiamo.* – we understand
(voi) amate.-you (fam. plural) they love	*vivete.*-you (fam., plural), they live	*capite.*-you (fam., plural) understand
(Loro, loro) amano.- you (pol., plural) love	*vivono.*-you (pol., plural) live	*capiscono.*-you (pol., plural) they understand

In the table below we have omitted the stem to emphasize the pattern of endings.

252

	-are	*-ere*	*-ire*
(*io*)	- *o*	- *o*	- *isco*
(*tu*)	- *i*	- *i*	- *isci*
(*Lei, lui, lei*)	- *a*	- *e*	- *isce*
(*noi*)	- *iamo*	- *iamo*	- *iamo*
(*voi*)	- *ate*	- *ete*	- *ite*
(*Loro, loro*)	- *ano*	- *ono*	- *iscono*

Note the invariance (Also valid for irregular verbs!) of the ending for *io*, *tu*, *noi*, and *voi*, i.e.

io:	- *o*, - *o*, - *o*
tu:	- *i*, - *i*,- *i*
noi:	- *iamo*, - *iamo*, - *iamo*
voi:	- *ate*, - *ete*, - *ite*

Note that *Lei* - you (pol.) complicates Italian in many ways, including the conjugation of verbs. The Fascist regime in 1938, under Mussolini, tried to eliminate *Lei* from the Italian language and replace it by *voi*. But the experiment never worked. It should be noted that some regular *-ire* verbs have a different conjugation than the one listed above. Thus there are two regular conjugation of *-ire* verbs. The two conjugations are illustrated with the verbs *soffrire* (to suffer) and finire (to finish).

soffrire - to suffer	*finire* - to finish
(*io*) *soffro*	*finisco*
(*tu*) *soffri*	*finisci*
(*liu, lei, Lei*) *soffre*	*finisce*
(*noi*) *soffriamo*	*finiamo*
(*voi*) *soffrite*	*finite*
(*loro, Loro*) *soffrono*	*finiscono*

Some other examples of common regular verbs are given below.

- *are* verbs

parlare - to speak	*lavorare* - to work
baciare - to kiss	*mangiare* - to eat
cantare - to sing	*visitare* - to visit

- *ere* verbs

conoscere - to know	respondere - to answer
leggere - to read	vedere - to see
perdere - to loseripetere - to repeat	

- *ire* verbs

"*capire*" type

costruire - to build	*pulire* - to clean
guarire - to heal	*punire* - to punish
obbedire - to obey	*spedire* - to send/to mail

"*soffrire*" type

dormire - to sleep	*servire* - to serve
offrire - to offer	*soffrire* - to suffer
partire - to depart/to leave	*vestire* - to dress

5. THE IMPERATIVE MOOD

The imperative mood is a conjugation that is used to command, persuade, suggest, etc. We will focus on *tu*, *Lei*, and *noi* since these are the most commonly used "persons" when commanding people to do things. The conjugation for *noi* is particularly simple because it is identical to that of the present tense. We have tabulated below the imperative-mood conjugation for some of the verbs introduced in the previous sections. For comparison we list below examples of the imperative with examples of the present tense.

amare - to love

Imperative	Present
(*tu*) *Ama*! - Love (you, fam.)!	*Ami*? - Do you (fam.) love?
(*Lei*) *Ami*! - Love (you, pol.)!	*Ama*? - Do you (pol.) love?
(*noi*) *Amiamo!* - Let us love!	*Amiamo*? - Do we love?

vivere - to live

Imperative	Present
(*tu*) *Vivi*! - Live (you, fam.)!	*Vivi*? - Do you (fam.) live?
(*Lei*) *Viva*! - Live (you, pol.)!	*Vive*? - Do you (pol.) live?
(*noi*) *Viviamo!* - Let us live!	*Viviamo*? - Do we live?

capire - to understand

Imperative	Present
(*tu*) *Capisci*! - Understand (you, fam.)!	*Capisci*? - Do you (fam.) understand?
(*Lei*) *Capisca*! - Understand (you, pol.)!	*Capisce*? - Do you (pol.) understand?
(*noi*) *Capiamo!* - Let us understand!	*Capiamo*? - Do we understand?

essere- to be

Imperative	Present
(*tu*) *Sii*! - Be (you, fam.)!	*Sei*? - Are you (fam.)?
(*Lei*) *Sia*! - Be (you, pol.)!	*È*? - Are you (pol.)?
(*noi*) *Siamo!* - Let us be!	*Siamo*? - Are we?

avere- to have

Imperative	Present
(tu) Abbi! - Have (you, fam.)!	*Hai*? - Do you (fam.) have?
(Lei) Abbia! - Have (you, pol.)!	*Ha*? - Do you (pol.) have?
(noi) Abbiamo! - Let us have!	*Abbiamo*? - Do we have?

fare- to do/to make

Imperative	Present
(tu) Fa! - Do/Make (you, fam.)!	*Fai*? - Do you (fam.) make?
(Lei) Faccia! - Do/Make (you, pol.)!	*Fa*? - Do you (pol.) make?
(noi) Facciamo! - Let us do/make!	*Facciamo*? - Do we make?

Examples of the imperative versus the present:

> *(Lei) Ami suo fratello*! - Love (pol.) your brother!
>> but
> *(Lei) Ama suo fratello*? - Do you (pol.) love your brother?

> *(Lei) Viva da solo*! - Live (pol.) by yourself!
>> but
> *(Lei) Vive da solo*? - Do you (pol.) live by yourself?

> *(Lei) Capisca che ho ragione*! - Understand (pol.) that I am right!
>> but
> *(Lei) Capisce che ho ragione*? - Do you (pol.) understand that I am right?

(Tu) Sii pronto! - Be (fam.) ready!
  but
(Tu) Sei pronto? - Are you (fam.) ready?

(Noi) Facciamo cena! - Let us make dinner!
  and
(Noi) Facciamo cena? - Are we making dinner?

To give a negative command simply put *non* before the positive command, e.g. *non facciamo la cena!* - let us not make dinner!

6. OBJECT PRONOUNS

In this section, we consider Italian pronouns that are objects of verbs. There are two kinds of objects, <u>direct</u> and <u>indirect</u>, and in Italian the object pronoun can be <u>stressed</u> or <u>unstressed</u>. In the stressed version, the pronoun appears after the verb, and in the unstressed before the verb. The term "stressed" is used to indicate that some stress is to be placed on the pronoun.

The tables below illustrate the various forms.

Direct Object

Stressed	Unstressed
(Tu) ami <u>me</u>. - You (fam.) love <u>me</u>.	<u>*Mi*</u> *ami.*
(Io) amo <u>te</u>. - I love <u>you</u> (fam.).	<u>*Ti*</u> *amo.*
(Io) vedo <u>Lei</u>. - I see <u>you</u> (pol.).	<u>*La*</u> *vedo.*
(Io) vedo <u>lui</u>. - I see <u>him</u>.	<u>*Lo*</u> *vedo.*
(Io) vedo <u>lei</u>. - I see <u>her</u>	<u>*La*</u> *vedo.*

257

(*Loro*) *amano <u>noi</u>.* - They love <u>us</u>.	<u>*Ci*</u> *amano.*
(*Loro*) *amano <u>voi</u>.* - They love <u>you</u> (fam.).	<u>*Vi*</u> *amano.*
(*Io*) *amo <u>Loro</u>.* - I love <u>you</u> (pol.).	*Amo <u>loro</u>.*
(*Io*) *amo <u>loro</u>.* - I love <u>them</u> (masc.).	<u>*Li*</u> *amo.*
(*Io*) *amo <u>loro</u>.* - I love <u>them</u> (fem.).	<u>*Le*</u> *amo.*

Indirect Object

Stressed	Unstressed
(*Lui*) *parla a <u>me</u>.* - He speaks to <u>me</u>.	<u>*Mi*</u> *parla.*
(*Io*) *parlo a <u>te</u>.* - I speak to <u>you</u> (fam.).	<u>*Ti*</u> *parlo.*
(*Io*) *parlo a <u>Lei</u>.* - I speak to <u>you</u> (pol.).	<u>*Le*</u> *parlo.*
(*Io*) *parlo a <u>lui</u>.* - I speak to <u>him</u>.	<u>*Gli*</u> *parlo.*
(*Io*) *parlo a <u>lei</u>.* - I speak to <u>her</u>.	<u>*Le*</u> *parlo.*
(*Loro*) *parlano a <u>noi</u>.* - They speak to <u>us</u>.	<u>*Ci*</u> *parlano.*
(*Io*) *parlo a <u>voi</u>.* - I speak to <u>you</u> (fam.).	<u>*Vi*</u> *parlo.*
(*Io*) *parlo a <u>Loro</u>.* - I speak to <u>you</u> (pol.).	*Parlo a <u>Loro</u>.*
(*Io*) *parlo a <u>loro</u>.* - I speak to <u>them</u>.	*Parlo a <u>loro</u>.*

With the imperative, familiar form, the object is attached to the end of the verb, e.g.

> (*Tu*) *Dimmi!* - Tell me!
> (*Tu*) *Parlami!* - Speak to me!
> (*Tu*) *Fammi domire!* - Let me sleep!

Note however that for the polite form we have:
> (*Lei*) *Mi dica!* - Tell me!
> (*Lei*) *Mi dia!* - Give me!

7. REFLEXIVE VERBS

Reflexive verbs are very common in Italian. The infinitive of a reflexive verb is easily identified by its *-si* ending, e.g. *alzarsi* (to get up), *sedersi* (to sit down), *vestirsi* (to dress). Listed below is the reflexive verb *sentirsi* conjugated with its associated object pronouns.

(*Io*) *mi sento.* - I feel.
(*Tu*) *ti senti.* - You (fam.) feel.
(*Lei*) *si sente.* - You (pol.) feel.
(*Lui, lei*) *si sente.* - He, she feels.

(*Noi*) *ci sentiamo.*-We feel.
(*Voi*) *vi sentite.*-You (fam.) feel.
(*Loro*) *si sentono.* - You (pol.) feel.
(*loro*) *si sentono.* - they feel.

8. SOME SPECIAL WAYS OF SAYING THINGS IN ITALIAN

•The use of the verb "to have" (*avere*) to mean "to be" (*essere*).

avere fame - to be hungry
avere sete - to be thirsty
avere caldo - to be warm
avere freddo - to be cold
avere fretta - to be in a hurry
avere dieci anni - to be ten years old
avere ragione - to be right.

•The use of the verb "to make" (fare) to mean "to let" (lasciare).

        Fammi morire! - Let me die!

        Fammi parlare! - Le me talk!

        Mi faccia un piacere! - Do me a favor!

•The way to say "I like."

In Italian to say "I like the books," you must literally say, "The books are pleasing to me," e.g. *i libri piacciono a me* (stressed) or *i libri mi piacciono* (unstressed). To say "you like me," you say *(tu) piaci a me* (stressed) or *(tu) mi piaci* (unstressed).

•Repeating a word to mean "very."

        poco poco - very little

        piano piano - very softly

•*Fare una bella figura* - to look good.

This expression, which literally means "to make a beautiful figure," explains a great deal about why Italians sometimes behave the way they do. They dress well to *fare una bella figura*. They bring nice presents to *fare una bella figura*. The worst thing that can happen to you in Italy is to *fare una brutta figura* - to look bad.

•Different meanings of *fregare* - to rub.

        Me ne frego. - I do not give a damn.

        Che te ne frega? - What do you care?

        Mi hanno fregato. - They cheated me.

        Mi hanno fregato il libro. They stole my book.

•Other meanings of *fare* - to do.

        fare il bagno - take a bath

fare il numero del telefono - to dial the telephone number

fare la spesa - to go shopping

fare male - to hurt

fare una domanda - to ask a question

9. PREPOSITIONS

We list below some common prepositions.

> *a* - to
>
> *con* - with
>
> *da* - from, by
>
> *di* - of
>
> *in* - in
>
> *per* - for
>
> *su* - up

Examples:

> *Luigi parla a me.* - Luigi speaks to me.
>
> *Vieni con me.* - Come with me.
>
> *Leonardo viene da Vinci.* - Leonardo comes from Vinci.
>
> *Questo libro è scritto da me.* - This book is written by me.
>
> *Parlo di questo libro.* - I am speaking of this book.
>
> *Il professore è in ufficio.* - The professor is in his office.
>
> *Partiamo per Torino.* - We leave for Turin.
>
> *Su questa strada.* – Up this street.

Note that when a preposition is followed by a pronoun, it is the stressed indirect-object form of the pronoun that is used, e.g. *parlo a te* (I am speaking to you), *vieni con me* (come with me).

When a preposition appears before an article, the two combine as indicated in the table below.

	_il_	_la_	_i_	_le_	_lo_	_gli_
_a_	al	alla	ai	alle	allo	agli
con	col	con la	coi	con le	con lo	con gli
_da_	dal	dalla	dai	dalle	dallo	dagli
_di_	del	della	dei	delle	dello	degli
_in_	nel	nella	nei	nelle	nello	negli
_su_	sul	sulla	sui	sulle	sullo	sugli

There are two particles that are often used in Italian that have numerous meanings. They are:

ne - of it, of him, of her, of them, some of it, some of them, etc.
ci - here, there is, there are, etc.

Examples:

Ne hai abbastaza? - Do you have enough <u>of it</u>?
Ne parlo sempre. - I always speak <u>of him</u>.
Ci sono molti libri qui. - There are many books <u>here</u>.
Ci vieni questa sera? - Are you coming <u>here</u> tonight?

10. FUTURE TENSE AND CONDITIONAL MOOD

The conjugation for the future tense and conditional mood are particularly simple because the endings are the same for all verbs, with only a slightly modified stem. The modified stems of the regular verbs _parlare_ (to speak), _vivere_ (to live), and _capire_ (to understand) are _parler_, _viver_, and _capir_ respectively. The endings are illustrated below for the verb _parlare_.

262

Future	Conditional
(*Io*) *Parlerò* - I will speak	*Parlerei* - I would speak
(*Tu*) *Parlerai* - You (fam.) will speak	*Parleresti* - You (fam.) would speak
(*Lei, lui, lei*) *Parlerà* - You (pol.), he, she will speak	*Parlerebbe* - You (pol.), he, she would speak
(*Noi*) *Parleremo* - We will speak	*Parleremmo* - We would speak
(*Voi*) *Parlerete* - You (fam.) will speak	*Parlereste* - You (fam.) would speak
(*Loro, loro*) *Parleranno* - You, they will speak	*Parlerebbero* - You, they would speak

The conditional mood is used often to make polite requests. For example to say you want (*volere*) something, it is considered impolite to say *voglio* (I want), instead one should say *vorrei* (I would like). The verb *volere* is irregular. Its stem for the future tense and conditional mood is *vorr*. The conjugation of this particular verb is listed below for comparison with regular verbs. Note that the endings in the future tense and conditional mood are exactly like those of regular verbs!

Future	Conditional
(*Io*) *Vorrò* - I will want	*Vorrei* - I would like
(*Tu*) *Vorrai* - You (fam.) will want	*Vorresti* - You (fam.) would like
(*Lei, lui, lei*) *Vorrà* - You (pol.), he, she will want	*Vorrebbe* - You (pol.), he, she would like
(*Noi*) *Vorremo* - We will want	*Vorremmo* - We would like

(Voi) *Vorr<u>ete</u>* - You (fam.) will want	*Vorr<u>este</u>* - You (fam.) would like
(Loro, loro) *Vorr<u>anno</u>* - You, they will want	*Vorr<u>ebbero</u>* - You, they would like

11. PAST TENSES

The two main past tenses are the *past imperfect*, often simply called the *imperfect*, and the *past definite*. The imperfect is used to describe actions that have taken place in the past but may be continuing, and the past definite is used to describe actions that have a unique occurrence in the past. The two conjugations are illustrated below for the irregular verbs essere (to be) and avere (to have).

Essere

Imperfect	Past Definite
(Io) ero - I was	*fui*
(Tu) eri - You (fam.) were	*fosti*
(Lei) era - You (pol.) were	*fu*
(lui, lei) era - He, she was	*fu*
(Noi) eravamo - We were	*fummo*
(Voi) eravate - You (fam.) were	*foste*
(Loro, loro) erano - You (pol.), they were	*furono*

Avere

Imperfect	Past Definite
(Io) avevo - I had	*ebbi*
(Tu) avevi - You (fam.) had	*avesti*
(Lei, lui, lei) aveva - You (pol.), he, she had	*ebbe*

(*Noi*) *avevamo* - We had	*avemmo*
(*Voi*) *avevate* - You (fam.) had	*aveste*
(*Loro*, *loro*) *avevano* - You (pol.), they had	*ebbero*

For regular verbs the imperfect tense is particularly simple to conjugate because all verbs have the same endings, with only slightly modified stems. For example, the modified stems for *parlare*, *vendere*, and *capire* are *parlav*, *vendev*, and *capiv* respectively. The endings are illustrated below for *parlare*.

Imperfect

(*Io*) *parlavo* - I was speaking.

(*Tu*) *parlavi* - You (fam.) were speaking.

(*Lei*) *parlava* - You (pol.) were speaking.

(*Lui*, *lei*) *parlava* - He, she was speaking.

(*Noi*) *parlavamo* - We were speaking.

(*Voi*) *parlavate* - You (fam.) were speaking.

(*Loro*, *loro*) *parlavano* - You(pol.), they were speaking.

The above endings - *o*, -*i*,-*a*, -*amo*, -*ate*, and -*ano* apply also to -*ere* and -*ire* verbs.

The past definite is a bit more complicated since the endings are not the same for all verbs. We illustrate below the past-definite endings for the regular verbs *parlare*, *vedere*, and *capire*.

Past Definite

Parlare	Vendere	Capire
Parl*ai* - I spoke.	Vend*ei* - I sold.	Cap*ii* - I understood.
Parl*asti* - You (fam.) spoke.	Vend*esti* - You(fam.) sold.	Cap*isti* - You (fam.) understood.
Parl*ò* - You (pol.) spoke.	Vend*é* - You (pol.) sold.	Cap*í* - You (pol.) understood.
Parl*ammo* - We spoke.	Vend*emmo* - We sold.	Cap*immo* - We understood.
Parl*aste* - You (fam.) spoke.	Vend*este* - You (fam.) sold.	Cap*iste* - You (fam.) understood.
Parl*arono* - They spoke.	Vend*erono* - They sold.	Cap*irono* - They understood.

The following example illustrates the distinction between the imperfect and past-definite tenses.

Imperfect
> *Parlavo sempre con lui.* - I always used to speak with him.

Past Definite
> *Parlai con lui l'ultima volta nel Marzo 1994.* - I spoke to him the last time in March of 1994.

The final past tense we will discuss briefly is the *compound past*. The compound past is formed with the *past participle* together with either the verb *avere* or the verb *essere*. The past participle of regular verbs is formed by adding -*ato* to stems of -*are* verbs, -*uto* to stems of -*ere* verbs, and -ito to stems of -ire verbs, e.g. the past participles for *parlare, vendere,* and *capire* are *parlato, venduto, capito* respectively. An example of a verb which uses avere in forming the compound past is *parlare*, and an example of a verb that uses *essere* is *arrivare*. We illustrate these two below.

266

Compound Past

Parlare	*Arrivare*
Ho parlato. - I have spoken.	*Sono arrivato.* - I have arrived.
Hai parlato. - You (fam.) have spoken.	*Sei arrivato.* - You (fam.) have arrived.
Ha parlato. - You (pol.) have spoken.	*È arrivato.* - You (pol.) have arrived.
Abbiamo parlato. - We have spoken.	*Siamo arrivati.* - We have arrived.
Avete parlato. - You (fam.) have spoken.	*Siete arrivati.* - You (fam.) have arrived.
Hanno parlato. - They have spoken.	*Sono arrivati.* - They have arrived.

Note that in verbs that use *essere* in the compound past, the past participle must agree in gender and number with the subject.

12. THE PRESENT SUBJUNCTIVE

The subjunctive mood is used to denote uncertainty, emotion, conditions, etc. It is probably the most difficult of all the grammatical forms to use correctly. However, it is important to know, since it is so often required in everyday speech. A key in recognizing the need to use the subjunctive is the word *che* (that), for example *penso che tu sia stanco* (I think you may be tired). In listing the subjunctive conjugation for regular verbs below we add the word *che* to stress this point.

Present Subjunctive

Parlare	Vendere	Capire
Che io parli. - That I speak.	*Che io venda.* - That I sell.	*Che io capisca.* - That I understand.
Che tu parli. - That you (fam.) speak.	*Che tu venda.* - That you (fam.) sell.	*Che tu capisca.* That you (fam.) understand.
Che Lei parli. - That you (pol.) speak.	*Che Lei venda.* - That you (pol.) sell.	*Che Lei capisca.* - That you (pol.) understand.
Che noi parliamo. - That we speak.	*Che noi vendiamo.* - That we sell.	*Che noi capiamo.* - That we understand.
Che voi parliate. - That you (fam.) speak.	*Che voi vendiate.* - That you (fam.) sell.	*Che voi capiate.* - That you (fam.) understand
Che loro parlino. - That they speak.	*Che loro vendano.* - That they sell.	*Che loro capiscano.* - That they understand.

Note the invariance of endings in the singular, e.g. *io parli, tu parli, Lei parli.*

13. DATES AND NUMBERS

For days of the week and months of the year see section 8 of Appendix II.

• Cardinal Numbers

1 - *uno*	16 - *sedici*	60 - *sessanta*
2 - *due*	17 - *diciassette*	70 - *settanta*
3 - *tre*	18 - *diciotto*	80 - *ottanta*
4 - *quattro*	19 - *diciannove*	90 - *novanta*
5 - *cinque*	20 - *venti*	100 - *cento*

6 - *sei*	21 - *ventuno*	101 - *cento uno*
7 - *sette*	22 - *ventidue*	102 - *cento due*, etc.
8 - *otto*	23 - *ventitré*	200 - *due cento*
9 - *nove*	24 - *ventiquattro*	300 - *trecento*
10- *dieci*	30 - *trenta*	500 - *cinquecento*
11 - *undici*	31 - *trentuno*	600 - *seicento*, etc.
12 - *dodici*	32 - *trentadue*	1000 - *mille*
13 - *tredici*	33 - *trentratré*, etc.	1200 - *milleduecento*
14 - *quattordici*	40 - *quaranta*	2000 - *duemila*, etc.
15 - *quindici*	50 - *cinquanta*	1,000,000 - *un milione*

For ordinal numbers, 1 - 10, see section 8 in Appendix II.

In writing numbers in Italian the comma and period have the opposite meaning as in English, e.g. in Italian "1,300.25" is written "1.300,25." Also when a large number is written out, as on a check (*assegno*), the numbers are slurred together, e.g. "one thousand three hundred and twenty one" is written, *milletrecentoventuno*. Finally we should note that in Italy it is important to be able to read Roman numerals, since they appear so often on monuments and buildings.

• Roman Numerals

1 - I	9 - IX	80 - LXXX
2 - II	10 - X	90 - XC
3 - III	20 - XX	100 - C
4 - IV	30 - XXX	200 - CC
5 – V	40 - XL	300 - CCC
6 - VI	50 - L	400 - CD
7 - VII	60 - LX	500 - D
8 - VIII	70 - LXX	1000 – M

Note the pattern in forming numbers. When a lower "number"

appears before a larger "number," the lower is substracted from the upper, e.g. XC = 100 - 10 = 90. When a lower "number" appears after a larger "number," the two are added, e.g. LX = 50 + 10 = 60. The year 1995 would be written as M CM XC V = 1000 + 900 + 90 + 5.

APPENDIX II. Elements of Piedmontese Grammar

1. NOUNS, ARTICLES, AND ADJECTIVES

Like Italian, Piedmontese nouns and articles have genders and number. However, many masculine nouns do not change endings between singular and plural. In the tables below, Italian translations are shown in parenthesis next to the Piedmontese words.

Articles

Masculine	Feminine
ël (*il*) - the (sing.)	*la* (*la*) - the (sing.)
ij (*i*) - the (plural)	*le* (*le*) - the (plural)
un, *'n* (*uno*, *un*) - a (sing.)	*na* (*una*) - a (sing.)

Examples:

ël fieul (*il figlio*) - the son	*ij can* (*i cani*) - the dogs
ij fieuj (*i figli*) - the sons	*la fomna* (*la donna*) - the woman
'n fieul (*un figlio*) - a son	*le fomne* (*le donne*) - the women
ël can (*il cane*) - the dog	*na fomna* (*una donna*) - a woman

Note that "dog" is the same, i.e. *can*, in the singular and plural, and that feminine nouns in Piedmontese are modified the same way as they are in Italian, e.g. *a* ending in the singular becomes an *e* ending in the plural.

For feminine nouns, adjectives agree in gender and number. For example:

na bela fomna (*una bella donna*) - a beautiful woman
le bele fomne (*le belle donne*) - the beautiful women.

However, for masculine nouns, special endings do not appear. For example:

271

un cit inteligent (*un bambino intelligente*) - a smart boy

ij cit inteligent (*i babini intelligenti*) - the smart boys.

The gender of a noun in Piedmontese is generally the same as in Italian, however this is not always the case. Some exceptions are given below.

English	Piedmontese	Italian
the smoke	*la fum*	*il fumo*
the wall	*la muraja*	*il muro*
the jug	*la doja*	*il boccale*
the sock	*ël caussèt*	*la calza*
the pencil	*ël crajon*	*la matita*
the apple	*ël pom*	*la mela*

2. PERSONAL SUBJECT PRONOUNS

The table below illustrates Piedmontese subject pronouns.

English	Piedmontese	Italian
I	*mi*	*io*
you (fam., sing.)	*ti*	*tu*
he, she	*chiel, chila*	*lui, lei*
you (pol., sing.)	----	*Lei*
we	*noi, nojàutri*	*noi*
you (fam., plural)	*voi, vojàutri*	*voi*
you (pol., plural)	---	*Loro*
they	*lor, loràutri*	*loro*

Note that the formal "you" does not exist in Piedmontese, and recall that although *noi* and *voi* are written the same as Italian, they are pronounced differently since the letter "o" in Piedmontese is pronounced like the letter "u" in Italian.

3. SOME IMPORTANT IRREGULAR VERBS - PRESENT TENSE

As in Italian, in Piedmontese all verbs have one of three endings - *é*, *-e*, and *-i*, corresponding to the Italian ending *-are*, *-ere*, and *ire*. We list below the conjugation of four common irregular verbs *esse* (to be), *aveje* (to have), *fé* (to do/make), and *vorèje* (to want).

English	Piedmontese	Italian
To be	***Esse***	***Essere***
I am	*Mi i son*	*(Io) sono*
You (fam., sing.) are	*Ti it ses*	*(Tu) sei*
He, she is	*Chiel, chila a l'é*	*(Lui, lei) è*
We are	*Noi i soma*	*(Noi) siamo*
You (fam., plural) are	*Voi i seve*	*(Voi) siete*
They are	*Lor a son*	*(Loro) sono*

To have	***Aveje***	***Avere***
I have	*Mi i l'hai*	*(Io) ho*
You (fam., sing.) have	*Ti it l'has*	*(Tu) hai*
He, she has	*Chiel, chila a l'ha*	*(Lui, lei) ha*
We have	*Noi i l'oma*	*(Noi) abbiamo*
You (fam., plural) have	*Voi i l'eve*	*(Voi) avete*
They have	*Lor a l'han*	*(Loro) hanno*

273

To do/make	Fé	Fare
I do	*Mi i faso*	*(Io) faccio*
You (fam., sing.) do	*Ti it fas*	*(Tu) fai*
He, she does	*Chiel, chila a fa*	*(Lui, lei) fa*
We do	*Noi i foma*	*(Noi) facciamo*
You (fam., plural) do	*Voi i feve*	*(Voi) fate*
They do	*Lor a fan*	*(Loro) fanno*

To want	Vorèje	Volere
I want	*Mi i veuj*	*(Io) voglio*
You (fam., sing.) want	*Ti it veule*	*(Tu) vuoi*
He, she wants	*Chiel, chila a veul*	*(Lui, lei) vuole*
We want	*Noi i voroma*	*(Noi) vogliamo*
You (fam., plural) want	*Voi i veule*	*(Voi) volete*
They want	*Lor a veulo*	*(Loro) vogliono*

Note that in conjugating verbs in Piedmontese, a letter is inserted after the pronoun, e.g.

Mi i	*Noi i*
Ti it	*Voi i*
Chiel, chila a	*Lor a*

As in Italian, in Piedmontese the subject pronoun is often omitted, however the inserted letter can never be omitted. For example, instead of saying "*mi i son stanch* (I am tired)" one can say "*i son stanch*," but one should not say "*son stanch*." This holds for both regular and irregular verbs.

4. REGULAR VERBS - PRESENT TENSE

Regular verbs are conjugated by adding to the stem (obtained by removing the endings *é*, *e*, and *ì*) appropriate endings. The three conjugations of regular verbs are illustrated below.

English	Piedmontese	Italian
To speak	*Parlé*	*Parlare*
I speak	*(Mi) i parlo*	*(Io) parlo*
You (fam., sing.) speak	*(Ti) it parle*	*(Tu) parli*
He, she speaks	*(Chiel, chila) a parla*	*(Lui, lei) parla*
We speak	*(Noi) i parloma*	*(Noi) parliamo*
You (fam., plural) speak	*(Voi) i parle*	*(Voi) parlate*
They speak	*(Lor) a parlo*	*(Loro) parlano*

To write	*Scrive*	*Scrivere*
I write	*(Mi) i scrivo*	*(Io) scrivo*
You (fam., sing.) write	*(Ti) it ëscrive*	*(Tu) scrivi*
He, she writes	*(Chiel, chila) a scriv*	*(Lui, lei) scrive*
We write	*(Noi) i scrivoma*	*(Noi) scriviamo*
You (fam., plural) write	*(Voi) i scrive*	*(Voi) scrivete*
They write.	*(Lor) a scrivo*	*(Loro) scrivo*

To finish	*Finì*	*Finire*
I finish	*(Mi) i finisso*	*(Io) finisco*
You (fam., sing.) finish	*(Ti) it finisse*	*(Tu) finisci*
He, she finishes	*(Chiel, chila) a finiss*	*(Lui, lei) finisce*
We finish	*(Noi) i finioma*	*(Noi) finiamo*
You (fam., plural) finish	*(Voi) i finisse*	*(Voi) finite*
They finish	*(Lor) a finisso*	*(Loro) finiscono*

The table below highlights the respective endings.

	-é	-e	-ì
(mi)	-o	-o	-isso
(ti)	-e	-e	-isse
(chiel, chila)	-a	-	-is
(noi)	-oma	-oma	-ioma
(voi)	-e	-e	-isse
(lor)	-o	-o	-isso

Note how similar the endings are for all three regular conjugations in Piedmontese. For example the endings for *parlé* (to speak) and *scrive* (to write) are identical except for the third person singular.

5. OBJECT PRONOUNS

Unlike Italian, in Piedmontese subject pronouns *mi, ti, chiel, noi, voi, lor,* may also be used as unstressed object pronouns. For example:

   Chiel a ven con mi. - He comes with <u>me</u>.

However, in the unstressed mode, where the pronoun appears before the verb, different words are required, as summarized below.

Italian (English)	Piedmontese
mi (to me)	*me, ëm, më*
ti (to you)	*te, të, ët*
gli (to him)	*je, ëj, jë*
le (to her)	*je, ëj, jë*
lo (him)	*lo*

la (her)	*la*
ci (to us)	*ne, ën, në*
vi (to you)	*ve, ëv, vë*
li, loro (them)	*je, ëj, jë*
a loro (to them)	*je, ëj, jë*

Examples:

Italian (English)	**Piedmontese**
Lui <u>mi</u> parla. (He speaks <u>to me</u>.)	*Chiel am (a+'m) parla.*
<u>Ti</u> parla. (He speaks <u>to you</u>).	*At (a+'t) parla.*
Lei <u>gli</u> dice. (She says <u>to him</u>.)	*Chila a-j (a+'j) dis.*
Lui <u>ci</u> parla. (He speaks <u>to us</u>.)	*Chiel an (a+'n) parla.*

In Piedmontese, apostrophes are used to replace a vowel when two vowels meet, e.g., *a ët* (to you) becomes *a + 't = at*. Note also the use of hyphens for similar combinations, e.g., *a ëj* (to him) becomes *a + 'j = a-j*.

6. PREPOSITIONS

A few Piedmontese prepositions are listed below.

Italian (English)	**Piedmontese**
a (to)	*a*
da (from)	*da*
di (of)	*dë*
su (on)	*su, së*

When these prepositions are combined with the articles *ël*, *la*, *ij*, *le* we obtain the following table.

±	ël	la	ij	le
a	al	a la	ai	a le
da	dal	da la	dai	da le
dë	dël	ëd la	dij	ëd le
su	sël	sla	sij	su le

The reader may want to compare these Piedmontese entries of this table with the corresponding Italian entries in section 9 of Appendix I.

The adverb corresponding to *ci* in Italian, meaning "here, there is, etc." becomes in Piedmontese *i* and often appears hyphenated, e.g. *chiel a-i ven* - he comes <u>here</u>.

7. OTHER TENSES/MOODS

We will not attempt to reproduce all other conjugations here. Instead we select the first person singular of the verb "to be" to illustrate some of the other tenses and moods in Piedmontese.

Italian (English)	Piedmontese	Tense/Mood
Io sono (I am)	*Mi i son*	present
Io sarò (I will be)	*Mi i sarai*	future
Io sarei (I would be)	*Mi i sarìa*	conditional
Io ero (I was)	*Mi i j'era*	past imperfect
Io sono stato (I had been)	*Mi i son ëstàit*	compound past

8. DATES AND NUMBERS

•Days of the Week

Italian (English)	Piedmontese
Lunedí (Monday)	*Lun-es*
Martedí (Tuesday)	*Màrtes*
Mercoledí (Wednesday)	*Mèrcol*
Giovedí (Thursday)	*Giòbia*
Venerdí (Friday)	*Vënner*
Sabato (Saturday)	*Saba*
Domenica (Sunday)	*Dumìnica*

•Months of the Year

Italian (English)	Piedmontese
Gennaio (January)	*Gené*
Febbraio (February)	*Fërvé*
Marzo (March)	*Mars*
Aprile (April)	*Avril*
Maggio (May)	*Magg*
Giugno (June)	*Giugn*
Luglio (July)	*Luj*
Agosto (August)	*Agost*
Settembre (September)	*Stèmber*
Ottobre (October)	*Otóber*
Novembre (November)	*Novèmber*
Dicembre (December)	*Dzèmber*

•Cardinal Numbers (1 - 10)

Italian	Piedmontese
1 *uno*	*un*
2 *due*	*doi*
3 *tre*	*trè*
4 *quattro*	*quatr*
5 *cinque*	*sinch*
6 *sei*	*ses*
7 *sette*	*sèt*
8 *otto*	*eut*
9 *nove*	*neuv*
10 *dieci*	*des*

•Ordinal Numbers (1 - 10)

Italian		Piedmontese
1st	*primo*	*prim*
2nd	*secondo*	*scond*
3rd	*terzo*	*ters*
4th	*quarto*	*quart*
5th	*quinto*	*quint*
6th	*sesto*	*sest*
7th	*settimo*	*sétim*
8th	*ottavo*	*otav*
9th	*nono*	*nòno*
10th	*decimo*	*décim*

9. A VERY SHORT PIEDMONTESE DICTIONARY

We include here a short listing of Piedmontese words, with translations into Italian (and English). The main purpose is to illustrate the significant differences that exist between standard

Italian and the Piedmontese dialect. The Frenchman Charles de Brosses wrote in 1740, "In Turin, French and Italian are spoken equally, but neither one nor the other is the language spoken by the common people: the language they speak is Piedmontese, a kind of Italian dialect completely bastardized, of which I cannot understand a single word."

PIEDMONTESE - ITALIAN (ENGLISH)

Adess-*ora* (now)

agiut - *aiuto* (help)

agnolòt - *agnolotti* (ravioli)

aj - *aglio* (garlic)

amont - *in alto* (high)

ancheuj - *oggi* (today)

ansima - *sopra* (on)

asil - *aceto* (vinegar)

avnì - *avvenire* (future)

barba - *zio* (uncle)

bagna - *salsa* (sauce)

basin - *bacio* (kiss)

basta - *abbastanza* (enough)

biciolan - *panino bislungo* (soft bread stick)

bin - *bene* (good)

boge – *muovere* (to move)

bondì - *buongiorno* (hello)

bòsch - *legna* (wood)

bota - *bottiglia* (bottle)

braje - *pantalone* (pants)

brav - *buono* (good)

buji - *bollito* (boiled)

buté - *mettere* (to put)

bzògn - *bisogno* (need)

cadrega - *sedia* (chair)

campé - *buttare* (to throw)

càud - *caldo* (hot)

cerea - *salute* (greetings)

ceresa - *cilliegia* (cherry)

cesa - *chiesa* (church)

cheur - *cuore* (heart)

chiel - *lui* (he)

chila - *lei* (she)

ciapé - *prendere* (to take)

ciòca - *campana* (bell)

cioca - *sbornia* (intoxication)

cioch - *ubriaco* (drunk)

cit - *piccolo, bambino* (small, young boy)

col - *quello* (that, masc.)

cola - *quella* (that, fem.)

colassion - *prima colazione*

(breakfast)

contacc – *meraviglia* (wow!)

còs - *che* (what)

cossa - *zucca* (pumkin)

cost - *questo* (this)

cotin - *gonna* (dress)

crajon - *matita* (pen)

crin - *maiale* (pig)

cunij - *coniglio* (rabbit)

davzin - *vicino* (near)

dcò - *persino* (even)

dé - *dare* (togive)

des - *dieci* (ten)

dëspers - *smarrito* (lost)

deurve - *aprire* (to open)

di - *giorno* (day)

disné - *pranzo* (lunch)

dné - *denari* (money)

doja - *boccale* (jug)

doss - *dolce* (sweet)

dzora - *sopra* (on top of)

ëd - *di* (from)

ëdcò - *anche* (also)

euj - *occhi* (eyes)

euv - *uovo* (egg)

eva – *acqua* (water)

feu - *fuoco* (fire)

fieul - *ragazzo, figlio* (boy, son)

fija - *ragazza, figlia* (girl, daughter)

fiòca - *neve* (snow)

fòl - *pazzo* (crazy person)

fomna - *moglie, donna* (wife, woman)

frisa - *un pochino* (a little bit)

ghërsin - *grissini* (bread sticks)

gnòch - *gnocchi* (potato dumplings)

gnun - *nessuno* (none)

goregn - *duro* (hard to chcw)

got - *gotto* (mug)

gram – *cattivo* (bad)

istà - *estate* (summer)

jer - *ieri* (yesterday)

leugn - *distante* (far away)

lòbia – *balcone* (balcony)

lus - *luce* (light)

mach - *sottanto* (only)

magna – *zia* (aunt)

marcé - *camminare* (to walk)

mare - *madre* (mother)

masnà - *bambino* (child)

mat - *pazzo, ragazzino* (crazy man, young boy)

mërluss - *baccalà* (dried cod)

mi - *io* (I)

mnestra - *minestra* (soup)

monsù - *signore* (mister)

nèh - *vero* (right)

neuit - *notte* (night)

nojàutre - *noi* (we)

Nosgnor - *Dio* (God)

òm - *uomo* (man)

pa - *non* (not)

paga - *salario* (pay, salary)

paisan - *contadino* (farmer)

pare - *padre* (father)

patanù - *nudo* (nude)

pes - *peggio* (worse)

pess - *pezzo* (piece)

pèss - *pesce* (fish)

pì - *più* (more)

pijé - *prendere* (to take)

piòla - *osteria* (tavern)

pocionin - *tesoruccio* (little sweetheart)

pogieul- *balcone* (balcony)

pom - *mela* (apple)

pròpi - *appunto* (exactly)

pruss - *pera* (pear)

ratin - *topolino* (little mouse)

risòt - *risotto* (rice)

sacòcia - *tasca* (pocket)

sagrin - *dispiacere* (sadness)

saré - *chiudere* (to close)

s-ciairé - *vedere* (to see)

s-ciass - *stretto* (tight)

s-cionfëtta - *tornellino* (little

heater)

scué - *spazzare* (sweep)

seugn - *sogno, sonno* (dream, sleep)

seurte – *uscire* (to go out)

sgnor – *signore, Dio*(mister, God)

sin-a - *cena* (dinner)

sinch - *cinque* (five)

sità - *città* (city)

smija - *sembra* (looks like)

sossì – *questo* (this)

spars - *asparagi* (asparagus)

spussé - *puzzare* (to smell)

strach - *stanco* (tired)

stansia – *camera* (room)

strass - *straccio* (rag)

svicc - *vispo* (lively)

tajarin - *tagliatelle* (flat noodles)

tempestà - *grandinata* (hail storm)

tisòire - *forbici* (scissors)

tòch - *pezzo* (piece)

toché - *toccare* (to touch)

tomàtica - *pomodoro* (tomato)

tòta - *signorina* (young woman)

travajé - *lavorare* (to work)

trifole – *tartufi* (truffles)

tucc - *tutto, tutti* (all)

uss - *uscio* (door)

vaca – *mucca* (cow)

vàire - *quanti, molto* (how many, much)

vej - *vecchio* (old)

venté - *essere necessario* (to be necessary)

vni - *venire* (to come)

vzin – *vicino* (near, neighboor)

APPENDIX III. Elements of Neapolitan Grammar

During the period 1266 - 1442, Naples was ruled by the French *Anjou* dynasty and french was the official court language. However, during the rule of the Spanish *Aragon* dynasty, which followed from 1443 to 1501, the Neapolitan "dialect" became the official court language. This was followed by the rule of Naples by Spain via viceroys, and the institution of Spanish as the court language. But by this time the Neapolitan language had been firmly established with the people of Naples. To this day Naples is one of the few large cities in Italy where one can here young people speaking their local dialect.

Since Neapolitan is not an official language, there are no real standards for the language. In our presentation of some of the elements of Neapolitan grammar, we have arbitrarily elected to follow the Neapolitan defined in Fierro's *Grammatica della Lingua Napoletana*.

1. NOUNS, ARTICLES, AND ADJECTIVES

Like Italian, Neapolitan masculine nouns end in "o" and feminine nouns in "a." For example:

Neapolitan (Italian)	English
ommo (uomo)	man
femmena (donna)	woman
sciummo (fiumme)	river
nennella (ragazza)	girl

However, some Neapolitan nouns end in "e", and the gender is defined only by the associated article. For example *giovane* (young boy, young girl) is the same for both genders; *'o giovane* and *'a giovane* then distinguished male from female. Sometimes masculine and feminine nouns have the "right" endings, that is: "o" or "a", but are spelled differently. For example *cuóco* (cook, male) and *còca* (cook, female).

Articles

Masculine	Feminine
'o (il) - the (sing.)	*'a (la)* - the (sing.)
'e (i) - the (plural)	*'e (le)* - the (plural)
nu, no (un, uno) - a (sing.)	*na (una)* - a (sing.)

Examples:

> *'a tazza (la tazza)* - the cup
> *'o cane (il cane)* - the dog
> *nu giovane (un giovane)* - a young boy
> *na cerasa (una ciliegia)* - a cherry
> *'e pisce (i pesci)* - the fish
> *'e mamme (le madre)* - the mothers

In Neapolitan, like Italian, adjectives agree in gender and number

Examples:

> *Nu buono guaglione (un bravo ragazzo)* - a good boy
> *'E buone guagliune (i bravi ragazzi)* - the good boys
> *Na bella casa (una bella casa)* - a beautiful house
> *'E belle case (le belle case)* - the beautiful houses

Note the change in spelling of the stem for boy in the singular and plural. This occurs only in Neapolitan. In some cases the adjective for a masculine noun takes on a "u" ending instead of an "o" ending. For example, *nu caru figlio* (a dear son).

2. PERSONAL SUBJECT PRONOUNS

The table below illustrates Neapolitan subject pronouns.

English	Neapolitan	Italian
I	*i', io*	*io*
you (fam., sing.)	*tu*	*tu*
he, she	*isso, essa*	*lui, lei*
we	*nuje*	*noi*
you (fam., plural)	*vuje*	*voi*
they	*isse, esse, loro*	*essi, esse, loro*

Note that, as in Piedmontese, the formal "you" does not exist in Neapolitan. This is a rather common feature of most Italian dialects. Note also, the "j" in *nuje* and *vuje*. The letter "j" is not in the Italian language, but does appear in various dialects, e.g. Piedmontese and Neapolitan. The letter "j" is pronounced roughly like the Italian "i."

3. SOME IMPORTANT IRREGULAR VERBS - PRESENT TENSE

English	Neapolitan	Italian
To be	***Essé'***	***Essere***
I am	*I' songo, so'*	*(Io) sono*
You (fam., sing.) are	*Tu sì*	*(Tu) sei*
He, she is	*Isso, essa è*	*(Lui, lei) è*
We are	*Nuje simmo*	*(Noi) siamo*
You (fam., plural) are	*Vuje site*	*(Voi) siete*
They are	*Loro songo, so*	*(Loro) sono*

To have	*Avè'*	*Avere*
I have	*I' aggio*	*(Io) ho*
You (fam., sing.) have	*Tu hai, hê, aie*	*(Tu) hai*
He, she has	*Isso, essa ha, ave*	*(Lui, lei) ha*
We have	*Nuje avimmo*	*(Noi) abbiamo*
You (fam., plural) have	*Vuje avite*	*(Voi) avete*
They have	*Isse hanno, aveno*	*(Loro) hanno*

To go	*Ji'*	*Andare*
I go	*I' vaco*	*(Io) vado*
You (fam., sing.) go	*Tu vaje*	*(Tu) vai*
He, she goes	*Isso, essa va*	*(Lui, lei) va*
We go	*Nuje jammo*	*(Noi) andiamo*
You (fam., plural) go	*Vuje jate*	*(Voi) andate*
They go	*Isse vanno*	*(Loro) vanno*

To do/make	*Fà'*	*Fare*
I do	*I' faccio*	*(Io) faccio*
You (fam., sing.) do	*Tu faje*	*(Tu) fai*
He, she does	*Isso, essa fa*	*(Lui, lei) fa*
We do	*Nuje facimmo*	*(Noi) facciamo*
You (fam., plural) do	*Vuje facite*	*(Voi) fate*
They do	*Isse fanno*	*(Loro) fanno*

Note that in Neapolitan, an apostrophe before or at the end of a word indicates a "cut-off" of letters, e.g. *i'* for *io* and *cantà'* for *cantare*. The accent grave (`) is used to indicate a stressed letter.

4. REGULAR VERBS - PRESENT TENSE

In Neapolitan, the endings of regular verbs corresponding to *-are*, *-ere*, and *-ire* in Italian are (cut off form) *-a'*, *-è'*, and *-ì'*. The three regular conjugations are illustrated below.

English	Neapolitan	Italian
To sing	***Cantà'***	***Cantare***
I sing	*Io canto*	*(Io) canto*
You (fam., sing.) sing	*Tu cante*	*(Tu) canti*
He, she sings	*Isso, essa canta*	*(Lui, lei) canta*
We sing.	*Nuje cantammo*	*(Noi) cantiamo*
You (fam., plural) sing	*Vuje cantate*	*(Voi) cantate*
The sing	*Isse cantano*	*(Loro) cantano*

To believe	***Credè'***	***Credere***
I believe	*I' credo*	*(Io) credo*
You (fam., sing.) believe	*Tu cride*	*(Tu) credi*
He, she believes	*Isso, essa crede*	*(Lui, lei) crede*
We believe	*Nuje credimmo*	*(Noi) crediamo*
You (fam., plural) believe	*Vuje credite*	*(Voi) credete*
They believe	*Isse credeno*	*(Loro) credono*

To feel/hear/smell	***Sentì***	***Sentire***
I feel	*I' sento*	*(Io) sento*
You (fam., sing.) feel	*Tu siente*	*(Tu) senti*
He, she feels	*Isso, essa sente*	*(Lui, lei) sente*
We feel	*Nuje sentimmo*	*(Noi) sentiamo*
You (fam., plural) feel	*Vuje sentite*	*(Voi) sentite*
They feel	*Isse sentono*	*(Loro) sentono*

Note that in Neapolitan the stem of verbs ending in *-ì'* does change in the second person singular, e.g. *tu siente* for the verb with stem *sent-*, another stem change unique to Neapolitan. The table below highlights the respective endings.

	-à'	*-è'*	*-ì'*
(io)	*-o*	*-o*	*-o*
(tu)	*-e*	*-e*	*-e*
(isso, esso)	*-a*	*-e*	*-e*
(nuje)	*-ammo*	*-immo*	*-immo*
(vuje)	*-ate*	*-ite*	*-ite*
(isse)	*-ano*	*-eno*	*-ono*

5. OBJECT PRONOUNS

Italian (English)	Neapolitan
mi (to me)	*me*
ti (to you)	*te*
gli (to him)	*le*
le (to her)	*le*
lo (him)	*le*
la (her)	*le*
ci (to us)	*nce*
vi (to you)	*ve*
li, loro (them)	*le*
a loro (to them)	*le*

Examples:

Italian (English)	Neapolitan
Lui mi vuole. (He wants me.)	*Isso me vo'.*
Io ti dico tutto. (I tell you everything).	*I' te dico tutte cose.*
Lui gli diede il libro. (He gave him the book.)	*Nce è rimasto 'o core.*
C'è rimasto il cuore. (Our heat remained.)	*Isso le dette 'o libbro.*
Vi siamo grati di ciò. (We are grateful to you for that.)	*Ve ne simmo grate.*

6. PREPOSITIONS

A few Neapolitan prepositions are listed below.

Italian (English)	Neapolitan
a, in (to)	*a*
da (from)	*'a*
di (of)	*'e*
con (with)	*cu*
per (for)	*pe'*
presso (near)	*addu*

Examples:

Italian (English)	Neapolitan
La tazza di caffè. (The cup of coffee.)	*'A tazza 'e caffè.*
Per campare (for survival).	*Pe' campà'*
Me ne voglio andare in Italia. (I want	*Me ne voglio jì' 'a l'Italia.*

to go <u>to</u> Italy.)

Con la scarpa (with the shoe)   <u>Cu</u> *'a scarpa.*

7. EXCLAMATIONS

Neapolitans are reputed to be very emotional, and there are many famous exclamations in the Neapolitan language. Below we list a few examples.

Examples:

> *'A faccia toja!* - In your face!
>
> *Maronna mia!* - Mother of mine!
>
> *Mena mo!* - Forget it!
>
> *P'ammore 'e Dio!* - For the love of God!
>
> *Frusta là!* - Away from there!
>
> *Povero a nuje!* - Poor us!
>
> *Oi Francì!* - Oh Francesco!

8. DOUBLE CONSONANTS

One last point about written Neapolitan, when certain consonants appear right after a vowel in a previous word, the consonants is doubled. The pronunciation of the consonants is not changed with this doubling.

Examples:

> *Stongo <u>cc</u>a.* - I am here.
>
> *Tu <u>mm</u>e faje murì.* - You let me die.

292

Sti <u>cc</u>arne. - This flesh.

Stive' <u>mm</u>iezo. - You were in the middle of.

9. A VERY SHORT NEAPOLITAN DICTIONARY

We include here a short listing of Neapolitan words with translations into Italian (and English). We have selected many of the words from famous Neapolitan songs, and have emphasized those words that differ significantly from their Italian counterparts.

NEAPOLITAN - ITALIAN (ENGLISH)

abbascio - *in giù* (below)

addó - *dove* (where)

addù - *verso* (towards)

addurà' - *adorare* (to smell)

ajere - *ieri* (yesterday)

allero - *allegro* (happy)

ammore - *amore* (love)

appiccià - *accendere* (to light up)

arreto - *dietro* (behind)

ascevulì - *venir meno* (to diminish)

ascì' - *uscire* (go out)

ascià' - *cercare* (to look for)

assaje - *tanto* (so much)

ato - *altro* (other)

avutà' - *voltare* (to turn around)

bonnì - *buongiorno* (good day)

ca - *che* (that)

cà - *qua* (here)

cagnà' - *cambiare* (to change)

capa - *testa* (head)

capille - *capelli* (hair)

carcioffolà - *carciòfo* (artichoke, bobby)

cardillo - *cardellino* (goldfinch)

cauro - *caldo* (warm)

cchiù - *più* (more)

cerasa - *ciliegia* (cherry)

chella - *quella* (that one, fem.)

chesta - *questa* (this, fem.)

chiagne - *piange* (cries)

chiano - *piano* (quietly)

chillo - *quello* (that one, masc.)

chino - *pieno* (full)

chiochiaro - *stupido* (stupid)

chista - *questa* (this, fem)

chistu - *questo* (this, masc)

chiù - *più* (more)

chiummo - *piombo* (lead)

ciardino - *giardino* (garden)

ciotola - *tazza* (cup)

ciuccio - *asino* (donkey)-

criature - *bambini* (children)

cu - *con* (with)

cuffià - *prendere in giro* (to make fun of)

damme - *dammi* (give me)

dinto - *dentro* (in)

doce - *dolce* (sweet)

dóje - *due* (two, fem.)

duje- *due* (two, masc.)

durmì'- *dormire* (to sleep)

essa - *lei* (she)

figliola - *ragazza* (girl)

giucà' - *giocare* (to play)

gnorsì - *signorsi* (yes sir)

guaglione- *ragazzo* (boy)

into - *dentro* (in)

isso - *lui* (he)

janca - *bianca* (white, fem.)

jesce - *esci* (to go out, to come out)

jettà' - *buttare* (to throw)

jucà' - *giocare* (to play)

jurnata - *giornata* (day)

lastra - *cristallo* (crystal, window pane)

malandrino - *furbo* (wise guy)

mazzacane - *sasso* (rock)

mico - *me* (me)

'mmiezo - *in mezzo* (in the middle of)

'mmocca - *in bocca* (in the mouth)

mo- *adesso* (now)

'mpastà' - *impastare* (to mix)

'mpuntato - *impuntato* (stuck)

munno - *mondo* (world)

murì' - *morire* (to die)

musso - *muso* (face, mug)

na - *una* (a, fem.)

'nanze - *avanti* (ahead)

'ncap'a - *dopo* (after)

'ncoppa - *sopra* (on, on top of)

'ncuccià -*sorprendere* (to surprise)

nenna- *fanciulla* (young girl)

nennella - *ragazza* (girl)

nepeta - *nepitella* (basil thyme)

'nfunno- *in fondo* (at the bottom, in the final analysis)

'ngrato - *ingrato* (ungrateful)

nisciuna - *nessuna* (no one, fem.)

ninno - *ragazzo* (boy)

nòmme - *nome* (name)

'nnanze - *davanti* (in front of)

nonna - *nina nanna* (lullabye)

nu - *un* (a, masc.)

nun - *non* (not)

'nzieme - *insieme* (together with)

'nzino - *in grembo* (in the lap)

'o - *il* (the, masc.) or *lo* (him)

ommo - *uomo* (man)

overo- *vero* (true)

paciona - *donna quieta* (quiet, peaceful woman)

paraviso - *paradiso* (paradise)

parite - *pari* (you seem like)

pazzià' - *giocare* (to play)

pe' - *per* (for)

pecundria – *ipocondria* (hypochondria)

piccerélla - *piccolina* (little girl)

piccerì - *fanciullo*(little boy)

pisce - *pesce* (fish, plural)

pittà - *dipingere* (to paint)

pizzo - *posto* (place)

pò - *poi* (then)

priezza - *allegrezza* (joy, happiness)

quanno - *quando* (when)

rezza - *rete* (fishing nets)

scapriccia - *scapricciare* (to satisfy one's whimes)

scetà'- *svegliare* (to wake up)

schiocche - *grappoli* (bunches of)

sciantosa - *cantatrice* (singer, fem.)

sciato - *fiato* (breath)

sciòre - *fiore* (flower)

sciummo - *fumo* (smoke)

scullata - *scollata* (low cut)

sfizio - *diletto* (dear one)

smerza - *sinistra* (left)

spià' - *domandare* (to ask)

spingola - *spillo* (pin)

sta- *questa* (this, fem.)

sto - *questo* (this, masc.)

suffrì' - *soffrire* (to suffer)

sunnà'- *sognare* (to dream)

suonno - *sonno* (sleep)

surdate - *soldato* (soldier)

tanno - *allora*(then, well then)

tirabusciò - *cavaturaccioli* (corkscrew)

toja - *tua* (your)

turnè - *torneo* (tournament, competition)

turzo - *stupido* (stupid, insensitive)

tuzzulià - *bussare* (to knock)

urdemo - *ultimo* (last)

vascio - *basso* (low, ground floor apartment)

vaso - *bacio* (kiss)

vierno - *inverno* (winter)

vocca - *bocca* (mouth)

vote - *volte* (times)

vucchella - *boccuccia* (tiny mouth)

vuto - *voto* (vow)

REFERENCES

David Abulafia, *Frederick II: A Medieval Emperor*, Oxford University Press, Oxford, 1988.

Harold Acton, *The Bourbons of Naples*, Prion Books Limited, London, 1998.

Richard D. Alba, *Italian Americans: Into the Twilight of Ethnicity*, Prentice-Hall, Inc., Englewood Cliffs, NJ 1985.

Dante Alighieri, *The Divine Comedy: Inferno*, Bantum Books, New York, 1980.

Raffaele Andreoli, *Vocabolario: Napoletano - Italian*, Arturo Berisio Editore, Napoli, 1966 (originally published in 1887).

Evelyn Barish, *Emerson in ITALY*, Henry Holt and Co., New York, 1989.

Luigi Barzini, *The Italians*, Atheneum/MacMillan, New York, 1964.

Laura Busini Birch, *Traditional Italian Food*, Fontana Paperbacks, William Collins Sons and Co., Glasgow, 1985.

Sergio Bittanti (Editor), *Count Riccati and the Early Days of the Riccati Equation*, Pitagora Editrice, Bologna, 1989.

Giorgio Bocca, *In Che Cosa Credono Gli Italiani*, Longanesi, Milano, 1982.

Ada Boni, *Italian Regional Cooking*, E.P. Dutton & Co., Inc., New York, 1969.

Sanford P. Bordeau, *Volts to Hertz....the rise of electricity*, Burgess Publishing Company, Minneapolis, Minnesota, 1982.

Camillo Brero, *Storia della Letteratura Piemontese - Primo Volume (da Sec. XII a Sec. XVIII)*, Editrice Piemonte in Bancarella, Torino, 1981.

Camillo Brero, *Vocabolario Piemontese - Italiano*, Editirice Piemonte in Bancarella, Torino, 1982.

Camillo Brero, *Vocabolario Italiano - Piemontese*, Editirice Piemonte in Bancarella, 1989.

Camillo Brero and Remo Bertodati, *Grammatica Della Lingua Piemontese*, Edizione "Piemont/Europa," Torino, 1988 (In Italian).

Placido Bucolo (Editor), *The Other Pareto*, Scholar Press, London, 1980.

W. F. Butler, *The Lombard Communes: A History of the Republics of North Italy*, Haskell House Publishing Ltd., New York, 1969 (originally published in 1906).

Filippo Burzio, *Lagrange*, Utet Libreria, Torino, 1993 (In Italian; Original Edition 1963).

Michele Cantarella, *The Italian Heritage*, Holt, Rinehart, and Winston, Inc., New York, 1959.

Linda Brandi Cateura, *Growing Up Italian*, William Morrow and Company, Inc., New York, 1987.

Marie Chay, *Pilgrim's Pride*, Dodd, Mead & Company, New York, 1961.

James Cleugh, *The Medici*, Barnes and Noble Books, New York, 1993.

Francesco Cognasso, *Storia di Torino*, Aldo Martello Editore, Milano, 1969 (In Italian).

Pietro Colletta, *Storia Del Reame Di Napoli*, Edizione S.A.R.A., 1992.

Mario Costantino, *Italian at a Glance (Phrase Book & Dictionary for Travelers),* Barron's, Hauppauge, NY, 1992.

Eugene L. Cox, *The Green Count of Savoy:Amadeus VI and the Transalpine Savoy in the Fourteenth Century*, Princeton University Press, Princeton, NJ, 1967.

Sebastian de Grazia, *Machiavelli in Hell*, Vintage Books, New York, 1994 (orginally published y Princeton University Press in 1989).

Luisa Del Giudice (Editor), *Studies in Italian American Folklore*, Utah State University Press, Logan, UT, 1993.

Luisa Del Giudice, *Italian Traditional Song*, 2nd Edition, Istituto Italiano di Cultura, Los Angeles, CA, 1995 (Text and cassettes).

Lorenza de' Medici, *Italy:The Beautiful Cookbook*, Harper Collins Pub., New York, 1996.

Vittorio Di Sant'Albino, *Gran Dizionario Piemontese-Italiano*, Edizione Anastatica, Torino, 1993 (originally published in 1859).

Charles Dickens, *American Notes and Pictures from Italy*, Oxford Univ. Press, Oxford, 1987.

Bianca Dorato, *Drere 'd Lus,* Amici di Piazza, Edizioni "Ël Pèilo," Mondovi, 1990 (In Piedmontese).

P. Dorato, C. Abdallah, V. Cerone, *Linear Quadratic Control: An Introduction*, Prentice Hall, Piscataway, NJ, 1995.

Orrin E. Dunlap, Jr., *Marconi, The Man and His Wireless*, Arno Press and the New York Times, New York, 1971.

George Eliot, *Romola*, Penguin Books, New York, 1981 (First published in 1862 - 1863).

W. S. Ellis, "Surviving Italian Style," *National Geographic*, February, 1984, pp. 185 - 208.

Aurelio Fierro, *Grammatica Della Lingua Napoletana*, Rusconi, Milano, 1989 (In Italian).

Raymond Flower and Alessandro Falassi, *Culture Schock, Italy* Graphics Arts Center Pub. Co., Portland, 1991.

David Forgas and Robert Lumley (Editors), *Italian Cultural Studies: An Introduction*, Oxford University Press, Oxford, UK, 1996.

J. Freund, *Pareto*, Plutarch Press, Washington, DC.

Roberto Gervaso, *La Bella Rosina*, Bompiani, Milano, 1991.

Paul Ginsborg, *A History of Contemporary Italy. Society and Politics, 1943-1988*, Penguin Books, London and New York, 1990.

J. W. Goethe, *Italian Journey*, Penguin Books, London, 1962.

R. Gore, "When the Greeks Went West," *National Geographic*, November, 1994, pp. 2 - 37.

Francesco Guicciardini, *The History of Italy*, Princeton University Press, New Jersey, 1984 (Originally published in Italian in 1561.)

Hermann W. Haller, *The Hidden Italy*, Wayne State University Press, Detroit, 1986.

Daniel Halpern, *Halpern's Guide to the Essential Restaurants of Italy*, Addison-Wesley Reading, MA, 1990.

George Bruce Halsted (Editor), *Girolamo Saccheri's Euclides Vendicatus*, Chelsea Pub. Co., New York, 1986 (In English. Original Latin version published in 1733.)

Valentina Harris, *Traveller's Guide To The Food of Italy*, (An Owl Book), Henry Holt and Co., New York, New York, 1988.

Ernest O. Hauser, *Italy. A Cultural Guide*, Atheneum, New York, 1981.

Harry Hearder, *Italy: A Short History*, Cambridge Univ. Press, Cambridge, 1991.

Mark Helprin, *A Soldier of the Great War,* Harcourt Brace Jovanovich Pub., New York, 1991.

Christopher Hibbert, *Garibaldi and his Enemies*, Penguin Books, New York, 1987 (First published in 1965.)

Paul Hofmann, *That Fine Italian Hand*, Henry Holt and Company, New York, 1990.

Paul Hofmann, *Cento Città: A Guide to the "Hundred Cities & Towns" of Italy*, Henry Holt and Company, New York, 1988.

Andrea Imperiali and Paolo Recalcati, *La Canzone Napoletana*, Antonio Vallardi, Editore, 1998 (In Italian).

Henry James, *Italian Hours*, The Ecco Press, New York, 1987 (First Published in 1909).

Nathaniel T. Kennedy, "United italy Marks Its 100th Year," *National Geographic*, November, 1961, pp. 593-649.

Edna E. Kramer, *The Nature and Growth of Modern Mathematics, Volumes 1 and 2*, Fawcett Pub., Inc., Greenwich, Connecticut, 1974.

Barbara M. Kreutz, *Before the Normans: Southern Italy in the Ninth and Tenth Centuries*, Univ. Pennsylvania Press, Philadelphia, 1991.

Herbert Kubly, *Easter in Sicily*, Simon and Schuster, New York, 1956.

Herbert Kubly, *American in Italy*, Grosset & Dunlap, New York, 1995.

D. H. Lawrence, *D.H. Lawrence and Italy*, Penguin Books, New York, 1985.

H. LaFay, "Sicily, Where All the Songs are Sad," *National Geographic*, March, 1976, pp. 407 - 436.

Alberta Lantermo, *La Cucina Delle Regioni D'Italia: Piemonte*, Edizioni Mida, Bologna, 1989.

Carlo Levi, *Christ Stopped at Eboli*, Penguin Books, London, 1982 (*Cristo Si È Fermato a Eboli*, first translated into English in 1947).

Primo Levi, *The Periodic Table*, Everyman's Library, Alfred A. Knopf Inc., New York, 1996 (First published in Italian in 1975).

Valerio Lintner, *A Traveller's History of Italy*, Windrush Press, Gloucestershire, England, 1989.

Sophia Loren, *Sophia Loren's Recipes and Memories*, G.T.Publishing, New York, 1998.

Niccolò Machiavelli, *The Prince*, The University of Chicago Press, Chicago, 1998.

Niccolò Machiavelli, *The Discourses*, Penguin Classics, London, 1983.

Frances M. Malpezzi and William M. Clements, *Italian-American Folklore*, August House Pub. Inc., Little Rock, 1992.

Alessandro Manzoni, *The Betrothed*, Penguin Books, New York, 1987.

Lauro Martines, *Power and Imagination. City-States in Renaissance Italy*, Alfred A. Knopf, New York, 1979.

Bruno Migliorini and T. Gwynfor Griffith, *The Italian Language*, Faber and Faber, London, 1966.

William Murry, *The Last Italian. Portrait of a People*, Prentice Hall, New York, 1991.

Benito Mussolini, *My Rise and Fall,* Da Capo Press, New York, 1998.

Gianni Oliva, *I Savoia-Novecento anni di una dinastia*, Arnoldo Mondadori Editore, S.P.A., Torino, Italy, 1998 (In Italian).

Lynn M. Osen, *Women in Mathematics*, The MIT Press, Cambridge, MA, 1984.

Vittorio Paliotti, *Storia Della Canzone Napoletana*, Newton Compton Editore, 1992 (In Italian).

Vilfredo Pareto, *Manual of Political Economy*, Augustus M. Kelly Pub., New York 1971 (originally published in Italian in 1906).

Armand Patrucco, *The Critics of the Italian Parliamentary System, 1860-1915,* Garland Pub. Inc., New York, 1992.

Giuseppe Pitrè, *La Lingua Parlata del Dialetto Siciliano*, Edizioni Librarie Siciliane, Palermo, 1991.

Lorenzo Polizzotto, *The Elect Nation: The Savonarolan Movement in Florence*, 1494-1545, Clarendon Press, Oxford, 1994.

Martha D. Pollak, *Turin 1564 - 1680*, The University of Chicago Press, Chicago, 1991.

Ernst Pulgram, *The Tongues of Italy*, Harvard Univ. Press, Cambridge, MA, 1958.

Mario Puzo, *The Fortunate Pilgrim*, Atheneum, New York, 1965.

Mario Puzo, *The Sicilian*, Bantam Books, New York, 1985.

Mary Renault, *The Mask of Apollo,* Vintage Books, New York, 1988 (Originally published 1966).

Peter Robb, *Midnight in Sicily*, Vintage Books, New York, 1999 (Originally published in Australia by Duffy and Snellgrove, 1996).

Ralph Roeder, *The Man of the Renaissance*, Garden City Publishing Co., New York, 1933.

Steven Runciman, *The Sicilian Vespers*, Cambridge Univ. Press, Cambridge, 1992.

Marianne Shapiro, *De Vulgari Eloquentia: Dante's Book of Exile*, Univ. Nebraska Press, Lincoln, NB, 1990.

Denis Mack Smith, *A History of Siciliy: Medieval Sicily, 800-1713*, Dorset Press, New York, 1968.

Denis Smith, *A History of Siciliy: Modern Sicily, After 1713*, Dorset Press, New York, 1968.

Denis Mack Smith, *Mussolini*, Vintage Books/Random House, New York, 1983.

Denis Mack Smith, *Italy and Its Monarchy*, Yale Univ. Press, New Haven, 1989.

Charles Speroni , Carlo L. Golino, and Barbara Caili, *Basic Italian*, Holt, Rinehart and Winston Inc., New York, 1993.

Paul Strathern, *Machiavelli in 90 Minutes*, Ivan R. Dee, Publisher, Chicago, 1998.

Giuseppe Tomasi di Lampedusa, *The Leopard*, Everyman's Library, Alfred A. Knopf, New York, 1991 (Originally published in Italian, *Il Gattopardo* in 1958).

Luca Torre (Editor), *Canzoni Classiche Napoletane Da Jesce Sole A Carmela*, Torre Editrice S.R.L., Napoli, 1993.

Antonio Traina, *Vocabolario Siciliano-Italian*, REPRINT S.A.S., Milano, 1991 (Originally published in 1868).

Pasquale Villari, *Life and Times of Girolamo Savonarola*, Volumes I and II, Haskell House Pub. Ltd., New York, 1969, (First Published 1888).

Pierre Van Paassen, *A Crown of Fire: The Life and Times of Girolamo Savonarola,* Charles Scribner's Sons, New York, 1960.

William Van Wyck, Savonarola: *A Biography in Dramatic Episodes*, Robert M. McBride, New York, 1927.

Pasquale Villari, *The Life and Times of Niccolo Machiavelli, Volumes I and II*, Haskell House Pub. LTD, New York, 1969 (First Published in 1892).

James J. Walsh, *What Civilization Owes to Italy*, The STRATFORD CO. Publishers, Boston, 1923.

Alethea Wiel, *A History of Venice*, Barnes & Noble, New York, 1995 (originally published in 1898).

D. J. Wilde, *Optimum Seeking Methods*, Prentice Hall International, Englewood Cliffs, 1964.

INDEX

A

abbacchio alla romana, roasted lamb, 57

Abulafia, David, 37, 229

Acton, Harold, 230

Adelaide di Susa, 224

Agnesi, Maria Gaetana - Mathematician, 109, 110, 124

Agnesi, witch of, 110

Al'Idrisi-Arab geographer, 224

Alba, Richard, 47, 60, 244, 246, 297

Albana di Romagna, wine, 62

Alessandro VI, 19

Alfonse of Aragone, 32

Amaretto di Saronno, liqueur, 63

Amedeo IV, 224

Amedeo IX, 226

Amedeo VI, 226

Amedeo VII, 226

Amedeo VIII, 226

Anafesto, Paolucio-Venetian doge, 34

Andeoli, Raffaele, 79

Anjou dynasty, 285

antipasto, 52

Antonelli, Alessandro, 38

aperitivo, 52

Aragon dynasty, 285

Arbore, Renzo, 157, 160, 166, 216, 219

Archimedes, 13, 100

arrabbiati, 19

Ars Magna, manuscript, 104

Asti Spumante, 61

B

bagna cauda, 58

Barbera, wine, 61

Barberesco, wine, 61

Bardolino, wine, 62

Barolo, wine, 61

Barzini, Luigi, 44

Beltrami, Eugenio - Mathematician, 113

Bertodatti, Remo, 79

bibita analcolica, non-alcoholic soft drink, 52

Birch, Laura Busini, 63

Birichin, journal, 92

bistecca alla fiorentina, steak, 52, 59

Bittanti, Sergio, 123

Bixio, Cesare Andrea, 216

Bocca, Giorgio, 46

Boccaccio, Giovanni, 75

bollito misto, mixed boiled meats, 58

Bordeau, Sanford, 124

Bourbon dynasty, 227

Bovio, Libero, 177

Brero, Camillo, 79, 97

Brooklyn Technical High School, 243

Brunelleschi, Fillipo, 15

Brunello di Montalcino, wine, 61

Bucolo, Placido, 123

buridda, fish stew, 58

Burzio, Fillpo, 124

Buti, Carlo, 216, 217, 220, 241

Butler, W.F., 37

Byzantine Empire, 38, 223

C

Caboto, Giovanni - John Cabot, 21
caffè corretto, 53
caffè granite, 53
caffè latte, 53
caffè lungo, 53
caffè macchiato, 53
caffè ristretto, 53
Calvo, Edoardo - Piedmontese poet, 97
Campanella, Fillippo, 182
campanilismo, 47
Canavese, 9
cannelloni, 58
Cantarella, Michele, 37
Canyno, Antonyo, 211, 219
Capoluogo, capital city, 7
Caporetto, city of, 29
capponata, 59
cappuccino, 53
Cardano. See Cardano, Girolamo - Mathematician
Cardano, Girolamo - Mathematician, 104
Carlo Alberto, 24, 34, 228
Carlo Emanuele IV, 228
Carlo Magno, Charlemagne, 223
Carthagians, 222
cassata alla siciliana, 59
Cateura, Brandi, 47
Cavour, Conte Camillo Benso di, v, 25, 27, 41, 81, 319
cena, 51
Central Park West, 241
Centro Studi Piemontesi, 98
Cesaro, Ernesto - Mathematician, 113
Charles of Anjou, 225

Charles V, 22, 46
Charles VIII, 17, 33, 46
Chay, Marie, 44, 85, 246, 299
Chianti, wine, 61
Cibo e vino, food and wine, 51
Cittadella, Turin, 227
Clements, William, 47
Cleugh, James, 41
Cognasso, Francesco, 229
Cola di Rienzo, 4, 15, 45
Colletta, Pietro, 230
Colombo, Cristoforo, 21
Columbia University, 243
commune, 9
condottieri, 17
Constance of Sicily, 71
Constantino, Mario, 79
contorno, 52
Copernicus, Nicolas, 115
Corvo, wine, 62
Costa, Nino - Piedmontese poet, 97
cotechino, pork sausage, 57
Cours d'Économique Politique, Pareto, 120
Cox, Eugene, 230
Crotone, city of, 13, 99

D

Dante Alighieri, 4, 15, 72, 297
De Divina Proportione, 102
de Grazia, Sebastian, 42
de' Medici, Catherine, 41
De Vulgari Eloquentia, 73
de' Medici, Cosimo, 15
de' Medici, Giovanni, 22
de' Medici, Giuliano, 20
de' Medici, Lorenza - cookbook, 64
de' Medici, Lorenzo, 4, 15, 17, 20,

Gothic Origin, 69
Lombard Origin, 69

J

James, Henry, 39

K

Kalman, Rudolf, 108
Kiefer, J., 102
Kingdom of Italy, 24
Kramer, Edna E., 123
Kreutz, Barbara, 38
Kubly, Herbert, 39, 303

L

l'Arvista dl'Acaemia, Piedmontese
   journal, 98
la Scala, 17
La Divina Commedia, 72
la dolce vita, 31
la Lega Nord, 32
Lachello, Rosina, 232
Lacrima Christi, wine, 62
Lagrange, Giuseppe Luigi -
   Mathematician, 111
Lagrangian function, 112
Lagrangian multiplier, 113
Langhe, 9
Langue d'Oc, 71
Langue d'Oil, 71
Lantermo, Alberta, 63
Laudi Sacre, 87
Laurea, 36
Lawrence, David Herbert, 39, 303
Leonardo da Pisa, 101
Leonardo da Vinci, 4, 15, 17, 100,

102, 119
Levi - Civita, Tullio -
   Mathematician, 113
Levi, Carlo, 43, 303
Levi, Primo, 43, 303
Liber Abaci, 101
liceo, 35
Limoncello, liqueur, 63
Linear Quadratic Control, book, 109
Lintner, Valerio, 38
Lobachevskian geometry, 106
Lobachevsky, 106
Logica Demonstrativa, manuscript,
   106
Lombards, 223
Loren, Sophia - cookbook, 64
Los Alamos National Laboratory,
   118
Lucera, city in Apulia, 225
Lumley, Robert, 36

M

Machiavelli, Nicolo, 19
Mafia, 40, 45, 46, 226
Malpezzi, Francis, vii, 47, 246, 304
Manfred, son of Federick II, 225
*Manin, Ludovico-*Venetian doge, 34
Manzoni, Alessandro, 1, 4, 22, 76,
   304
Marconi, Guglielmo - Engineer, 122
Mario, E.A., 179
Martines, Lauro, 37
Mazzini, Giuseppe, 4, 24
Méchanique Analytique, book by
   Lagrange, 112
Mezzogiorno, 29, 46
Michelangelo, 15
Migliorini, Bruno, 78

315

Credits

Graphics

Maps 5, 6, and 7 in Chapter 1 are reprinted, with permission of Cambridge University Press, from Harry Hearder's *Italy: A Short History* (originally maps 3, 4, and 7).

Line drawings of Mazzini, Garibaldi, Vittorio Emanuele II, and Cavour in Chapter 1 are by John Hoste (in Valerio Lintner's *A Traveller's History of Italy*).

Lyrics to Songs

The lyrics to the songs *Mamma, Mi Scappa la Pipi, Parlami D'Amore Mariu,* and *Vivere* in Chapter 6, are reprinted with permission of the Bixio Music Group (Bixio Music Group, c/o IDM Music, 111 East 14th Street, Suite 140, New york, NY 10003.)

The lyrics to the songs *L'Italiano* and *Guaglione* in Chapter 6, are reprinted with permission, as follows:

L'Italiano © Copyright 1983 by NUMBER TWO EDIZIONI MUSICALI S.R.L./EDIZIONI CURCI S.R.L./STAR S.R.L.-Milano (Italy). Printed by kind permission of Number Two Edizioni Musicali S.r.l./Edizioni Curci S.r.l./ Star S.r.l.-Milano (Italy).

Guaglione © Copyright 1956 (Renewed 1958) by ACCORDO EDIZIONI MUSICALI S.R.L. – Milano (Italy). Printed by kind permission of Accordo Edizioni Musicali S.r.l., - Milano (Italy).

The lyrics to the song *Dla Del Pont* in Chapter 4, are reprinted with permission of UNIVERSAL MUSIC ITALY S.R.L., Edizioni, Musicali.

The lyrics to the song *Ortigia in Blues* in Chapter 6, are reprinted with permission of *Antonio Canino*.

The lyrics to the song:

Uno Per Tutte (I Like What I See)

By B. Kaye, T. Renis and Mogol,

© WB Music Corp. (ASCAP) All Rights Reserved, used by permission of WARNER BROS. PUBLICATIONS U.S. INC., Miami, FL. 33014.

Poem

The poem *Per Son* is reprinted with kind permission of the author, *Bianca Dorato,* from the collection of poems *Drere 'D Lus (*Edizioni Mondovi, Italy, 1990).

About the Authors

Peter Dorato was born in Manhattan, NY, December 17, 1932. He received a BS degree from the City College of New York in 1955, an MS degree from Columbia University in 1956, and his Doctorate from the Polytechnic Institute of Brooklyn in 1961, all in Electrical Engineering. He has been a faculty member at the Polytechnic Institute of Brooklyn and the University of Colorado at Colorado Springs. Since 1976 he has been a faculty member in the department of Electrical and Computer Engineering at the University of New Mexico in Albuquerque, NM, where he also teaches a course on Italian Culture, through the Division of Continuing Education. During the academic year 1991-1992 he spent a sabbatical year at the Polytechnic Institute of Turin, and is a frequent visitor to Italy and Villadeati, his parents hometown. He is the author of two engineering books, co-authored with Italian colleagues.

Sylvia Dorato, daughter of Peter and Madeleine Dorato, was born in Forest Hills, Queens, NY, August 23, 1960. She received a BS degree in Chemical Engineering in 1982 and an MS degree in Electrical Engineering in 1987, both from the University of New Mexico, where she is currently working on her Ph.D. in Electrical Engineering. She is a branch chief in the Laser Division at the Air Force Research Laboratory in Albuquerque, NM. She also visits Italy and Villadeati often.